RELIGION
IN
GREECE AND ROME

*the text of this book is printed
on 100% recycled paper*

RELIGION IN GREECE AND ROME

H. J. ROSE

with a new Introduction by the author

HARPER TORCHBOOKS ❦ The Cloister Library
HARPER & ROW, PUBLISHERS
NEW YORK, HAGERSTOWN, SAN FRANCISCO, LONDON

RELIGION IN GREECE AND ROME
Introduction to the Torchbook Edition
Copyright © 1959 by Harper & Row, Publishers, Incorporated
Printed in the United States of America

Originally published as *Ancient Greek Religion* (1946) and *Ancient Roman Religion* (1948) and reprinted here in one volume by arrangement with Hutchinson and Company, Limited, London.

First HARPER TORCHBOOK edition published 1959

Library of Congress catalog card number 59-11124

ISBN: 0-06-130055-1

78 79 80   12 11 10

CONTENTS

INTRODUCTION
TO THE TORCHBOOK EDITION

THE TWO small books combined in this volume sketch an important part of the history of the two outstanding peoples in European antiquity, the Greeks and the Romans; namely, their religious development from the earliest times of which we have any knowledge, or even plausible guesses, down to the disappearance of the ancient cults before the rising tide of the new world religion, Christianity. When we look at the early history of these worships, we cannot but be struck by a decided difference between them, not the less marked because it is combined with real and considerable resemblances. Thus, both Greek and Roman cults were polytheistic, both were creedless, neither was attached to any system of ethics, both admitted, though neither required, the use of cult images and other visible objects of worship, both had their holy places and, sooner or later, their holy buildings, both had priests and priestesses, yet neither developed a powerful priesthood which could, as such, make its influence felt in politics or even in governing the life of the individual in any great detail; and, perhaps most important of all, both were closely attached to the organisation of the State and, before that existed, to the family, clan, or tribe. Yet the difference is striking and outstanding. The Greek religion, at all events the religion of those Greeks who were articulate enough to have left us records of what they felt and imagined, was that of a people intellectually lively to an extraordinary degree, inspired with a boundless curiosity which extended to the objects of their worship and the ritual with which their cult was conducted. Their most characteristic gods were clear-cut figures, described to us, alike in art and literature, under unmistakable forms (no one for instance would confuse a statue or a legend of Aphrodite with one of Athena), and each attended with a body, often very considerable indeed, of traditional tales, telling how this or that god or goddess was born, who the parents were, through what adventures the deity passed in childhood and later, what were his, or her, likes and dislikes, loves and hates. Such myths were by no means always edifying or to the credit of the divine being of whom they were told.

Zeus is on occasion tyrannous and often selfishly lustful, as are sundry other gods; Ares is a bloodthirsty swashbuckler, although divine; Artemis can take a cruel revenge for a trifling slight, Athena use her intelligence to cheat. In other words, these tales, where they are not the frivolous inventions of late writers who believed in the traditional deities hardly more than we do, are older than the great advances in ethics which convinced at least the more thoughtful Greeks that right and wrong are absolutes and the moral law binding on all rational creatures alike, whether mortal like ourselves or immortal. But like the scientific and philosophical discoveries which are due to that remarkable people, they result from their native curiosity, which was not content with the supposed fact that there existed supernatural beings potent to help or harm, but must needs consider, imaginatively or by some process of reasoning (but that was to come later) what manner of beings they were both in their outward forms and in their dispositions and tastes. A Greek must needs fancy or theorise concerning everything which came within his range of experience or belief and did not appear immediately obvious to him.

The Romans, on the other hand, were a singularly incurious folk. Their exploits in peace and war resulted from strong practical good sense and great industry, combined with sturdy fidelity to a few elementary principles, for example, that of loyalty to the existing constitution, whether of family, clan, tribe, or State. Thus, they early developed and step by step improved a military system better than that of any contemporary people, yet they wrote hardly anything on tactics or strategy. They constructed admirable buildings, roads and other public works, but made not the smallest contribution to such departments of learning as physics, or even the theory of structure. It would seem that they put up their bridges and constructed their highways by a sort of inspired rule of thumb. They were respectable land surveyors, yet even the most elementary mathematics remained something of a mystery to them. They conquered and governed a large part of the then known world, but the very name of geography is not of their language, and the works on that subject which have come down to us are either in Greek or obviously dependent on Greek models for their form, Greek collections of facts for their contents. Even in their greatest contribution to civilisation, jurisprudence, the fundamental maxims from which such works as Justinian's *Institutes* start are taken from Greek ethics.

This being so, it is quite understandable that they showed no curiosity about religious matters, save in so far as was necessary to secure proper means of intercourse with the gods in whom, in early times at all events, they firmly believed and whom they reverenced deeply. A god was a being possessed of that superhuman power which in Latin is called *numen*, at least from the second century B.C. onwards. The name of the deity was generally (not always, at least originally) of either masculine or feminine gender, and this was a useful guide in such matters as determining the sex of the victims to be offered. The divine functions extended to this or that sphere, which experts might seek to define closely; one appealed, for instance, to Ceres for a good crop of corn, to Mars for defence against foes visible or invisible who might endanger the homestead, to Juppiter for rain in season. Tradition, however originated, bade the worshipper approach the power in a certain way, generally with some fixed form of words to reinforce the ritual gestures and the approved offerings. This done with no omissions or mistakes, the divine response, in other words, the employment of the *numen* in the desirable way, might be looked for with some confidence. The divinity was not indeed compelled in any way to do as his worshippers asked, but there existed friendly relations between the two parties, the "peace of the gods" (*pax deorum*) as it was called, and there seems to have been a deep-seated conviction that as long as this was not broken by some offence on the part of the human beings concerned, the same reasonable and fair dealing might be expected as would be forthcoming from an honest fellow citizen or a foreign State which faithfully kept its treaty with the Roman people. But further than this the Romans in early days did not enquire. It was no business of theirs what their deities looked like, how they passed their time when not listening to their worshippers and attending to their wants, or punishing their offences, whether they were in any real sense male and female, and so forth. Hence the apparently total absence of Roman myths concerning their own or any other gods. The many stories about divine activities which we find in Roman authors such as Vergil and Ovid are without exception either taken directly from Greek sources with substitution of Latin for Greek divine names (Mars for Ares, for instance), or not even that (Apollo was taken over name and all), or else are new tales made up out of Greek materials, which represent nothing specifically Roman whatever. This lack of imaginative curiosity was not shared by all the ancient inhabitants of Italy. We find for instance Etruscan pictures plainly mythological and yet not representing any Greek story, which therefore presumably illustrate an Etruscan myth. But there is no evidence that the other peoples who spoke languages akin to Latin, such as Oscan, Umbrian, or Faliscan, were any more curious concerning the doings of the gods than the Romans themselves.

But another characteristic of the Romans, despite their intense pride of race and consciousness of superiority to other peoples, was their quick and intelligent readiness to learn, and especially to learn from the Greeks, little though they valued Hellenic abilities in practical things and deeply though the more conservative of them suspected Greek, and indeed all foreign, ways of living. By the time (the third century B.C. and afterwards) that Rome became well acquainted with the Greeks, especially with the Greeks who lived in Italy and Sicily, her own religion had absorbed sundry foreign elements and had developed in outward form in a manner not at all unlike that of Greece. It seems also to have been a regular, if tacit, assumption in antiquity that all peoples worshipped about the same gods, and identifications between the deities of different nations began early and continued throughout the historical period. Hence if the Greeks, purveyors of so much curious information on so many topics, told strange and fascinating tales about the doings of Zeus and Hera, Ares and Aphrodite, and so forth, clearly something of the kind was credible concerning Juppiter and Juno, Mars and Venus. That the new learning spread rapidly is plain from Plautus, for instance (died 184 B.C.), in one of whose plays, the *Cistellaria*, probably a rather early work, one character corrects the mistakes of another in the genealogy of some of the principal gods (*Cist.* 512-15). As this, starting from pure Roman presuppositions, is wholly artificial and foreign, and as the blunders are meant to be understood and laughed at by a Roman audience, evidently it had not taken Rome very long to learn the new tales. Rather more remarkable is the evidence, again from Plautus, that the irreverent attitude towards even the greatest gods which some of these stories imply gave little or no offence. In his *Amphitruo*, Plautus does not hesitate to make comic figures not only of Mercurius (Hermes) but of Juppiter, i.e., Zeus, himself.

It is therefore easy to understand that well before the beginning of the Empire Roman religion was no longer an entirely distinct phenomenon, but rather the local variety of Graeco-Roman cult, which was spread over much of the ancient world, absorbing more or less completely the worships of various European nations, whose native gods were identified to a great extent with those of Rome and consequently with Greek deities also. There were many local varieties in the manner of approaching these gods, and many local names remained unchanged. For example, a Roman worshipping Juppiter or Quirinus did so with a fold of his cloak pulled over his head, to shut out ill-omened sounds and sights, but when he invoked Apollo or Saturnus, he did so in Greek fashion (*Graeco ritu*), with the head uncovered. A Gaul, though he might call one of his native gods Mars or Mercurius, continued to pay his respects to the local "Mothers" (*Matronae*), as his ancestors had done. There were also barbarous rites, including human sacrifice, which the central government forbade and managed as a rule to stamp out. But the general pattern was fairly uniform, a temple for instance being substantially the same kind of building whether it stood in Athens, Rome, North Africa, or Britain. Like polytheisms generally, this kind of worship was hospitable, and readily admitted new gods from all manner of sources. Hence the flood of Oriental deities with their strange rites; hence also the growth of new "mysteries", not least those of Dionysos, which sprung up all over the Greek and Roman worlds. The language of most of these cults was Greek, which was the lingua franca of the Mediterranean, even in Italy, and the vehicle of the new Christian teaching. I have pointed out [1] that the two earliest communications to the young Church of Rome, the epistles of St. Paul and St. Ignatius, are in that tongue and not in Latin. Hence as the great new faith spread, it was aided not only by the existence of a civilisation mostly under one government and enjoying comparatively rapid and safe means of transport, but also of a general similarity in ideas of what constituted religion and the general knowledge, for purposes both of everyday life and of worship, of a single language. In time, Latin took the place of Greek for the West, but that was not till later, and even then it was

[1] *Ancient Rom. relig.*, p. 275 below.

primarily for those provinces of the Empire which were not directly in touch with districts where Greek was the native tongue. Even so, a traveller needed but two languages to be perfectly understood by at least most people whom he met, wherever he went in the countries which now make up western Europe, much of the Near East, and a wide strip of North Africa; a sharp contrast to their polyglot condition to-day.

Thus we find that the history of antiquity shows us the coming together of two main currents of religious custom, feeling, and experience, with additions it is true from other sources, some of them well known, some obscure, and the resultant blending of these different materials into one composite, but fairly self-consistent body, which in turn gave way to a new and higher development spreading gradually throughout the whole mass during the first centuries of our era, until it imposed its form and colour upon it all and resulted, at a time of increasing political chaos and break-up, in that religious unity which lasted, in Europe at least, until new divisions were brought about by the Reformation. I have tried, in the two little works brought together in this volume, to sketch the curious history of what I have styled the two main currents, from what we can discover of their springs down to the great stream formed by their union and the tributaries which flowed into it.

H. J. ROSE

St. Andrews, Scotland
March, 1959

ANCIENT
GREEK RELIGION

PREFACE

Many Greek names occur, of necessity, in a book of this kind, and they have been transliterated exactly, not into their Latinized forms, for the book is not written in Latin, but in English. A few exceptions have been made, however. Some names have an English form, as Athens, and this has been used. One or two are so familiar in the Latinized form as to have become English, as Thucydides. Here again, consistency has gone by the board. It may be noted that in the transliterations, *u* represents what Greek wrote and writes with a diphthong, as French does. To write it *ou* might suggest the sound which those letters have in the English word *house*, but never had in any Greek word at any period. A Greek *u*, which in the classical language was generally (not in all dialects) pronounced like the French one, is written *y*. In words transliterated from modern Greek, *dh* is the sound of English *th* in *then*, *gh* is the modern Greek gamma, pronounced a little farther back in the mouth than the English or German "hard" *g* (as in *go, gehen*), but like our consonantal *y* if it comes before *i* or *e*. An accent over a syllable of a modern word denotes stress; in antiquity, it meant a rise in the pitch of the voice. In the modern words, again, *ĕ* and *ai* are pronounced alike (like English *e* in *let*), but *aï* is English *I*. *Ē, i, oi, y*, are all like English *ee*.

H. J. Rose.

CHAPTER I

INTRODUCTORY

A STUDENT acquainted only with the faiths professed by civilized nations of to-day must begin by ridding his mind of several ideas of what constitutes religion, if he is to understand the beliefs and practices of classical Greece. A Christian or a Jew who takes his religion seriously is committed to belief in a number of advanced and subtle propositions concerning the nature of God and His relations to humanity. Also, he regards a number of actions of moral importance as dictated by his religion; thus, he must live either single or the faithful husband of one wife, because that is commanded; he must be strictly honest in money matters, for the same reason. If he neglects these duties, he is behaving like a bad Christian, or Jew, and if he disbelieves some of the doctrines he has been taught, he is to that extent heretical. In brief, his is a credal religion which embodies an ethical code. But the religion of ancient Greece had no creed and, although certain actions were irreligious and therefore generally condemned as displeasing to the super-natural powers, there was nothing like a code or system of morality which must be accepted by everyone who worshipped Athena or Zeus. Furthermore, a man's private beliefs were no concern of any ecclesiastical authority, provided they did not result in his trying to upset the established forms of worship or introduce new and unauthorized ones, and that they stopped short of denying that any such beings as the gods of the popular faith existed at all. It was, for example, perfectly allowable to go on worshipping Hera while accepting and teaching the philosophical doctrine that she was a personification of the air, or to consult the oracle of Apollo yet hold strongly that he was no other than the sun. The very words which signify, to us, a religious opinion, as "dogma," "faith," "heresy," "theology," have, in classical Greek, completely different associations. A dogma is the opinion of a philosopher or a philosophic school. Faith (*pistis*) is either trustworthiness and loyalty or acceptance of the truth of what someone says, or of his reliability in practical matters. A heresy (*hairesis*) is a philosophic, not a religious sect. Theology is much more nearly what we call mythology, often coupled with an attempt to discover some sort of philosophical belief concealed in the traditional opinions about the gods and their doings.

Ancient and modern religion come somewhat closer to each other on the ceremonial side. A modern Christian, Jew or Muslim, especially one who holds to the more ancient and traditional forms of his religion, has sundry observances which in themselves have no moral value, or only a very indirect one. He sets apart one day in every seven to be devoted principally to religious exercises of prescribed type. He abstains, always or at certain seasons, from various kinds of food. He will not perform sundry actions, perfectly innocent in themselves, at certain times; thus, if he is an orthodox Jew, he will not travel or transact any business on the Sabbath. On entering his place of worship he subjects himself to certain rules regarding dress, posture and gestures. All these things find their parallels, often close, in antiquity. For example, anyone wishing to handle sacred objects, which were very numerous, must first wash his hands. The worshipper who entered the sacred precincts on the Akropolis at Athens must leave his dog behind. Anyone praying to a celestial deity lifted his hands towards the sky; if he prayed to one of the powers of the underworld, he held his hands, palm downwards, towards the ground. If he offered sacrifice, the kind of beast to be killed, its sex and colour, the attitude in which it was to be held when its throat was cut, and many other details were prescribed more or less minutely. If he would deck the shrine of a deity with wreaths, a very common form of offering, not all plants, however ornamental, were allowable; for example, at Thebes no ivy might enter the temple of Aphrodite. A festal day recurring at short intervals, like the Christian Sunday, was no part of his calendar, but other festivals were common enough and occupied no small part of the year. We shall see presently that they attached themselves for the most part to the rhythm of the seasons.

But perhaps the greatest difference between classical Greek religion and the highest modern cults was that the latter are transcendental, holding out to their adherents hopes, not so much of prosperity in this life, as of future and eternal happiness. They have indeed their connexions with everyday routine, witness the various ceremonies such as prayer for rain or fine weather, for a blessing on some public or private undertaking, and the like; but even here, in the formulæ used at the great crises of life (birth, marriage, sickness, death) the emphasis is placed not so much on material as on immaterial things. In classical Greece it was not so. For instance: a baby was put through a ceremonial corresponding in some measure to baptism. But there was no idea of ridding it of purely spiritual ills, corresponding to original sin, or giving it new spiritual strength or purity. A little analysis of the rites in use makes it clear that the child was being cleansed, by material means, from the strangeness which in naïve belief clings to any newcomer, and so made a fully human being; to this day, a Greek infant not yet baptized is sometimes referred to as a drak, an ogre-like monster common in folktales. Also, it was ceremonially brought into contact with the family to which it would hence-forth belong, and thus made a proper object for all the care which a young child needs. Till then, nothing in the opinions of the average man prevented the new-born boy or girl from being exposed, i.e., simply left on the ground in some more or less lonely spot to take his chances of being picked up by a stranger or dying of hunger and cold. This was not the murder of a young member of the family, but merely refusal of admission into it and the society of which it formed part. The frequency of such an incident in Greek drama is enough to assure us that it was by no means unheard of, even at the height of Hellenic civilization; to take two examples out of scores, the *Ion* of Euripides and the *Arbitration* of Menander turn on the exposure, rescue and ultimate recognition of a child. Ceremonies reminiscent of our harvest festivals were very common in Greece, but here again, it is quite easy to see that their object was primarily to set going beneficent processes of a magical nature with the intention of continuing the fertility of the land. To bury the dead was an act of piety incumbent upon all, alike for friend and foe, kinsman and stranger, only the vilest criminals being refused formal sepulture; but the reason was that the dead belong to another world with which the living, and the gods of the living, have no concern, and the sooner they are dispatched to their own place, the better for the quiet of those left behind, for a restless, houseless ghost is formidable.

Being thus material in most of its objects, Greek religion was decidedly a thing of every day. The gods were not confined to their temples or to their heaven or nether realm, but were in the streets and houses of the people. Every hearth-fire was sacred; Hestia is the name alike of the place at which the fire was lit and of the rather vague and impersonal goddess who governed it. Before the house generally stood a little shrine, perhaps of Apollo of the Roads (Agyieus) or of Hermes, patron of all wayfarers and bringer of luck, sometimes of Hekate, not infrequently of a *héros*, or powerful and well-disposed ghost. In the house itself, the store-room was not complete without a large jar, containing portions of various foodstuffs, which was Zeus Ktesios, the divine guardian of the family's possessions, while Zeus Herkeios (He of the garth) watched over the court-yard. The blacksmith was the votary of Hephaistos, the herdsman adored Pan, Apollo Nomios (Him of the pastures) and the Nymphs, the farmer a multiplicity of deities, chief of whom was Demeter, the corn-goddess, the sailor others again, especially Poseidon (see pp. 50, 54-9). The great ceremonies in honour of the gods, at their own official residences, the temples and other shrines, might be comparatively rare; but for every-day happenings, the gods were about everyone's path and might be invoked at any moment, to confirm an oath, avert evil, heal sickness, or bless all manner of actions. There was a certain etiquette in dealing with them, as was natural, con-sidering their superiority to mankind, but it was simple for the most part, and connoted no very profound awe, still less servility. A Greek would say that he reverenced or tended this or that god, but very seldom that he was his slave; that is an oriental expression.

With this absence of other-worldliness in normal Greek religion went the choice of gods to be worshipped. A classical Greek acknowledged without demur the deity of sundry powers to whom he addressed neither prayer nor sacrifice. These included, not only such a grim figure as Hades, the Unseen

One who is lord of the nether world (his one cult in Greece is probably due to confusion with Pluton, giver of the wealth, *ploûtos*, of the fertile earth), but conspicuous and harmless or beneficent beings, such as the sky itself and the various heavenly bodies. Uranos (Heaven) is purely a mythological figure, whom no one worshipped; the Sun had no cult in Greece proper, the moon and stars none at all. And the reason is quite plain. These high and mighty ones stay in their own region, never descending to earth to meddle with the affairs of human beings. Therefore, as they show no concern for men, men need show none for them. It is very different with Zeus, the weather-god, the "cloud-gatherer," who can be seen gathering his clouds on the tops of high hills; with Kore, the Corn-Maiden, whose embodiment is the new harvest as it comes year by year; Hermes, who makes his power felt along roads and in wrestling-schools where young men congregate; the Nymphs, to whose influence is due the movement of streams and the growth of trees, and innumerable little local gods on whom the prosperity of small communities was traditionally thought to rest and to have rested for generations. All these and many more showed their powers and occasionally manifested their presence in visions to specially favoured worshippers in places where the ordinary man or woman commonly resorted for business or pleasure, in the houses where people lived and the fields or workshops where they earned their bread. They were members, however exalted, of the same communities, and so relations with them were inevitable and it remained only to know what sort of relations they preferred, with what words and actions they should be approached, what manner of gifts pleased them best, and what displeased them and so should be avoided in dealing with them.

For man had something to give in return for divine favours. It may be that few Greeks consciously thought what Aristophanes in one of his best comedies, *The Birds*, assumes, that the gods were dependent on their worshippers for sustenance, living somehow on the animal and other foods which were burned on their altars or otherwise offered to them, but certainly it was felt that they welcomed human gifts and human honours. According to some modern Greek peasants, the earth says to those that till it, "Give me, that I may give thee," and a very similar attitude seems to have been credited to the classical gods. How this may have been supposed to "work" is a question which will be discussed in a later chapter.

Another point which must be clearly grasped to start with, and will be explained in more detail later, is that the Greeks, like every other people we know anything about, were of mixed origin, and different elements in the population may well be supposed to have contributed different factors to the complex total of classical religion. Sometimes it is possible to trace some of these contributions to their source, but often we must confess our ignorance and content ourselves with avoiding over-simplified or too neat and symmetrical theories which the facts do not warrant. For example: there is no doubt that Greek gods fall into two main classes, Olympians, whose proper home is the sky and the highest mountain of the Greek region, Olympos in Thessaly, whose top visibly touches the heavens, and chthonians, dwellers in the *chthon*, an old word for "earth"; deities of the sea are in some sense intermediate. An old myth explained it by saying that when the ancient god Kronos ceased to be lord of the universe, his three sons cast lots for his former domain, and Zeus thereby got heaven, Poseidon the sea and Hades the nether world, the earth and Mt. Olympos remaining their common property. It is also generally acknowledged that the chthonians show rather more primitive features, in other words are somewhat nearer the kind of gods adored by savages, while the typical Olympians are more developed and more closely associated with the usages of a civilized people. It therefore was for a while a popular theory that the chthonians were gods of the old, pre-Greek population of the country, while the Olympians were brought in by the more progressive people who introduced the Greek language and some of the most characteristic features of Greek organization and general culture. That there was a pre-Greek population archæology shows clearly, for the remains of their rather backward communities have been examined and a few of their settlements, speaking a language wholly different from Greek, remained in historical times. That a new element, the people whom Homer calls Achaians, came into the country fairly early in the second millennium B.C. is likewise an established fact; it is probable that they created the culture called Mycenæan, certain that they brought with them the classical tongue and the rudiments at least of classical institutions, political and other. There is no reason to doubt that they likewise brought gods of their own, different from those worshipped by the earlier inhabitants, whom Greeks of the historical period knew as Pelasgians. We can actually point to holy places where a typically Greek divinity is worshipped along with one who either has no name or none that can be explained from Greek. There is no reasonable doubt that the newcomers included the greatest of the celestial gods, Zeus himself, nor that the "Pelasgian" deities were some of them chthonian. But to imagine that the Achaians worshipped only gods of the sky, the earlier natives only gods of the earth, is flying in the face of some of the clearest evidence. No chthonian is more important than Demeter, whose name is plain Greek; Athena is an important Olympian, and her name is not Greek at all, but of a form which is known to belong to the ancient and forgotten tongue of the earlier population.

On the whole, the religion we are discussing had its origins among a people who still lived simply, depending for their sustenance chiefly on what they could grow in their fields and gardens. Trade on a comparatively large scale and anything like organized industry came later. Hence, when the city-state became the normal Greek community, a certain amount of change in their religious rites was inevitable; with their increased wealth and greatly enhanced technical skill, they could give their gods more splendid festivals, and elaborate temples instead of rustic shrines to live in. At the same time, an element of unreality was imported into some of the holiest and most ancient rites, for what was essentially the worship of country folk had to adapt itself as best it could to the needs of town-dwellers. The progressive sense of this unreality and the attempts to find new reasons for old customs (for religion is conservative and does not take kindly to altering its established expressions) will occupy us later. One change certainly took place, for it became markedly the function of the gods, "saviours" as many of them were characteristically called, to save, not a small farming community against famine, but a comparatively large and complex state against political dangers. When the conventional gods showed themselves less and less able to do this, faith in their efficiency was bound either to decline to vanishing point or to take another, less material form.

At the same time that the community became larger, the individual's importance to it decreased. Obviously, to be one of a group of a few hundreds is to be a larger factor in the commonweal than if the population is counted in tens of thousands. But together with this went a vastly increased individual consciousness. With simple men, the individual is thought of and apparently thinks of himself mostly as a member of a group which regularly works together for its common ends, and therefore worships normally as a group, not as so many single persons. Thus all the early religions we know are congregational, not individual; the powers which are the objects of their cult are approached, in the most characteristic expressions of the religious life, by a whole community, performing rites of some sort in common. At least, the members of the community attend in a body when they are performed by the recognized experts, priests or medicine-men, and by means of them they seek to gain, it may be, good harvests, increase of their cattle, success in war with another tribe, or the like. Later, however, the individual, more important to himself and less important to the body of which he is a member, is increasingly apt to bring his personal wants and aspirations to the attention of whatever god or gods he may believe in. Therefore we expect, and in the religion of classical Greece we find, a development of individual worship. For example, one of the most popular gods in all Greece from the later years of the fifth century B.C. till the extinction of paganism before the rising power of Christianity was Asklepios, who, although he was abundantly honoured by various communities, was characteristically in receipt of appeals from individuals who came to him to have their illnesses cured by his superhuman medical skill. Since there was no official creed and no central authority to regulate belief, the individual could put what interpretation he chose on the rites, corporate or other, in which he took part, and that interpretation, in many cases, tended towards a belief far more other-worldly than we can find in earlier times. Lofty ideas borrowed from philosophies, little influenced in their origin by any properly religious tendencies, were read into ceremonials whose authors would have been much astonished to find themselves credited with any such intentions. Thus the way was paved for elaborately transcendental theologies, capable for a while of competing for the support of intelligent and pious men with the new faiths and their developed dogmas which were taking possession of the world. To trace this long and interesting process in its main features will be the object of this book; to discuss it in detail would need many volumes.

CHAPTER II

THE PLAIN MAN'S GODS

GREEK religion, as we find it in historical times, is a polytheism. Its gods are fairly numerous, and most of them are clearly defined figures, whose functions are less sharply differentiated than their personalities. Thus, while Ares is the war-god, a number of deities have warlike functions, notably Athena, while the Dioskuroi are helpers on occasion not only at sea but in battle. Demeter is the corn-goddess, but one of the titles of Zeus is Georgos, "Farmer". Apollo and Zeus alike give oracles, but oracular shrines of other gods are quite common, while several heroes have a similar function. Asklepios is the divine specialist in medicine, but miracles of healing are reported from shrines with which he has nothing to do. Artemis is generally the hunters' goddess, but we hear of hunting magic in connexion with Pan, and Artemis has another and an important duty, that of helping women in labour. These facts, even without many others which point the same way, would be enough to make it clear that the Greek gods were not the result of systematic division of the activities which most interest man between a number of figures imagined to have power over the world, but the fruit of a long growth, involving not only the development and modification of this or that deity but the combination into a kind of system of several different cults, some brought, as the last chapter mentioned, by the Greek-speaking immigrants into the peninsula, some existing before they came, while again we are justified in saying that different groups both of the newcomers and of the older inhabitants worshipped different gods originally. Polytheism is tolerant, as a rule, and when its adherents learn of deities other than their own, one of three things happens. Either they adopt them and worship them side by side with those they know already, or they acknowledge them as the proper objects of other people's cult (so a Hebrew of the older, pre-prophetic age, seems to have been quite ready to admit that Chemosh or Ba'al-Peor was a god, and to be worshipped by certain foreigners, while he and his compatriots maintained their adoration of Yahweh[1] and exalted him as being more powerful than the strange deities), or finally, they identify the new powers with their own supernatural beings, perhaps adopting the foreign name as a title of the native god, or contenting themselves with saying that such a people worship one of the deities they know, but call him by a different name. So various authors assure us that the Egyptians worship Hermes and Demeter, meaning Thot and Hat-hor. We can find examples in Greece of all these processes. There is good evidence that Dionysos came from abroad, probably from Phrygia, in historical times, and he seems to have brought his name with him. Kybele, Anaitis, and various Anatolian mother-goddesses are known to classical writers, but for the most part, Greeks left them to their own worshippers. When the Dorians came to Sparta, about 1,000 B.C., they brought a new goddess, Ortheia or Orthia, who in some ways resembled the old native deity Artemis. Before long, public opinion had decided that Ortheia was Artemis under a new name, or title, and Artemis Orthia, or Orthosia, for the unfamiliar word was modified, is a not uncommon figure.

But polytheism also, like every kind of religion, develops as the people practising it develop, from a simpler and ruder to a loftier and, generally, more complicated cult. The ancestors of the classical Greeks, like every other people, were once savages and their descendants retained some few traces, fossilized and harmless for the most part, of that stage of development in their worship as in their other customs. Barbarism, the next stage above savagery, left more and clearer traces on the classical civilization. Furthermore, since the basis of ancient culture was not industrial but agricultural, no region of the ancient world having anything comparable to our immense and complex factories, however much city life developed, a very large proportion of the population consisted of peasants, who, living in small communities with little opportunity for

---

[1] It is perhaps worth mentioning that there is no such name as Jehovah, which is a mixture of the consonants of Yahweh (Jahveh) with the vowels of *adonai*, "my lord," the phrase substituted for the unmentionable divine name in reading aloud.

self-improvement, kept the ways of their ancestors to a much greater degree than the less conservative townsfolk, and so continued to worship in a fashion very similar to that of earlier generations. Thus there survived among them, even to very late times, much of the ancient and simple approach to humble local deities, who might or might not be identified with the glorious figures of the great temples and festivals familiar to an inhabitant of such places as Athens. If we would learn what the earliest recoverable forms of Greek worship were like, we must go, not to our earliest written document, the Homeric poems, for they were composed for an aristocracy, much more advanced in its thought and practice than the poorer people over which it ruled, but to what authors of various dates tell us concerning the ways of the countryside. Fortunately, our material is fairly abundant, one of the chief documents being also one of the latest, the guide-book to Greece composed by Pausanias (second century A.D.), an intelligent and inquisitive man, for the benefit of tourists who, like himself, had antiquarian interests and a respect for the religion of the land whose language they spoke. Modern anthropology teaches us what to look for, in other words to recognize elements comparatively primitive when we find them.

Whatever may be the ultimate origin of religion, a question which it is fortunately unnecessary to go into for our purposes, two phenomena are certainly early, originating in a lower stage of civilization than any which we can now trace in Greek lands. These have been given the somewhat pretentious names of dynamism and animism, but they are perfectly simple and easy to understand, as one would expect, seeing that they are ideas of simple people.

The former is the notion, generally vague and hardly expressed in any definite words, that there exists a kind of power, not necessarily belonging to any particular sort of being, but most likely to be found in the possession either of a noteworthy man or woman, or of something which is not human at all, but more potent than mankind, a god, a spirit, a beast or bird (often credited with strange powers, because of the real strength or cunning which many of them have, or simply because their habits are imperfectly known). It may manifest itself in quite unlikely forms, dwelling, for example, in a stick or stone which is fancied to have peculiar properties, in magic regalia, or in forms of words, or ritual gestures. The best-known word describing it is perhaps the Polynesian and Melanesian term *mana*. Originally meaning no more than "strength," or, for it is both substantive and adjective, "strong," it tends to specialize. It works, says Bishop Codrington, who first brought *mana* to the attention of European investigators, "to effect everything which is beyond the ordinary power of men, outside the common processes of nature . . . When one has got it he can use it and direct it, but its force may break forth at some new point; the presence of it is ascertained by proof . . . This power, though itself impersonal, is always connected with some person who directs it; all spirits have it, ghosts generally, some men." "All Melanesian religion," he adds, "consists, in fact, in getting this Mana for one's self, or getting it used for one's benefit."[1]

The other phenomenon is animism, which is simply that attitude of mind that is unwilling to conceive of anything as really inanimate. It is as the result of many centuries' scientific thought that we now realize that a river, for example, is nothing but a quantity of water, an inorganic compound totally incapable of having any sort of life, set in motion by the mechanical action of gravity. How near the surface the older conception of it as a living thing lies is clear from the ease with which we speak of it as angry, gentle, furious, sluggish or the like, and that not simply in fanciful or poetical works of literature, but in speech which rises very little above the level of the most ordinary, everyday talk. To man at an earlier stage of his development, before any such great effort of exact and abstract thought had yet been made, even by the ablest of the race, it seemed perfectly obvious that a river was alive, for it behaved in many ways like a man or a beast. Like them it moved, and like them it uttered sounds; it might work harm or good, and at times it did strange and unaccountable things, such as disappearing underground to rise again farther on, or vanishing in summer to reappear in winter. Furthermore, rivers are not all alike, since some flow swiftly, others slowly, some have

[1] R. H. Codrington, *The Melanesians*, Oxford, 1891, p. 118 foll.

clear and some muddy water, and so forth. The conclusion was obvious, given the very limited knowledge of nature then available; a river was a powerful living being, possessed of much *mana*, either the body or the habitation of someone greater than man—this was the usual Greek way of regarding it—or in some other and mysterious fashion having a life and a will of its own, and so much power that it was well to treat it with respect and avoid making it angry. It is not a matter for surprise that in early Greek thought and, later, Greek poetical imagination, rivers were holy and every river had its indwelling god, often thought of as having something of the shape of a bull, the strongest and, when bellowing, the most noisy beast known to their zoology. To men whose occupations made them on occasion ford large streams swollen by winter rains, the tale of how the river Acheloos once did battle with Herakles and was overcome only after a hard struggle was nothing incredible. The unusual feature of the story was that the river-god appeared in visible form, or rather in several forms, now as a bull, now as a serpent. But Herakles was an unusual man, half-divine, and might be expected to see the very persons of gods when an ordinary mortal would see nothing but those parts of nature which they immediately controlled. And this tendency to animism, coupled, it would seem, with a belief in something very like *mana*, credited life and power to many things further removed from any appearance of life than flowing water. No human beings can long be ignorant of the force of sexual passion, and it is therefore not surprising that Desire (Eros) had his worshippers at Thespiai in Boiotia. But the curious thing is, not that they recognized the existence of such a power, but that they seem to have concluded that his *mana* was centred in so unlikely an object as a rough stone. This is but one of many such holy stones which were honoured up and down Greece, and continued to be held in much reverence long after they had been supplemented in most places by images of the deities supposed to have their seats in them. For instance, Orchomenos, another Boiotian city of great age, venerated the Charites, goddesses whose name, the Gracious or Lovely Ones, seems to refer originally to their power of making the fields take on the "lovely" appearance which a good harvest gives them. Greek artists found them promising subjects and visualized them as young women, slender and graceful, and statues of them, no doubt of that kind, were at Orchomenos when Pausanias visited it. But these were modern dedications of his own day, and not the chief objects of worship. The really venerable things were again certain unshaped stones, which may well have been meteorites, since the story went that they had fallen from heaven in the days of the mythical king Eteokles. Here we perhaps have one of the reasons for the cult of rude stones; a meteorite is rare and impressive enough to give rise to a belief in its supernatural powers, especially among people who have no idea whatever of its actual nature. Others again of these ancient holinesses may have been old standing stones, similar to those which are found in many parts of Europe to this day, relics of a neolithic population. Be that as it may, such cults were quite common in antiquity, and the ultimate explanation would seem to be that for some reason which appeared to them sufficient the inhabitants concluded that the stones were either the abodes of invisible beings or contained *mana*.

It need not follow that they proceeded to identify the shapeless objects of their worship with any of the greater or lesser gods familiar to them and, through the numerous works on ancient mythology, to us also. True, such identifications were not unknown; thus, at Pharai in Achaia, alongside a statue of Hermes, whose temple was in their market-place, there stood some thirty stones, not quite unwrought, for they had been squared, and the inhabitants associated the name of a god with each. But not only were there altars frankly dedicated to unknown gods, for instance at Athens and Elis, but several deities locally venerated seem to have had no names. Thus, not far from Megalopolis in Arkadia there was the shrine of a power known simply as the Good God (Agathòs Theós), while in the region of Bulis, near Phokis, although the inhabitants knew of and worshipped some of the generally recognized gods and goddesses, their chief veneration was for a being whom they called by no name but only by a title, Mégistos, the Very Great. This and like facts may underlie the theory of Herodotos that the Pelasgians knew no divine names at all till they were instructed from abroad; to us it proves one of two things, either that the local conception of deity was somewhat vague—there was some one spot in the district where the presence of divine power was recognized, and the *mana* which showed itself there was given a complimentary title but nothing more—or else the name of their deity was a secret too precious to be revealed, and they would tell it to nobody. This last involves a very old idea indeed, that the name is part of the person and he who knows the correct name has power over its owner. It is a persistent notion, showing itself in countless charms, when the wizard claims to invoke the power he wishes to press into his service by its one true name, but its origins go far back in the history of mankind. When, whichever of these explanations is the true one, we find some obscure and unnamed power the chief object of a little Greek community's adoration, we get a glimpse into the origins of their elaborate polytheism; the great Olympian family of which, in the orthodox mythology, Zeus is the head has received contributions from many quarters, and this is one reason why the functions often overlap, as they would not do if originally the gods had all been conceived by the same group of worshippers at the same time. Naturally, any society which believed in such beings at all would ask much the same favours from them, sufficiency of food, safe delivery for their women, increase of their flocks and herds, protection against enemies, human or bestial. Therefore, when a deity belonging to another group was, for any reason, adopted it did not by any means follow that he or she was credited with the power to give different gifts, but might have been called in to provide more efficiently the blessings which the power or powers already worshipped seemed unable or unwilling to bestow in sufficient measure.

Looking again at these gods of the simpler Greek communities, we find them often vague in their nature and sometimes limited in their functions to a far greater degree than the better-known deities. Pan has been mentioned already in another context; it is noteworthy that some at least of his worshippers were none too certain whether he was one or many; at all events, Aristophanes and Plato, to say nothing of later authors, have heard of the plural, Panes. But this is exactly what, under the circumstances, we should expect, and indeed find in several like cases. It is probable on the whole that his name means the Feeder or Pasturer. We can easily imagine that in Arkadia, where he was originally worshipped, many little groups of herdsmen devoutly adored each its divine Pasturer, perhaps represented by some stick or stone set up in a holy place, and quite possibly each group was ready to proclaim the superiority of its own Pan to everyone else's. This might well be so, whether the god had originally been conceived as a single being or a plurality, for local cults tend to break up in this way. Nothing can be more certain than that the Virgin Mary is one person in every kind of Christian theology, and no cult is more widespread in modern Greece than hers; but I have read of a Chian peasant who proclaimed in emphatic and not over-delicate language that the Panaghià (the All-Holy One, her popular name) of his village church could outdo all other Panaghiès whomsoever.

This same divine Pasturer was never a very exalted figure, nor always treated with profound respect, or what we should regard as such, even by those who worshipped him in all sincerity. His business (a god has his duties; even Zeus is commended for "doing well" when he sends seasonable rain) was to keep his herdsman-worshippers well supplied with meat. The obvious way to do this was to make their flocks and herds increase abundantly, and theirs were mostly small cattle, sheep and goats, especially, it would seem, the latter. Now the obvious increaser of a herd of goats is the he-goat, and a divine he-goat is essentially what Pan was supposed to be. When represented by an image at all, he regularly has goat's legs and a shaggy beard, and his few legends make him out to be as lustful as his prototype. His power was not unfailing, and, like that of not a few gods of sundry religions, might need stimulation and renewal at times. We know how this was done; if the meat supplies, whether got from the flock or by hunting, were scanty, the boys used to beat Pan (i.e., his statue or whatever object represented him) with squills, a plant supposed to have the virtue of driving away evils. Thus they at once roused the god to further efforts and rid him, to the best of their ability, of whatever unlucky influence had hindered his activities. That children should be the officiants in this quaint rite is characteristic of many magical processes.

Magic, indeed, of a simple and unlearned kind, very different from the complicated sorceries of later days, with their elaborate charms, formidable lists of outlandish names of power, and extraordinary recipes, such as must be briefly discussed later in this book, was much in vogue among these early communities. We get a glimpse of this from Hesiod, the first surviving writer who set out, not to entertain his audience simply, but to give them good advice and information. His home was Askra in Boiotia, a little country town, his status that of a small yeoman farmer and his date perhaps the eighth century B.C. Side by side with directions for making a plough, the dates proper for sowing and other agricultural processes, and such obviously practical matters, he sets forth, with exactly the same intention of giving useful counsel, a number of precepts which are apt to sound odd and superstitious to a modern, but certainly were taken seriously in his day. Here is one of them:

"Do not ford the fair-flowing water of perennial streams till thou hast prayed, turning thine eyes towards those fair currents, and washed thy hands in the clear water. For he who crosses a river evilly, with unwashen hands, with him the gods are wroth and send him woes thereafter."

This is an excellent example of that animism which was discussed on page 21. The river is a living thing, which will hear the wayfarer's prayer, no doubt for leave to trouble it by crossing. It is powerful and influential, for an insult to it is resented by "the gods" generally, to whose exalted company it belongs. Therefore the proper etiquette must be observed in dealing with it. First, the traveller should wash his hands in the water, thus at once getting rid of any pollution which may defile them and coming into contact with the stream, as it were shaking hands with it. Then, politely asking it to excuse the liberty he takes, he may venture across. Politeness must be observed likewise in dealing with all manner of powers, whether visible or not. The humbler bodily wants ought not to be attended to, another precept tells us, where the sun can see us, nor in an open place at night, "for the nights belong to the Blessed Ones," but in all possible seclusion. Someone, whether Hesiod himself or another, adds at the end of the poem (hence a part of its usual title, *Works and Days*) a curious list of lucky and unlucky days of the lunar month. For example, a boy born on the twentieth will be intelligent; the tenth, too, is a good birthday for a boy, the fourteenth for a girl, and also the fourteenth is an excellent day to start training a dog or breaking in a mule or ox, whereas the fourth days from the beginning and end are alike hopeless for work of any sort, as they bring nothing but trouble. It is likewise a fact, though this is known to but few, that the last day of a lunar period is the very best time to launch a ship. The nineteenth has its good points, especially in the morning and the late afternoon, but the fifth is to be avoided, for that is the birthday of Horkos, the grim power which punishes those who break their oaths (*horkoi*).

From about the time of Hesiod onwards, the number of powers to be revered was augmented by the widespread worship of "the gentry" (*héroës*), generally known to us as hero-cult. The original meaning of the word *héros* is simply a man of good family, a gentleman, especially, it would seem, a member of one of the old Achaian families whose exploits form the theme of Epic poetry for the most part. In Homer there is no indication that such men, though honoured "even as gods" in life, if they were worthy of their high position in society, were invoked after their death to help the living, but later this is exceedingly common. Perhaps the intervening Dorian invasion, which completely changed the political complexion of a great part of Greece and gave the poorer people a new and not too popular set of lords, had surrounded the older aristocracy with a halo of regretful glory, obscuring their weak points and lighting up their virtues. Certainly the views concerning the fate of man after death had changed. For Homer and his audience, this life is all that really matters; death is not annihilation, but for all alike, a few special favourites or enemies of the gods alone excepted, it means passing into a mere shadow of existence, in which the soul can do no more than engage in a kind of pale reflexion of its earthly activities. It would seem that the common people believed that

anyone powerful or otherwise remarkable in life continued to
be so after death. At all events, historical Greece was full of
the tombs, real or supposed, of such persons, and the cult given
them differed from that of chthonian gods only in being on
the whole less important and more strictly local; a "hero" was
not able, it would seem, to do either good or ill far from the
spot where his bones lay. Hence there was on occasion keen
competition for the possession of these relics; Athens brought
back from the island of Skyros some bones supposed to be
those of Theseus, Sparta attributed an important success to
the recovery from Tegea of certain gigantic remains confidently
identified with those of Orestes, while Thebes boasted the
possession of Hektor's body, fetched from Troy in obedience
to an oracle. An oracle also bade the remains of Theseus and
Orestes to be acquired, for Delphoi warmly supported this
popular cult of the great dead, and even sanctioned the honouring as a "hero" of an occasional person merely notorious.
Also, this wide-reaching form of worship caused not a few
minor local deities of the earth and its fruits to be confused
with the venerated ghosts, as happened for example at Amyklai
in Lakonia, where a very old deity, Hyakinthos, was fitted
with a comparatively new legend which told how he had been
a boy favoured and accidentally killed by Apollo. Even the
greater deities were subject to such a confusion now and then;
there is no reasonable doubt that the "heroine" Kallistó,
venerated in Arkadia, is no other than Artemis herself, whose
title Kallíste (Fairest) had taken on independent existence.

Besides all these, Hesiod is of opinion that there are innumerable, though invisible, beings who do good or evil to
mankind. In the Golden Age there lived men far superior in
every way to us; when they died they became *daímones*—
possessors, we might say, of *mana*—who walk invisible on the
earth, guarding mankind and bringing prosperity. On the other
hand, spirits of disease flit about, both by day and by night,
bereft of the power of speech but not of the power to harm us.

The plain man, then, in ancient Greece lived in a world
full of all manner of supernatural powers, great and small,
friendly and unfriendly, and naturally tried to get and maintain
right relations with them. This was done partly, as we have

seen, by avoiding unlucky actions and days as much as possible.
Such avoidance was not wholly a matter of magic and superstition, for quite early, not least in Hesiod himself, the idea was
current that at least some of these beings, and above all Zeus,
cared for the morality of mankind. If men will do justly both
by fellow-countrymen and strangers, he teaches, the gods will
reward them with prosperity; their fields will yield bounteous
harvest, the oaks will bear plenty of acorns and wild bees make
their hives in them, the flocks and herds will increase, the
women will bear healthy children. But for those who practise
hybris, wanton disregard for the rights of others, there are
none of these blessings, but rather plague, famine, sterility, and
disaster in war, or shipwreck at sea. We must not, however,
suppose all Greek country folk to have had so advanced an
idea of divine morality. Again and again we hear that it was
commonly supposed that the gods could be coaxed or bribed
into overlooking offences, that they are very long-suffering
and so forth, while throughout antiquity, and not only among
the humbler minds, the problem is discussed why, if there are
gods and they care anything for justice, the good are by no
means always prosperous nor the wicked always unfortunate.
Indeed, to believe as Hesiod did was never part of ancient
religion, which, as already pointed out, had neither a creed nor
a moral code, but the fruit of private reflexion on the data
available.

The average person, then, might mend his ways lest Zeus
or some other god be angry with him, but he certainly would
engage in the prescribed rites to win the favour of the powers,
great or small, whom he and his fellows supposed likeliest to
bless or ban him and his community. From a number of
sources we can put together a sort of composite picture, perhaps not exactly true for any one place or time, but accurate
enough in its main outlines, of how ordinary Greeks behaved
towards their deities. A little has been said in the first chapter
about the household observances; something can now be
added, especially regarding the great crises of life, birth,
marriage, and death.

The birth of a child, especially a son, was normally a welcome event, in ancient Greece as elsewhere. For a son's duties

included, not only care for his parents' old age, when they could no longer work for themselves, but tendance of their ghosts when they died. The dead of the family or clan (*génos*) had not ceased to be members of it, and being senior members, they were entitled to respect and good usage. This is a different thing from the hero-cult already described, although allied to it; it would seem that the care bestowed on the ghost of a father or mother did not differ essentially, in intention at least, from that given to the aged and infirm. Ghosts, in popular belief, continued to live vaguely in the nether world; as usual, the details of the belief were self-contradictory, for the departed seem to have been thought of as continuing to exist both in their graves and in a land of the dead, governed by Hades (the Unseen One; much later, the name is used for his realm instead of himself) and his queen Persephone, or Persephassa, and cut off from our world by water, most commonly by the river Styx (the Abhorrent), which is a real stream in Arkadia, but apparently was thought to continue its course somewhere underground. Wherever they might be, however, they had much the same wants as in life, food, drink, clothing, and water to wash in, for the Greeks were a very cleanly people. Hence foods and drinks were the commonest of offerings at graves. Aeschylus preserves a list of these *meiligmata*, or things calculated to win the good graces of the departed; they are milk, honey (reputed to be a great preservative of life, hence doubtless acceptable to those who have lost their normal lives), pure water, wine and olive oil. All these being liquids, they are often called *choaí*, substances which can be poured, and they were emptied into a pit dug on or near the grave, to ensure their reaching their proper destination. Occasionally, to make quite sure, the body was provided with a kind of tube running down to it from the outside of the tomb.

To return, however, to the arrival of the baby, the mother when her pains came on her would invoke Artemis or Eileithyia, the divine specialists in midwifery, to help her, and the mortal women, professional midwives or sympathetic neighbours, who attended her might use charms or medicines reputed to hasten delivery. The newborn child was in need of a proper rite of reception into the family and human society generally, and we have some idea of how this was done. The Athenians called it "the running around," *amphidrómia*, and it took place, says one ancient authority, on the fifth day, others say the seventh or tenth, after the birth. All who had attended the mother ceremonially cleansed their hands and so purified themselves; for parturition is a magically dangerous business besides its physical perils, and those who have anything to do with it are *tabu* in the opinion of practically every people on earth below the highest levels of modern civilization. So dangerous was it, in Greek opinion, that it might not take place on consecrated ground, any more than that equally ominous process, death. But the baby needed something more elaborate. Therefore the officiants in this homely rite stripped themselves naked and one of them, picking up the child, ran with it around the family hearth. The object of this performance is plain enough. The child, held against the naked body of one of the family, is brought into the closest possible contact with its kinsfolk. At the same time it is moved quickly through the air, in hopes of blowing off its strangeness, and exposed, though not so nearly as to hurt it, to the heat of the fire, which purifies, being the holy fire of Hestia, and also presumably burns away any ill-luck which the newcomer may carry. Now the child is one of the household, and further to cement the new relationship, presents were made it by friends and relatives; curiously enough, they normally consisted of octopods and cuttlefish, which were and are commonly eaten in Greece but are hardly suitable infant diet. The tenth day after birth, whether or not it was the date of this ceremony of reception, was the name-day of the baby, though here again some preferred the seventh, and friends and neighbours were invited to the Greek equivalent of a christening feast. A sacrifice regularly took place, and the meat of the victim furnished the staple of the meal. Meat, then as now, was something of a luxury to the average Greek, whose more usual diet was bread, salads and vegetables, olive oil, cheese, honey, and, when he could get it, fish. The gods shared the tastes of Achaian nobles, who disliked fish and were hearty eaters of meat. More presents to the child were the rule on occasions when people saw it for the first time, whether soon after the birth or not, and birthdays were observed, much as with us.

Marriage was celebrated with more observance of its essential ritual than we are accustomed to, for with us the real ceremonial is overlaid, often displaced altogether, by a religious or civil formality, or both. The fundamental parts of a true wedding ceremony are three; the bride must cease to be her father's daughter, she must be protected against evil influences during the short time when she is neither daughter nor wife, and therefore has no household gods of her own, and she must be assimilated to the family of the bridegroom. The first part of the ceremony we know little about, but it was proper for her to make a great show of reluctance; "to cry like a bride" seems to have been a proverbial saying. In some places a symbolic action marked the final departure from home; the axle of the wagon on which she was brought to her new house was solemnly burned, signifying that she was never to go back again. On the way, she was accompanied by friends and well-wishers of both parties, singing, joking, and raising the ritual cry ô hymèn hymenaîe, whose meaning, if it ever had one, was so thoroughly forgotten in classical times that the traditional words were commented upon in more or less ingenious stories about someone called Hymen, man or god, who had done something connected with married happiness. On arrival at the bridegroom's home, she was received with a shower of katachŷsmata, i.e., nuts, fruits and sweetmeats, which were flung over the bridegroom also. Whatever the ultimate reason for this, a point not settled among modern students of ancient ritual, it was a recognized way of ushering in a newcomer who was henceforth to belong to the household, for it was done also on the arrival of a newly bought slave. But there is little doubt of the reason for the noisy procession, especially the broad jokes which were proper on such occasions. Such merrymaking, the more indecent the better, is very offensive to the powers of infertility and evil generally, which appear, the world over, to be great prudes. Therefore it keeps them away, or drives them off if they are already present. Both bride and bridegroom had their attendants, corresponding to our best man and bridesmaids; hers were girls of about her own age, and part of their business

was to sing the epithalamium which accompanied the retire-
ment of the newly-married pair to their bedroom. Fragments
of other ceremonials have come down to us, mostly through
the good offices of ancient scholars who interpreted the names
of them to ages which used other rites or at least called them
something else. One of the bride's protections consisted of a
sieve which she carried; the reason is easy to suggest, for it is
a thing used up and down Europe to baffle evil spirits. They
cannot, it appears, resist trying to count the holes in it, and while
they are doing that, they are out of mischief. In some modern
forms of the belief, they are unable to pronounce "three," because
that is the number of the Trinity, and so go on saying, "one,
two, one, two," till they are hopelessly confused. We may guess
that whatever evil things plagued a Greek bride were stopped
in like manner at one of the ancient sacred numbers, possibly
seven, Apollo's number. We also know a little of the ritual
which the bridegroom went through when he formally made his
newly-married wife's acquaintance; it involved the removal
of her veil and the presentation to her by him of the "gifts of
uncovering" (*anakalyptéria*), in itself a rite of union, for to
give part of one's property is to give a piece of one's self and
therefore a kind of communion with the recipient. On another
occasion, when sometime after the wedding the bridegroom
formally called on the bride's family and spent the night there
without her, he and she gave one another gifts, hers being a
cloak, perhaps of her own weaving, for him to wear. But the
whole affair, from betrothal till after the consummation of the
union, was girt about with ceremonial, no doubt intended to
secure divine protection and favour. One rite was of a kind by
no means peculiar to weddings, but found in many contexts.
Before her marriage, the girl cut off some of her hair and dedicated it to an appropriate power. At Athens, Hera, Artemis and
the Moirai, the "Apportioners" who attended (and, in popular
belief, still attend) a birth and decide what the future destiny
of the child is to be, were the recipients. At Troizen, or Trozen,
in the Peloponnesos, the hair was left at the supposed tomb of
Hippolytos, the unfortunate son of Theseus whose untimely
death furnished Euripides with the subject-matter of two
plays. It is obvious enough that a lock of hair is a thing of little

value; but if we remember that sorcerers have often been supposed to work magic against a person if they had some of his hair in their possession (a belief attested from classical antiquity), we can see a reason for it. The goddess or the hero was thus enabled to work kindly magic upon the dedicatress. For a very similar reason, boys when they were coming to manhood gave some of their hair, generally, to the local river. Without water there is no life, and with the hair in his possession the good river-god was in a position still to infuse life into his former nurseling. But, although this was probably the original meaning of such offerings, their beginning lies so far in the past that even the earliest Greek writings we have seem to regard them as nothing more than acknowledgements of past favours, thank-offerings and not quasi-magical performances.

Male or female, members of a family, and therefore of the clan or *génos* to which it belonged, had, as such, their religious duties. Occasionally we find a priestly clan, such as the Eumolpidai of Eleusis, who had their definite functions in connexion with the Mysteries, but quite apart from this there can have been few if any families, and pretty certainly no clans or local organizations such as villages or demes (a *dêmos* is the Attic unit of population and land, which corresponded more or less to our parish) without their own cults, of some minor god or hero, or of one of the greater gods, recognized, it might be, as ancestral (*theòs patrôos*), which commonly meant that descent from him was claimed. Of the details of such worship, however, we know little, but we are informed to some extent concerning the cults which every household had. It has already been mentioned that some of them were associated with the great name of Zeus and that the hearth, Hestia, was a goddess receiving her due worship from those who cooked and warmed themselves at her fire; when hero-cult was established, not a few houses had each its *héros oikurós*, the friendly ghost who "kept the house," and commonly appeared in the form of a harmless snake, such as still haunts Greek country houses and is often known as the "master," *aphentikó*, and treated kindly in the belief that he will bring luck. Snakes generally were regarded by the ancients as uncanny and, because of their habit of living in holes of the earth or the crannies of walls, as belonging to the lower world, and so very fit vehicles for spirits of the dead, though it would be a gross mistake to suppose that every serpent treated with respect by an ancient Greek was supposed to be a ghost. It would be still more unjustifiable to fancy that they venerated all snakes; on the contrary, most of them were simply regarded as noxious creatures, to be killed at every opportunity. But some species were known or supposed not to be venomous, and if one of them appeared in a house, its owner would take more or less notice, according to his degree of religiosity. The fussily pietistic man (*deisidaímon*, he who dreads the supernatural; the word usually has a bad sense, though it can correspond to our "God-fearing") in Theophrastos, if he finds a snake of the sort called "holy" in his house, at once sets about making a hero-shrine for it. It is a fair deduction that the average householder would not jump to any such conclusion, but would watch to see if the creature came again or behaved in any remarkable way.

Since the gods were about everyone's path, indoors or out, it is no wonder that signs of their presence and intentions were common. A belief in omens was and continued to be universal among the general run of people throughout antiquity; indeed such a belief is by no means dead in our own day. Theophrastos' pietist again differs from his fellows not by believing in such things but by seeing them everywhere. Even a mouse nibbling at a leather sack is an omen to him, and he is very dissatisfied when an official interpreter of portents is unimpressed and tells him he had better get the sack mended again; while if a weasel runs across the road he waits for someone else to go along it before he dare tread on such a dangerous spot, or at least he performs a little counter-magic to nullify so terrible a sign. The average ancient had more common sense than to be frightened by every small creature he saw, but some kinds of animal behaviour attracted general attention, notably the cries and flight of the larger birds, especially the birds of prey which, not flying in flocks, are easier to observe. Hence the name for this kind of bird, *oionós*, or even "bird" in general, came to mean "omen," and instances of public and private observation of these signs are abundant. A bird-watcher in antiquity was not a naturalist but a professional interpreter of the warnings they gave, and there was a traditional science of augury, at least as old as Homer's day, which found favourable portents or the reverse in such details as the kind of cries the birds uttered, the direction in which they flew, their position (right or left, the former being generally the lucky side) relative to the observer, and so forth. Indeed, the universal itch to know the future in advance was rife throughout the ancient civilizations, Greek and other, and this kind of omens was only one of the many ways in which they tried to discover what was to happen, and especially whether any enterprises they had undertaken or planned were likely to succeed or fail. As was natural, one of the commonest ways of looking for information was to ask a god, for the gods know and can control events, both present and to come. The great oracles will be spoken of later, but any god might send a warning dream or other sign, and one at least, Hermes, was, at his shrine at Pharai in Achaia, a practitioner of a kind of divination known as the *kledón*, a word which persists into modern Greek and still means a sort of popular fortune-telling. The consultant went to his statue where it stood in the temple, in the evening, filled and lit the lamps which stood before it, burned incense in the hearth, laid a bronze piece of the local coinage on the altar, and whispered his question into the ear of the image. Then, stopping his own ears with his fingers, he left the temple, and as soon as he had got outside the market-place where the shrine stood, he unstopped his ears and listened to the talk of any chance passers-by. The words he overheard were his answer. It was a general belief that on occasion ordinary people were prompted to use words which meant more than they knew; this is a *kledón*, and doubtless at Pharai it was Hermes who put it into the minds of those about the neighbourhood of his temple to mention, for instance, the great profit which someone had made by trading if the enquirer had asked if he should venture his capital in the enterprise he had in mind, or to speak of shipwreck if the question was, "Shall I make a voyage?"

Quite apart from divination, the average ancient Greek was never far from the visible signs of the gods' presence, for their holy places, statues and the like were everywhere, and must be treated with respect. Again Theophrastos' pietist shows us by his exaggerations what a normal person would do. If he finds a holy stone at a cross-roads (a likely place for them; cross-roads are uncanny in most countries, and so the more divine help can be got there, the better), he will oil it, drop on his knees and adore it. Probably almost everyone would show respect in one way or another; a common gesture was to kiss one's hand to the holy thing. Even the most casual would avoid injuring or defiling it in any way; when the Hermai in Athens, upright stones improved by carving a human head at the top and a phallus half-way up, and usually dedicated to the god after whom they were named, were found one morning mutilated, the whole city was in an uproar and a long series of trials for impiety followed. To this day we are not sure whether the business arose out of the foolish and drunken freak of a few young men, or was a political plot to "spread alarm and despondency" at a critical moment in the history of Athens. Moralizing writers are full of tales of the terrible things which befell rash individuals who, under stress of wartime conditions or for some other reason, robbed or otherwise insulted shrines, and other stories were current of images which had shown by miraculous movements, closing their eyes or the like, their indignation at impious deeds committed in their presence.

At stated seasons, usually having a relation to the various activities of the farm, such as sowing, spring and autumn ploughings and harvest, a festival of some kind would engage the activities either of the whole community or of some considerable part of it, for example, all the women, or all married women. Something more will be said of these holy-days when we discuss the religion of Greek cities; for the present it is enough to explain the normal central rites which belonged to all of them. To approach a god in due form it was proper always to bring a gift, and, apart from dedications of statues and other ornaments for the shrine, the commonest gifts were food, either cereal, animal or both, drink, and incense. The gods were not unreasonable, and did not exact costly offerings from those who could not afford them; again to consult current ancient tales, we are told of offerings of a handful of meal or

some other trifle from a poor man which were declared highly
acceptable because they were presented with sincere piety.
But the characteristic sacrifice was a head of larger or smaller
cattle, usually, though there are exceptions, of the same sex
as the power to whom it was offered. Whatever may be the
ultimate origin of such rites, there is no doubt that to the
average ancient the object was to give the god good food, and
when worshipping an Olympian, the sacrificer and his friends,
which in the case of a communal sacrifice meant the members
of the community, or at least some of them, shared the meal,
indeed took the best of the meat for themselves. An old story,
known to Hesiod, told why this was so. Prometheus, the fire-
god who was consistently the friend of man, had beguiled
Zeus in ancient days by killing a sacrificial ox, making up the
meat into two parcels, and asking the god which he would
have. One parcel contained the offals, disguised with a coating
of fat outside; the other had all the best cuts, inconspicuously
packed. Zeus took the richer-looking bundle, and saw too late
that he was befooled. To a modern, it seems probable that the
most essential thing about sacrifice was originally to give the
life of the victim to the gods, to increase their *mana*, and therefore the vital organs were their especial portion. But be this
as it may, the beast was slain with due ritual. The altar itself
and the hands of the worshippers were purified with water
(*chérnips*, literally "handwasher"; to share the same *chérnips*
constituted a sacral bond). The beast was led up to the altar,
where it was thought a good omen if it seemed to go willingly,
a bad one if it struggled. Barley was formally sprinkled, apparently on the ground, the beast was knocked down and stunned
with an axe, then its muzzle was pointed upwards and its
throat cut. The women, if any were present, raised the ritual
cry called *ololygé*, a high-pitched, tremulous sound ending on
a yet higher note and apparently expressing joyous excitement.
Then the beast was skinned and cut up; the entrails, with portions cut from every limb, were wrapped in fat and laid on
the altar-fire. The rest formed the material for the feast, the
inedible parts being disposed of in one way or another. Often
the hide was the perquisite of the priest, if one had officiated,
which was neither invariable nor necessary, and not infrequently

such remnants as the bones were buried in the holy ground of the precinct where, generally, the rite took place, though there was nothing that we know of to prevent an altar being erected and a sacrifice offered on any ground which was not in some way polluted or otherwise supposed to be offensive to the deity. In later times at all events, if there was more flesh than could be eaten on the spot, it might be taken to the nearest market and sold like any other meat. If the victim was an ox or bull, its skull was often fastened up outside the temple, or, if the offering had been made by a private individual on his own property, outside his house.

This procedure was what the Greeks called a *thysía*, or burnt-offering. If the god approached was not an Olympian but a chthonian, the ritual was different in several ways. The victim, normally white for an Olympian, must now be black or dark-coloured. Its head was pointed down, not up, when it was killed, and not infrequently its body was not burned but disposed of in some other way. In any case, the god normally was given the whole of it, and the reason for this is fairly obvious; though the gods of the earth and the nether world were not evil, they were formidable, and the close communion with them implied in the shared meal was not wanted. A sacrifice to them was not called a *thysía*, but generally an *enágisma*, which means simply consecration. Finally, the proper times for the two kinds of offering differed; for the sky-gods, morning, at any rate daylight, and the full moon or the waxing moon were appropriate; for chthonians, night, or at least afternoon, and the wane of the moon. Special restrictions and prescriptions were not rare; there were a few altars on which no blood might be shed, the offerings being such things as cakes, and numerous chthonian cults which did not allow libations of wine, but only of water, milk and honey. This in all probability marked them as old, for wine, though the Mediterranean peoples of antiquity were perfectly well acquainted with its use and making, is yet a foreign drink, its name being a loan-word from some Anatolian speech. The native term for an intoxicating drink is cognate to English "mead" and, like it, probably meant originally a beverage made by fermenting honey, although in classical times the recipe for this was quite forgotten. Hence some of the more old-fashioned gods would not use the comparatively new substance, and perhaps the common offering of honey is a reminiscence of the days when it was used for mead-making.

When one of the ancient Greeks came to die, his funeral ceremonies might be quite elaborate; we hear of sundry laws forbidding extravagant shows of grief and ostentatious expense at a burial. The funeral followed the death quickly, partly no doubt because the climate of Greece is warm and decomposition would soon set in, but perhaps even more because a dead man or woman has no business in this world, and the sooner he goes to his own place the better. The ceremonies began with the "laying out" (*próthesis*) of the corpse, which was neatly dressed and placed on a bed. Around it took place one of the most ancient of rites, the formal wailing, conducted by the women of the family, who might be led by specialists in the art of lamentation; regularly they had a leader of some sort, and the rest joined in a sort of chorus of grief. To-day such laments are called *moirológhia*, and consist partly of traditional verses, partly of improvisations. In antiquity, when a wealthy or important man died, the relatives might employ a professional poet to write a dirge (*thrênos*), which was performed by a choir some time during the rites in honour of the departed; Simonides, the great lyric poet, was especially skilled in composing such laments. The next stage was the funeral procession (*ekphorá*, literally carrying out), when the body, still on the bed, dressed usually in white and wearing a garland of some plant considered appropriate to the occasion, was carried to the burial-place, oftener than not outside the settlement. Here it was either burned and the ashes stored in an urn, which was then buried, or put unburned into a tomb or grave, often enclosed in a coffin. No difference of belief concerning the other world seems to attach to this difference of rite; the essential thing was that the remains should be shut away from the world of the living and covered over. If an unburied corpse was found, the finder could discharge his minimum duties towards it by sprinkling it with a little dust. Once entombed, the dead man, if he had left any kin, was entitled to that tendance of which mention has already been made. At the time of the burial, some kind of grave-goods were usually put with him, the amount varying greatly at different epochs. The Mycenæan nobles had much wealth buried with them, as we know from the discoveries in their tombs; later ages were more economical, but it was not usual for the corpse to be left quite without possessions of any sort to serve him in the next world. For instance, we hear more than once of a dead woman's clothes being burned, to pass to where her soul was. In Aristophanes' time, at Athens, it was usual to give the dead a kind of cake made with honey; whatever the original reason may have been, one was found for this usage, as commonly happens when a custom is established but the object of it not clearly known. The lower world was guarded by a formidable, many-headed dog, Kerberos, which might interfere with the newcomer's entrance, as he most certainly would prevent his exit. A sweet cake would engage his attention for a moment while the ghost slipped by to his future home. A custom more famous in modern times is really not very common in antiquity; a piece of money was sometimes put into the mouth of the corpse, to pay the fare of the infernal ferryman, Charon (probably an old death-god; he has survived the other deities of the underworld and is still believed in), who took souls across the water lying between this world and the next.

Returning from the funeral, the mourners ate the funeral feast (*perídeipnon*) and purified themselves, washing off the taint of death. Their regular offerings at the tomb followed on the third and ninth days after the death, and in some places at least there was an annual rite, called at Athens *genésia*, the clan-feast. We know little about it, but the name makes it at least likely that the kin gathered, possibly near their burial-place, and, making the regular offerings to the dead, which, besides those already mentioned, might include animal victims, joined in a common meal. We shall see later that an All-Souls' day was part of a Greek ecclesiastical calendar. Such festivals were not so much sacrifices, still less worship, as renewals of the table-fellowship which had existed while the dead members of the kin were still alive.

Indeed, Greek ghosts seem for the most part to have been

taken as quite a matter of course; we do not get the impression that the living were much afraid of them as a rule, if they had been given the due rites to get them into the next world and keep them there in reasonable comfort and honour. When stories are told of their haunting the living, it is regularly the spirits of those dead by violence, or not properly buried, who plague the survivors. In the case of a murdered man or woman, his or her natural desire for vengeance might be reinforced by the more formidable visitations of supernatural powers; if death or any grievous wrong had been inflicted by a blood relative, very terrible beings might be expected to take a hand in punishing the guilty. These are the Erinyes, a sort of personified curses, imagined as women of frightful aspect, with serpents entwined in their hair, carrying torches or whips, who might appear to the criminal or, by a horrible magic of their own, so charm him that he wasted away to a mere shadow of himself and finally died, "and after death," the Erinyes grimly add in Æschylus' *Eumenides*, "he is not too free." Occasionally, too, the victim of a particularly foul outrage was thought to show some ability to trouble those who were not of his own blood, if they were guilty of the offence. But for the most part, it would seem that a Greek of that age regarded ghosts as nothing to be much feared if one had done them no wrong, though they were best left alone.

But if supernatural visitations, from ghosts or any other powers, did trouble an individual or a family, they had their remedies. There seem to have existed in most places and at most times specialists in rites of purification and aversion, who could be appealed to at need. We have, in a fragment of Sophron, a Syracusan writer of the fifth century B.C., an indication of the sort of thing which was done. A house is troubled by Hekate, one of the most formidable of the infernal deities, who, starting apparently as a power of fertility, degenerated into a kind of witch-goddess, capable of sending horrible phantoms and other manifestations of her power. The inhabitants call upon a woman skilled in such things to "lay" the hauntings. She gets the necessary materials, a puppy (chthonian deities not infrequently preferred a dog to other victims), laurel (Apollo's own plant, and so very potent against unwelcome visitants), bitumen to fumigate the house (strong smells are common means of aversion), salt, incense and a torch. The hearth-fire is carefully put out, all doors are opened, and the family sit around the expert in reverent silence. She kills the puppy and in a formal prayer tells the goddess that she has had her due feast and must now begone. Other and simpler means were often employed, notably appeals in various forms, spoken and other, to such gods and heroes as were thought especially able and willing to ward off evil; Apollo and Herakles had a good reputation for this, hence their common title of *alexikakos*, "averter of ill." A statue or a little shrine of Apollo often stood outside a house, thus keeping off invisible foes; Hermes often had the same function, Hekate herself on occasion might be so used, for once her favour was gained, it was not likely that any lesser powers of the underworld would hurt those whom she saw fit to spare. We have instances of an inscription over the house door, stating that "the glorious victor, Herakles, lives here," and forbidding any ills to enter; for evil things are often stupid, and to claim the presence of so great a hero might be enough to cause them to keep away without testing the truth of the statement. Often an oracle would be asked what rites should be performed, or on occasion the ghost, if one was involved, might be summoned by necromancy and bidden to explain itself. Something could be done by wearing amulets, and a widespread precaution was to avoid the use of any ill-omened words, such as the mention of death. This left its mark on the language in some rather quaint ways. For instance, the left hand was usually unlucky, and consequently was seldom called by its name, but styled "the better" or "the well-omened" hand. In general, it was well not to give offence; he who adopted this prudent course might indeed believe most fervently in the existence of all manner of powers, many of them terrible on occasion, but did not live in great fear of them. The average Greek was neither devil-ridden nor priest-ridden, and a little examination of the facts will explain why this is so.

Greece lies outside of that large section of the earth's surface (it extends from the Iranian plateau across central Asia, thence over the sea to North America) where there seems

to be an ancient and deep-seated tendency to dualism, i.e.,
to a religion which divides the powers it worships into good
and bad, the latter being nearly as strong as the former, and
gives each faction a divine head, whether Ormuzd and Ahriman,
as in Persia, or Glooscap and his wicked brother, as among the
Indians of Nova Scotia. Elsewhere, although a belief in some
kind of devil may be found, Satan, or Ahriman, or Eblis is a
foreigner, and often laughed at as well as feared, for all foreigners are funny, even when they are also hateful. No such figure
had reached classical Greece at all, and not even the grimmest
phantoms of its imagination are wantonly malignant. They may
inexorably punish the guilty, or pursue their own revenges
relentlessly, or go to great lengths to vindicate their dignity,
but they never do evil for evil's sake. Therefore people of
innocent and quiet life have little or nothing to fear from them,
at any rate if they avoid the company of wrong-doers, for
punishment may overtake these at any minute, and perhaps
will involve those who are near them. When Horace says that
he will not have under his roof one who has offended grievously
against Demeter, nor sail in the same boat with him, he is
expressing an idea as popular as it was old. What he pretends
to fear and men of a simpler age really had feared was that
the house might fall on the criminal, or the boat be wrecked,
to the great danger of innocent people who might be in one or
the other. That is why the guilty were so commonly separated
from their community, either by death or by life-long exile.
The reason was not so much moral indignation as avoidance
of a kind of infection, the same motive which impels us to
segregate sufferers from an infectious disease. If the criminal
could be rid of his pollution of combined sin and ill-luck, by
some of the numerous rites which existed for that purpose,
he could again be received into human society, and there are
many instances of a man-slayer doing this very thing. Once
the *miasma*, or pollution, as it was called, was off him, he was
no longer liable to vengeance from any ghost or Erinyes, and
therefore those who spoke or ate with him were safe also.

The reason why there was no dominant priesthood in
Greece is that there never was a caste or closed corporation of
priests. Their duties were little more than an intensification of

what the ordinary householder did every day of his life, when he laid a garland on the statue or altar of a household deity, or made some little sacrifice to him, pouring perhaps a few drops of wine or burning a small amount of incense. Generally speaking, apart from certain special functions reserved for particular clans, anyone could be a priest or priestess, and the office need not be held for life, but might be for a year or some other predetermined period. Few, while they held a priesthood, were cut off from ordinary secular activities, though they often had to observe sundry restrictions as to costume, avoidance of particular acts, and so forth. Also, a magistrate, however secular his office might be, usually had some priestly functions as well. In the earliest times of which we know anything, a king's office combined both kinds of activity, and that elected Athenian magistrate who still bore the name of king during the twelve months that he was in power had, besides much ordinary public business, a leading part to play in one of the holiest ceremonies of the year, and was assisted by his wife, for that occasion at least dignified with the title of queen. Nor were any special qualifications beyond professional knowledge required in order to be a diviner (*mántis*). Clearly, individual priests or prophets might exert considerable influence, if they were regarded as persons unusually wise or holy, but they were no more enveloped by a mysterious aura than are our doctors and lawyers, and they could have little or no class consciousness which might have moved them to take combined action towards influencing their fellows.

Finally, the average Greek was optimistic in his attitude towards his gods. One of their commonest epithets is "givers of good," and good was what was expected of them. It is plain fact that not only ghostly visitations, be they real or imaginary, but also such material ills as epidemics, drought and floods are abnormal; when they do occur, a reason is sought for them, while their absence is more likely to be taken as a matter of course. Therefore, the plain man much oftener than not saw the rites, for instance, which he performed to secure a good harvest followed by a sufficient yield from his land, and naturally was the readier to believe that they were efficacious. He tended the family dead, and no ghosts disturbed him; again the rites were plainly efficient. A good omen encouraged him as he went about his business; thanks to that and his own industry and shrewdness (qualities Greeks of all ages have generally possessed) the business succeeded; therefore the omen was valid, sent by some well-disposed god to guide him. On the whole, he was a reasonable person, neither cruel nor grossly unjust, and he believed in gods who were very like himself. That they should be much better, morally perfect, was an idea which occurred only in comparatively late times and to thoughtful minds.

As to what might happen to him when, after not many years, his life came to an end, that seems not to have been a question to which very much thought was given, so long as the affairs of the present world went reasonably well. As already mentioned, the underworld was a gloomy, shadowy place, to which ordinarily no one had any wish to go. On the other hand, yearnings for immortality were not characteristic of the general run of Greeks. It was not only Pythagoreans and other philosophers who associated the infinite or boundless with evil; the usual taste was for something finite and well-proportioned, and so, in the case of a human life, for such completeness as can be achieved by living to a good old age in tolerable prosperity, leaving descendants and dying honourably. Few would have disagreed with the reported dictum of Solon that Tellos the Athenian was the most blessed of all mankind: "Firstly, his city prospered, and he had noble sons, and saw them all with children of their own, all surviving; secondly, he was wealthy, as we Greeks count wealth, and his end was most glorious, for in a battle between the Athenians and their neighbours at Eleusis, he came to the rescue, put the enemy to flight, and died very valiantly, and the Athenians gave him a funeral at public expense on the spot where he fell and did him great honour." Such were the blessings an average decent ancient prayed for to his gods; he who wished for anything more, and especially for immortality, would probably be reminded of the sage counsel, given more than once by their poets, "Seek not to become Zeus."

CHAPTER III

THE ORIGINS OF GODS

ALTHOUGH, as we have seen, it is not always possible to trace the origin of any Greek cult to its beginnings, it is worth while to set down what is known with certainty or a high degree of probability about the history of some of the deities who made up the classical pantheon. From the earliest times of which we have any knowledge at all to the disappearance of the non-Christian worship in Greece is something like two millennia and a half, and in so long a period it was inevitable that many changes should take place, including the introduction of foreign deities and their rites.

To begin with, we have a considerable amount of evidence concerning the gods whom the Greeks found when first they entered the country. This is contained in the rich archæological discoveries made both in Crete, where the civilization we call Minoan flourished for about fifteen hundred years, and in Greece proper, which had a high culture, known as Mycenæan from the name of the place where the first important excavations were made. Who the bearers of this culture were is a disputed point, but on the whole it seems most likely that they were the invaders, the ancestors of Homer's nobles, who had adopted much of the art and refinement of the Cretans; it is, however, possible and maintained by some scholars that they were Cretan colonists, attracted presumably by the prospects of trade with the people of the mainland. Whichever theory is true, there are clear signs that they worshipped some deities at least similar to those of Minoan Crete, and that these cults left their traces behind, in the shape of several divine names inexplicable from anything in the Greek vocabulary, and in ceremonies and legends resembling each other but easily distinguishable from normal Greek myths and rites.

Briefly, we have good reason to suppose that goddesses were the principal objects of Minoan worship, and prominent also on the mainland. Many at least, if not all, were mother-goddesses, a type very common in the eastern Mediterranean

47

countries and often found elsewhere. For it is a widespread idea that the earth, which bears food-plants of all kinds, is a sort of woman and the vegetation her offspring. Quite frequently this woman, the Earth-Mother, is the wife of the Sky-Father, who sends her the rain that fertilizes her. Zeus is a sky-father of this kind, and his many matings with goddesses and women are easily explained as variants of this old and very natural myth. But it is not always so. The Earth-Mother may be so important as to make the question who her husband or lover may be quite uninteresting; indeed, in some of the earlier stages of man's thought it is not realized that every child has a father, and stories of virgin births are nothing unusual. It need not, therefore, surprise us that among the many works of Cretan or Mycenæan art which give us a glimpse of their religion, we seldom find any figure which might be that of a god, while goddesses (we have no right to say they are all the same goddess) are very common, occasionally naked, generally dressed in the elaborate costume of a Minoan lady, and in one case at least half-hidden behind a great shield which she carries, in a manner reminding us of the many classical statues of Athena which show her armed like a Greek infantryman. While we find little trace of a divine husband for any of these deities, we do find what seems obviously to be a divine child.

The Cretans had in antiquity a reputation for being great liars, and one of the reasons for it was that they said Zeus was dead and could show his tomb. This naturally seemed very ridiculous to Greeks, whose conception of a god was that he was not only powerful but immortal. The latter word meant normally, not that he was a spiritual being which could not die as living things which have bodies do, but that his soul and body were never separated. Consequently a dead god, especially a dead Zeus, was a contradiction in terms. But examination of a little more evidence, also from Crete, shows us more clearly what the supposed lie really meant. Not only was Zeus said to be buried in that island, but he was alleged to have been born there, and strange things were supposed to happen yearly in the holy cave of his nativity, suggesting that that was not a thing which had happened once in the past, but a recurrent miracle. Furthermore, there exists a hymn in Greek, of a relatively late date, in which Zeus is called upon as the "greatest of the young men," and asked to join in a rite meant to bring prosperity to the land. We find him, then, as a baby just born, a young man and a corpse. Parallels from various parts of the world make it evident who he is; not the Greek weather-god at all (why he was called Zeus is a puzzle, perhaps because he was the most important god the Greeks heard of in Crete and they therefore identified him with the chief of their own deities), but what may be styled a year-god. That is, he is an unconscious personification of the year, not as a period of time but as a cycle of seasons, in which all things that the earth bears come into being, mature and die. As such, he is naturally the child of the Earth-Mother, and as such he grows, decays and dies, only to come to life again the next year. That such a figure survived into the days of Minoan civilization and its derivatives indicates that it is a tough and long-lived conception. Among the Greeks, who had nothing of the kind in their own beliefs, it faded and took disguised forms; the divine child becomes a mortal infant who is exposed, but survives because he is tended by a beast or by some supernatural being such as a nymph. He then grows and has a distinguished, but human career. Or he may never reach maturity, but die either in infancy or while still young. The most famous instance of this has already been mentioned in passing. Hyakinthos of Amyklai was, beyond any reasonable doubt, a god of the type just described. His name proves that he is no Greek, for the suffix -*nth*- is characteristic of old names, inexplicable from any Greek word, which are found here and there in the classical vocabulary; sometimes names of places, such as Corinth (Korinthos), which pass, generally with some change of pronunciation, from one stratum of population to another, sometimes names of flowers and plants or other unalterable features of the surroundings in which the newcomers found themselves; we may compare place-names like Temiskeming, which dot the map of Canada and belong to the Amerindian speech, not to English or French, and words such as ouananiche, caribou, signifying respectively a fish and a quadruped not found in Europe but common enough in North America.

His legend describes him as a boy, but he was not shown so in the sculptures decorating the great throne on which stood an archaic image of Apollo in the precinct shared by the two divinities in historical times, for that represented him as a grown man with a beard. The same carving showed him being brought to heaven by a group of deities, mostly goddesses. The Dorians, who after a long struggle conquered Amyklai and introduced their own cult, evidently could make little of the native god, but respected him, as they respected the stubborn fighters who worshipped him, and tried to fit him somehow into the religion they knew. On the whole, then, although this Cretan and pre-Greek worship is interesting historically, it puzzled the Greeks of classical times too much to influence them profoundly.

It was different, however, with the goddesses. The invaders knew something of supernatural beings who were female and mothers of children, for they worshipped at least one such being themselves, Demeter. Her origin is assured by the fact that her name is Greek; the last two syllables are simply the Greek for "mother," and the first is most plausibly explained by supposing it to be a by-form of the word for spelt, that inferior grain which was the earlier form of wheat. She is therefore the Spelt-mother, or Corn-mother, and her daughter is Kore, the Maiden, the divine equivalent of the new grain which grows and is reaped and stored away. On coming to the land they were to occupy, therefore, the invaders were quite ready to recognize the divinity of such venerable figures as the great goddess of Argos. If she ever had a name, they do not seem to have learned it, for they called her Hera, which appears to be nothing but the feminine of *héros*, and therefore to mean no more than "lady." She was a ruler over all that concerned women, from childhood to old age, and so was a mother herself. Therefore, to so logical a people as the invaders, it was clear that she must have a husband, and no husband august enough for her was known save their own great god Zeus. Thus it came about that the Greek divine family had at the head of it a husband and wife of entirely different origins. The proper and original consort of Zeus was pretty certainly an earth-goddess, which there is no proof that Hera ever was, and her name, to judge by what she is called in the god's very old cult at Dodona, was a feminine form of his own, Dione.

Artemis was a little harder to fit into the Greek scheme of things. There is small doubt that she was originally a mother-goddess of that type which, not knowing what the Cretans called her, we name the Lady of wild things. Her province was the uncultivated land and the creatures that live in it; she also had women under her charge in two very important ways, for she could help them at childbirth and when a woman died suddenly, it was Artemis' arrow which killed her. A being so associated with fertility would herself naturally be fertile. But, unlike some goddesses otherwise resembling her, she had no consort. Now to Greek ideas, gods and goddesses should behave like great nobles; their ways might differ from those of men, but they had rules of their own, and, being the deities of a mono-gamous people, they clearly would set store by the chastity of their wives and daughters, though their males might allow themselves considerable liberty, as an Achaian noble did. A Homeric "king" (the word is rather too grand for such men as Homer describes; "baron" would be less misleading) had but one wife, but he might have children by other women also, and neither they nor their mother were outcasts; a *nóthos*, the son of one of these unions, was a member of his father's house-hold and had some part in the succession to his father's estate, though his share was smaller than that of a legitimate son. But the women of the baron's own kin are regularly shown as chaste; it was a most grievous offence when Agamemnon's wife took a lover in his absence, and Helen's leaving her husband to go to Troy with Paris was excusable only because she was under the influence of Aphrodite and could not help herself. In like manner, Zeus might have his concubines, but his daughter, if she was not married, must be a virgin. That Artemis was his daughter is a doctrine which must have arisen very early, and presumably it resulted from an attempt to fit so important a goddess into the scheme of which he was the head. Therefore Artemis could be no one's mother. That the original goddess was a figure of many local, pre-Greek legends of motherhood and birth is strongly indicated by the tales of women associated with her, or nymphs who attended her, forming unions generally, though not always, irregular. Kallistó, whom we have already mentioned, is a case in point, the more so as in some forms of her legend she turns into a bear, a creature closely associated with Artemis. So the old goddess of the wild was in time idealized into a gracious figure of maidenhood, retaining, however, something of her old vigour, in that she and her associates are huntresses.

There is not sufficient proof that Athena was ever a mother-goddess, but clear evidence that she also was in the country before the Greeks came. Like Hyakinthos, she has a name of a typical pre-Greek form, the suffix -na- being one of the characteristics of the old, unknown tongue which the "Pelasgians" spoke; it appears, for instance, in the very ancient place-name Mycenæ. Her behaviour in some passages of Homer suggests a feature of Minoan and Mycenæan religion, as shown in their art; that presents numerous scenes in which it is plain that birds, shown in holy places and associated with holy objects, are the visible forms of deities, and Homer's Athena, after appearing in human shape among men, more than once reveals her divinity by taking the form of a bird and flying away. Indeed, a bird, the owl, is her constant associate. If we would know what kind of goddess she was originally, before Greek imagination and piety transformed her into the noble figure of the patroness of wisdom and skill which she is in the surviving literature, we have several hints. Her oldest known cults are associated with natural strongholds, such as the Akropolis, or Citadel, at Athens, where the castles of Mycenæan lords once stood and traces of their foundations are still to be discovered. She is consistently warlike, reminding us of the female figure, already mentioned, which holds a great Mycenæan shield on a limestone plaque found at Mycenæ itself. This at once raises the problem why a goddess should be so concerned with war, especially when the Greeks had in classical times a recognized war-god, Ares. We can find something of a parallel, however, if we look to ancient Italy, for there the great goddess Juno is shown, at Lanuvium, carrying a spear and shield. The chief deity of any place in antiquity may assume warlike functions, in accordance with the continual struggles against neighbouring communities which were so prominent a feature of their whole history. Now when we find a deity armed and associated with the palaces of warlike Mycenæan barons—for everything we know about that culture tells us that its history was a stormy one—the conclusion is reasonable that Athena began as the guardian goddess of these princes and their houses, and when her worshippers passed, she remained, attached to the natural strong points where the fortified dwellings of the one-time lords had stood, and still an object of veneration to the newly arrived inhabitants of the Greek-speaking towns which grew up around the old sites. That an industrious and intelligent population should make her something more than a strong defence against its enemies, and that therefore she should be protectress of arts and handicrafts as well as of fighting men and their weapons, is nothing surprising. Indeed, we may say that so far as she is a war-goddess, she is a goddess of civilized warfare, with its intelligent discipline, whereas Ares, who in the opinion of some was originally a god of death, remained associated with slaughter, war-madness and violent ends of all sorts, including death by plague.

Another goddess of the mother-type, Aphrodite, can be traced to the island of Cyprus, which is a very old centre of trade and industry, the metal copper being named *aes Cyprium* or *Cyprum* from it in Latin; it is well known that at the end of the Stone Age the trade in copper, of which the island has deposits, became increasingly important. Here also archaic idols, exaggerating the sexual characteristics after the manner of such primitive things, have been found. The Greeks planted a settlement in Cyprus at an early date, as is shown by the fact that a variety of the very old-fashioned speech of Arkadia is found there, and naturally became acquainted with the chief goddess of the place. Coming to Greece proper, Aphrodite found herself faced by serious rivals, notably Hera, and consequently her activity came to be largely confined, not to the sober business of marriage and childbirth, but rather to all that concerns the passion of love, which no doubt is why she is commonly said to be the mother of Eros, a deity with whom, originally, she had nothing whatever to do. The moral tone of her cult varied very much at different shrines. Thus, in Athens and elsewhere she was worshipped as Pandemos, in whose power lay the loving and marrying of "all the people," and our evidence goes to show that her worship was of a perfectly unobjectionable type. But at Corinth and elsewhere, the goddess not only kept her old Cyprian title of Urania (Celestial) but had temple-harlots to serve her, like some of the goddesses of Asia Minor. A side of her nature which is apt to surprise those who know the goddess only from literary fancies is that she, like Athena, is on occasion warlike, being the Spear-bearer in her own island, Areia (the Martial) on Kythera, off the southern Peloponnesos, and very often associated with Ares, who in sundry well-known tales is her lover, her husband being generally Hephaistos, the smiths' and craftsmen's god. Yet another connexion, inexplicable if we start from a love-goddess but easily enough understood if we remember her original nature, is with death. At Delphoi, says Plutarch, who knew that place well, there is a little statue of her called Aphrodite by the Tomb, where they call upon the dead to accept offerings made them. The Great Mother, who gives birth to all things that live, in the end also receives them again when they die.

Finding as they did so many goddesses in Greece, the Achaians either brought but few with them or identified them so completely with the local divinities that they disappeared as separate entities. Unlike the Minoans and Mycenæans, they had generally male powers for their chief objects of worship, and adopted readily from the other peoples they came into contact with any whose favour it seemed advisable to win. There is but one god of whom we can say with perfect certainty that they had always worshipped him since their language separated out from the common ancestral tongue known variously as Indo-Germanic, Indo-European or Wiro. This was Zeus, "the Bright One," etymologically the same deity as the Latin Iuppiter and the Germanic Tiu. He is lord of the sky, regarded here not as the solid floor of the celestial gods' home, which was how most Greeks imagined it before their science developed, but as the place from which the weather comes. "Sometimes Zeus is clear, sometimes he rains," says Theokritos, and this at once describes his main activities and marks a common tendency to identify him with his particular portion of the universe. It is natural enough that he has a long string of titles denoting the sending of thunder, lightning, rain, wind and so forth, and, since a farmer's interest in the weather is practical, another series setting forth his connexion with agriculture. But this is very far from exhausting his complex nature. Being so high up, yet near enough to the earth to influence it, he must know everything and be very wise, as is the way of sky-gods the world over, since they see and hear all that goes on. Furthermore, things continually fall from the sky, not only rain, but also thunderbolts and meteorites. As these evidence the power, the *mana*, of the sky-god, they take his name on occasion; we hear now and then of a cult of Zeus Kappótas, Zeus Who-came-down; for instance, near Gythion, the port of Sparta. The object venerated was a stone, probably once known or supposed to be a meteorite, though in later times people had forgotten exactly why it was so holy. If in the form of a stone or a shower of rain, clearly Zeus might also descend in bodily shape, or invisibly, and tales of his doing so for all manner of purposes are innumerable. Very many stories and not a few titles assure us that he was interested in the conduct of the human beings whom he beheld from his lofty abode. Thus, he is Xenios, God of the Stranger, and to strangers hospitality is due. "The gods," says Homer, "in the likeness of strangers from foreign parts, taking all manner of shapes, wander about the towns, beholding the frowardness and the lawful dealings of men", and legends not seldom tell how Zeus himself did this very thing, rewarding or punishing on occasion those who regarded their duties towards the supposed petitioner for food and shelter or those who rejected his claims. Other journeys to the earth were for amorous purposes, as this or that woman caught his fancy. Several such myths are but thin disguises of the ancient tale, how Father Sky wedded Mother Earth, but apart from this, his conduct is much like that of the Achaian nobles whose sexual relations we have discussed. We must speak later of the comments which such stories excited in more sophisticated days. To their first tellers, there was nothing in them derogatory either to the majesty of the god or the character of the women whom he thus favoured. Another and a very important feature of this great deity is that he was early recognized as the chief of the gods, more powerful than the rest put together, and thus the first step was taken towards monotheism. What philosophical consequences later thinkers drew will be discussed when we come to speak of personal religion; but in the opinion of many from Homer onwards Zeus was the "father (i.e., natural ruler; the word need not signify physical relationship) of men and gods."

Zeus was one of three brothers, the next being Poseidon. He proved less capable of moral development than his greater brother, but is a grandiose figure none the less. Whether he is of Greek origin is a question not quite settled, for we are not sure of the etymology of his name; but he is probably Greek. If that is so, he can hardly have been a sea-god originally, as he is in the usual legends about him and in much of his classical cult, for wherever the Achaians came from, it was not a region with a sea-coast. Poseidon, therefore, would not be lord of an element of which his worshippers knew nothing. Rather he was a god of water in general, of rivers and springs and not least of underground waters, real or supposed, for he was god of earthquakes, and these may well have been thought in early times due to the movement of water somewhere underground, though that was not the only cause which popular speculation assigned to them. As a water-god, then, Poseidon comes, like Zeus, into relations with the Earth, which cannot be fruitful if it is dry. Hence the force of one of his oldest titles, Gaiáochos, the Holder or Embracer of Earth, in other words, the husband of the earth-goddess. That he is, in mythology, not her husband but her grandson is nothing against this, for such genealogies, the first attempts to make the scattered traditions into a system, are unstable things and at best rather artificial. For some reason which we can no longer fathom, he is also god of horses, sometimes himself taking the shape of a horse, often said to have made the first horse ever seen emerge from the ground, occasionally becoming the father of beings wholly or partly of horse-shape. But when his followers got acquainted with the sea, that became Poseidon's chief province, and the older sea-deities, certainly there before the Achaians came, were more or less completely displaced. One of them, Amphitrite, became the rather insignificant wife of the great god. Another, Nereus, although he himself sank into the background, maintained a place in the beliefs of the folk, since he is the father of the classical mermaids, the Nereids (i.e., daughters of Nereus), and they are still believed in about the Greek countryside, though to-day their name has been altered to Neraïdhes and they are by no means confined to the sea. Like his realm, Poseidon remained of a rough and forbidding character, subject to outbursts of furious rage, and his human children, for like Zeus he had his favourites among mortal women, were regularly men of violence. As was natural among a seafaring people whose country has a coastline enormously long in proportion to the size of the whole, he was much worshipped, but he commanded respect rather than affection.

Of the third brother, Hades, not much need be said. We have seen that the living did not worship him, and the only important rite with which he has any connexion, the Eleusinian Mysteries, will be discussed later.

The most typically Greek god, Apollo, probably was not a Greek to begin with. It is a disputed point where the Achaians found him, for many things about his cult and legends point to the Near East, while others indicate a northern origin. But, wherever he came from, he was thoroughly naturalized before the date of our earliest documents. His genealogy is, like that of all popular gods from abroad, completely Greek; he is son of Zeus by the Titaness Leto, a representative of the older race of gods who were before the Olympians, and Artemis is his twin sister. Why these two, whose origins are utterly different, should ever have been given this intimate connexion, no one can say; possibly the circumstances that both are archers and both connected with creatures of the wild had something to do with it. In his earliest form, Apollo seems to have been a god of herdsmen, hence his title Nomios (He of the pastures). Greek gods, like those of most nations, are apt to resemble their worshippers; indeed, it is not rare for a Greek deity to have titles which really signify the condition of those who pray to him. Thus Zeus is on occasion Hiketes, that is to say, "the suppliant," because those who come to beg for help from another, being strangers or guests, are under his protection, and to injure them is a wrong against him. Hera was worshipped as Maid, Wife and Widow, since she was a goddess of women and all women fall into one of those three classes. Hence Apollo of the Pastures would naturally behave like a human herdsman. This at once explains why he is armed with a bow; the modern herdsman in rough country carries a firearm to keep off wild beasts or cattle-stealers. It gives a reason for his interest in medicine; herding on mountain pastures is a lonely business, and those who engage in it must have some knowledge at least of how to treat their own ailments or those of the stock. It makes it perfectly clear why he is Lord of Wolves (Lykeios), for wolves, now extinct in and near the Balkans, were then the chief danger to cattle small and large. It may help to explain his interest in music, although his chosen instrument is the lyre, and a Greek shepherd or cattleman carried a pipe, not any stringed instrument. But where he got his powers of prophecy we do not know, any more than we can trace to its beginnings his expertize in all matters of purification. However, it is a well-known fact that the most celebrated of all Greek oracles, that at Delphoi, was Apollo's in historical times, though the temple-legend, confirmed by some archæological evidence, informs us that before he came, it was a shrine of the Earth-Goddess (Ge-Themis), though already oracular. Apollo, unlike most givers of Greek oracles, did not send warning dreams to those who consulted him, nor use mechanical means such as drawing lots, nor even omens, but directly inspired his prophetess, the Pythia (Woman of Pytho, the old name of Delphoi) to answer the question asked. In a state of possession, she would utter words probably quite unintelligible to the enquirer, who was afterwards handed by one of the temple clergy a written reply, usually in hexameters, the official version of what she had said. No doubt fraud on occasion entered into the composition of these writings, but there is not the least reason to suppose any Pythia to have been other than a genuinely "mediumistic" or "psychic" woman, who no doubt fully believed that the god entered into her and spoke through her unconscious lips, like the "control" at a modern spiritualistic séance. In person, Apollo was conceived as a handsome and graceful young man; in disposition, he was kindly, though his wrath was no light thing if he was offended. The favourite son of Zeus, he gave true oracles because he knew the will and purposes of his father.

For reasons which escape us, there grew up in the fifth century B.C. a philosophical theory that he was a personification of the sun. It became extremely popular, hence, for instance, the many passages in Latin and modern poetry in which "Phœbus" (Phoibos, the Bright or Pure One, is a title of Apollo) is said to rise or set, meaning that the sun does so. Perhaps as a corollary of this, many fancied that Artemis was the moon.

Of Ares something has already been said. The ancients generally regarded him as closely connected with Thrace, whose inhabitants, much more backward than those of Greece, were divided into a number of wild and turbulent tribes, perpetually at odds with each other. It may well be that he was a Thracian god originally, although he is provided, like the rest, with an Olympian pedigree, being the son of Zeus and Hera. He never developed into anything more than a supernatural cut-throat, having no connexion with any moral ideas, such as many of his alleged kinsmen, notably Zeus, Athena and Apollo, came to have. An unpopular god, for the Greeks, despite their constant feuds with one another, never liked war, he receives more uncomplimentary epithets in literature than any other deity. In equating him with the Italian Mars, theologians did him more than justice, for Mars is a good deal more than a war-god.

Hephaistos was undoubtedly a foreigner, as is shown not least by the position of his places of worship, for they spread out from Asia Minor. He probably began by being the god of volcanic fires, and came from what the Greeks called the "burned" region of Asia, which shows, and showed even more clearly then, traces of former volcanic activities. He is associated with Lemnos, which also showed traces of being volcanic, or at least was thought by the ancients to do so. But on arrival in the more progressive parts of Greece, those which were comparatively industrialized, such as Attica, he became a god of craftsmen who use fire for their trades. Moving farther west, as

Greek civilization sought an outlet for its surplus population in Italy and Sicily, he became once more associated with his old element, for one of the popular explanations of the activity of Mt. Etna was that he had a forge somewhere underneath it. Son, in mythology, of Hera without father, he remains something of an outsider in the Olympian circle, a rather comic deity. As far back as Homer's *Odyssey* (or perhaps an early insertion by an unknown hand into the poem) he is the central figure of a funny story, how Aphrodite his wife played him false with Ares and he took an ingenious vengeance on the lovers. Possibly we can guess at a reason for this. Greek gods as a rule are thought of as possessing more than mortal beauty, but Hephaistos is lame, very likely in this respect corresponding to the human smiths of little communities, where the man who could not walk far but was otherwise healthy must needs make himself useful by mending and making tools and weapons for the rest. Therefore he is somewhat grotesque. Also, we may suppose, he is much more distinctly foreign, despite his artificial genealogy, than other adopted gods, for when the Achaians came into Greece they found there craftsmen whose skill far exceeded their own. Hence, besides Hephaistos, there are other supernatural smiths in their beliefs, the Telchines, for example, who were reputed to be very clever, but also malignant and given to evil magic. In any case, a worker in metals has little time for the characteristic occupations of a Greek gentleman, and the Greek traditions were aristocratic, however democratic or socialistic their politics might become. Busy in his forge or his workshop, he neither hunts, farms, fights nor performs athletic feats such as running and jumping, and it is but natural that he should worship a rather queer god, not a normal Olympian like Apollo.

One of the most important foreigners was relatively a very late arrival, Dionysos. He can be traced to Phrygia, where his name is Diounsis, and also to Thrace, a region whose population and language were related to the Phrygian people and tongue, and where his rites flourished, as they did also in the neighbouring country of Macedonia. Phrygia too yields the names of what seem to be a divine pair, Dios and Zemelo, probably Sky and Earth, who, there is little doubt, are the

originals of Dionysos' parents in the Greek tradition, Zeus and
Semele, though the latter becomes a mortal woman, daughter of
Kadmos, the legendary founder of Thebes. A deity of the
powers of nature, his ritual in the countries of his origin was
marked by features strange to the sober Greek cult. His votaries,
especially women, worshipped him in wild places, with frantic
dancing, loud cries, and the rending in pieces and devouring
raw of certain animals, especially bulls and goats, which are
closely associated with the god and often his incarnations.
The object of all this seems to have been to induce a state of
ecstasy in which the human personality vanished and the
worshipper became for the time being one with his or her god;
hence the very common use of his titles to designate those who
had accomplished this mystical union with him, he being very
often called Bakchos, they Bakchoi or Bakchai, according to
their sex. While Homer has no more than heard of Dionysos,
his cult made its way into Greece and was established there
by about the seventh century B.C., although some of its more
savage features were reduced to mere decorous semblances of
the original actions. Even so, some of the ritual was ecstatic
enough, including, at Delphoi, where the new god was warmly
welcomed and given a quarter of the year for himself, revels at
night on the heights of Mt. Parnassos by torchlight. A minor
development was that, since other powers of the fertility of
nature were already well known, Dionysos tended somewhat to
specialize, not so much in ritual as in art and literature, into a
god of wine. Around him gathered, besides his human following, various lesser powers of the countryside and the wilds.
These included the Satyrs and Seilenoi, minor embodiments of
fertility, of whom the former were conceived as grotesque and
lustful little men with the tails of horses, and Nymphs, female
beings who haunted or animated trees, hills, streams and other
natural features. The word *nymphe* means " bride " or " young,
marriageable woman," and they are often represented as
amorous, and regularly, like the material objects with which
they are associated, as long-lived but not immortal. Furthermore, all manner of little local gods were swept up in the
newcomer's triumphant progress, becoming men whom he had
favoured, or the like, in popular beliefs and stories.   The

characteristic hymn to the new deity, called a dithyramb, became in time a literary form, being given its classical shape by the musician Arion of Corinth; we shall see later what interesting developments, very unlike Thracian savageries, the worship of the god assumed at Athens.

A much less important god, but always popular, was Hermes. So far as we can trace his history, he is Arkadian and pure Greek. His name is connected, according to the most likely theory, with *herma*, which means stone ballast. Now to mark a spot supposed to be haunted or in any way "uncanny" by a heap of stones is a very common custom. Such places often lie along roads or paths, and it is very understandable that "He of the stone-pile" should become a power familiar to way-farers. If this is so, most of Hermes' characteristics are easily enough explained. Haunting roads, he would naturally be interested in the doings of those who used them, whether for honest or dishonest purposes. The most respectable travellers were heralds, *kérykes* in Greek, messengers sent on public business from one community to another and universally regarded as inviolable, even in time of war. Hermes is their patron, although not their only one, for at least in Sparta Talthybios, Agamemnon's herald in Homer, interested himself from his grave in his younger colleagues and on occasion showed his anger when their sanctity was violated. Being a divine herald, Hermes goes on the errands of the gods, including those to the lower world, and thus is the escort of the souls of the dead, with the title Psychopompos (Guide of souls). But heralds are not the only users of roads; merchants pass along them to get foreign goods (travel for pleasure was still far in the future when the cult of Hermes began), and so Hermes is patron of merchants also, and bringer of good luck in trade or otherwise. Less reputable than the merchants are the robbers who prey on them; Hermes was little troubled by moral scruples, and thus was also the patron of thieves, being represented as a master-thief himself, who began his career the day he was born, by stealing the cattle of his half-brother Apollo. It is less clear how Hermes became the divine guardian of gymnasia and wrestling-schools, and also god of eloquence; perhaps the former resulted from his being thought of as an active young man, the latter from a herald's need of sufficient rhetoric to state his errand clearly and persuasively. In all these capacities, Hermes was brought into close contact with man, and generally was a kind and friendly god, a bringer of good fortune to all manner of people, and therefore of one of the most desired forms of it, fertility. At all events, the phallus was one of his commonest emblems, and marked his "herms," as already mentioned (p. 37). He had, as usual, an Olympian pedigree, being son of Zeus and Maia, daughter of the Titan Atlas, who in the shape of a mountain upholds the sky. She was identified with one of the Pleiades.

Any of these and the other, less-known deities might be worshipped separately or in small groups, or in conjunction with one or more of the heroes. Some of these groups were so familiar that it was not necessary to mention the names of the gods composing them; thus, if a Spartan swore "by the Two Gods," everyone knew he meant Kastor and Polydeukes, often called the Dioskuroi, i.e., Sons of Zeus. They are, either both or one of them, his sons, their mother is Leda, wife of Tyndareos, King of Sparta in legendary times, and in different accounts one, both or neither is immortal; evidently both were so in historical Sparta. Pairs of divine twins are not unexampled in Greece, though they tend to become heroes instead of gods. Other groupings were for certain formal purposes, such as solemn oaths; at Athens the usual deities were, according to an ordinance ascribed to the ancient law-giver Drakon, Zeus, Poseidon and either Athena or Demeter. Some preferred longer lists; if the oath was an important one, taken on behalf of a state by its plenipotentiaries when making a treaty, a dozen or more divinities might be invoked. Physicians, when they took the famous Oath of Hippokrates, swore by the gods of their art, Apollo, Asklepios and his family. In the casual asseverations —they are hardly real oaths—of everyday like, men tended to swear by gods, women by goddesses. But the largest permanent group of divinities was the Twelve Gods, who quite often were worshipped together. They are Zeus, Poseidon, Apollo, Ares, Hephaistos and Hermes; Hera, Athena, Artemis, Aphrodite, Demeter and Hestia. If a group of male and female powers of such different origins could share the same liturgy, the fusion between cults of various nationalities and dates was obviously complete in the mind of the average worshipper, who was little troubled with the history of his religion, much concerned with the practical benefits to be got by observing its rites.

CHAPTER IV

THE GUARDIANS OF THE CITY

So far, we have been considering chiefly the individual worshipper or the small rustic community. But the most characteristic developments of Greek religion, as of their civilization
generally, took place in cities and not up and down the countryside. A city without its public cults would have been an
unheard-of thing to any Greek of the classical period, as unheard-
of as one without churches would be to the present inhabitants
of Greece. Since Greek cities, though the biggest of them were
small compared to the huge size of our largest municipalities,
still were much greater, wealthier, and more advanced in culture
than the villages of a purely agricultural population, they could
and did worship with far more splendour and formality, and
appealed to their gods for more complicated gifts, though
ultimately they were the same as before, deliverance from want,
from conquest by an enemy, and from plague. Also, the more
conspicuous nature of the city's achievements called for more
imposing services of commemoration and thanksgiving; and
finally, the worship of a god was the commonest occasion for a
great assembly to which not only citizens but foreigners were
invited, and such assemblies were excellent advertisements
for the power and glory of the State. One result of all this is
very welcome to the historian. Such conspicuous pieties tend
to be recorded in some detail, and consequently we know
far more of the religious life of a city than of the country, and
most of that city which was the most articulate, Athens.
Athenian literature, like that of all Greeks, is full of mentions
of the gods and their festivals, and the lasting admiration which
it excited and the assiduous study of it in later times produced
abundance of explanatory matter, commentaries, lexica and so
forth, of which a considerable portion has come down to us.
The result is that we can construct, for Athens if for no
other Greek city, a fairly complete ecclesiastical calendar, and
give comparatively detailed accounts of the majority of the
festivals whose names and dates we know.

Before sketching the festivals, however, it is necessary to explain how the years and months were reckoned in Greece. Whereas we use the solar year, dividing it conventionally into twelve months, any one of which may happen to begin at any phase of the moon, the ancients used, until much later times than those of classical Greece, lunar months, reckoned from one new moon to the next. This is approximately 29½ days, but, since it is very awkward to have a month which consists of any but an integral number of days, months had alternately 29 or 30; in the latter case they were called "full," in the former "hollow." Twelve of these make 354 days, and it was very soon noticed that a few years of this kind put the calendar at variance with the seasons, spring months for instance coming some time before the spring began. This was put right by the rather clumsy method of intercalating months at intervals, i.e., letting a month come twice over in the year. So at the end of a cycle of years, generally eight, the extra months had lengthened the years enough to make the next cycle start on approximately the correct day; but any given year was too long or too short, and so more or less at odds with what was happening in nature. Therefore a sowing festival, for example, celebrated according to the official calendar of a city might be quite noticeably too early or too late, and practical farmers would pay little attention to the subtleties of townsfolk, but plough, sow and reap according to the real seasons, their guides being such phenomena as the appearance on the horizon at morning and evening of certain constellations, or the return of migratory birds and the flowering of wild plants. This in itself was enough to make a gap between the ceremonies of the town and the facts of the country, and so to bring an element of unreality into the official religion. It should be clearly grasped that the existence of the gods and their activities was very real to the average Greek. That Apollo, Demeter and the rest were the products of popular imagination and that their worship produced not the smallest effect upon the processes of nature, which would have gone on in exactly the same way had all the people of the land been atheists, could not and did not occur to any but very advanced and critical minds at that date or any other. To do without religion entirely is an idea which the mass of ancient humanity never considered for a moment, and when paganism finally collapsed, its place was at once taken by a new ritual, not by cessation of worship. But when the farmer saw the official clergy of the city performing the traditional rites which should accompany harvest, for instance, and were as much a part of it as the actual reaping of the corn, at a time when the grain was still unripe or was already gathered, it must have struck him as very strange and rather meaningless, though it might not seem so to the townsman who got his living, not by ploughing and sowing, but in a workshop which fashioned vases, it might be, or tools and weapons. Aristophanes, who always understood the plain man, puts into the mouth of his chorus of Clouds in the play of that name a complaint against the muddled calendar of Athens:

"The moon," they say, "sends her compliments to the Athenians and their allies, and adds that she is much annoyed at the abominable treatment she gets in return for all her benefits. . . . You will not reckon the days aright, but get them all topsy-turvy, so that the gods often threaten her when they must go home without the feast they expected on the proper date. When you ought to be sacrificing, you put witnesses to the question and decide law-suits, and when we gods are holding a fast-day, you pour drink-offerings and laugh."

However, the official calendar was the received framework of the official ritual, and all Athenian months have the names of festivals, great or small, which fell in them. The year began, approximately at midsummer, with Hekatombaion, the Month of the Great Sacrifice (*hekatómbaia*; a "hecatomb" is supposedly an offering of a hundred head of cattle), of which we know nothing save that it was in honour of Apollo and so probably on his day, the seventh. A more interesting day is the twelfth, the Kronia, or feast of Kronos, an old god (his name means nothing in Greek), whom popular tradition made the father of Zeus. It is pretty clearly a harvest-festival; indeed, the god is shown in art carrying a curved implement which may well have been originally a reaping-hook, though the myth gave a very different explanation of it. On that day masters served their slaves and ate at the same table with them, thus furnishing part of the material for yet another legend, that in the days when

Kronos was the supreme god there were no social distinctions, but all alike enjoyed peace and plenty. Yet more important was the great festival of the twenty-eighth day of Hekatombaion, the Panathenaia, or Feast of All Athenians. Every year on this, the birthday of Athena, a festival was held in her honour, and every fourth year the ceremony was especially splendid and known as the Great Panathenaia. The festivities then started on what we should call the evening of the 27th, for by ancient Greek reckoning a day begins at sunset, with songs and dances on Athena's holy hill, the Akropolis, and probably a torch-race. At dawn a great procession began to move up to her temple; it was headed by the "basket-bearers," *kanephóroi*, girls of good family who carried on their heads things necessary for the ritual. Next came the victims for the sacrifices, cattle and sheep, next numerous other attendants and officiants, then a great body of the citizens, on foot and on horseback, all in due order according to traditional arrangements, and in festal costumes. In the centre of this brilliant spectacle came a strange mixture of old and new. The goddess was given a new mantle by her faithful people, a very old act of worship (Dione at Dodona had a large wardrobe) inspired by nothing more transcendental than the thought that the deity, whether represented by a statue or some shapeless but holy object, must not go naked for fear of the cold. But this mantle was carried like a sail on the mast and yard of a ship on wheels, an emblem of the naval power of Athens, which in its great days saved Greece from Persia and secured an imperial position for the city. As might be expected, so sacred a garment was not made casually or by impure hands. Women, married and unmarried, of respectable Athenian families, wove it, assisted by two little girls, the *arrhephóroi*. It was gorgeously embroidered, the subjects represented including the wars of the gods against Titans and giants, with Athena herself shown doing valiantly in battle.

The next month, Metageitnion, may serve to remind us how incomplete our knowledge of the details of Greek religion is. It is obviously named from the festival called Metageitnia, and the etymology of this shows that it had something to do with relations between neighbours, *geitones*. But beyond the fact that a sacrifice was made then to Apollo, who bore in that connexion the title Metageitnios, we know nothing about it, not even on what day it fell. A little better known is another feast of this month, the Eleusinia. This had nothing to do with the Mysteries of Eleusis, though it was in honour of Demeter and Kore, nor did it occur every year, but biennially, with every second celebration especially brilliant and so called the Great Eleusinia. These four-yearly celebrations were one of the many Greek festivals of which athletics formed a part; the Great Panathenaia were another. This is not the place to go into the problems connected with Greek athletic sports; on the whole, the events did not differ very much from our own, save that team-games corresponding to our football, cricket and so forth, hardly existed and were never important. The most striking outward difference was that, except in early times, the contestants were entirely naked—the Greeks soon rid themselves of the pruderies and false modesties in regard to the human body which are a relic of savage superstitions concerning the sexual functions. More important is the association of the sports with religious ceremonials. All the greatest athletic "meets," the so-called Great or Holy Games, were in close connexion with festivals held in honour of gods. The greatest of them all, the Olympic Games, took place at the quadrennial feast of Zeus at Olympia in Elis; the Pythian Games were at Delphoi, Apollo being naturally the god honoured there, the Isthmian at the Isthmus of Corinth, in the worship of Poseidon, and the Nemean, again in honour of Zeus, at his ancient shrine at Nemea. The victor was crowned with a wreath of a plant associated with the local deities, at Delphoi, for instance, with laurel, which is Apollo's tree, and was held to enjoy their favour. From this it has been somewhat hastily concluded that the actual events were originally rites, but on further examination it becomes clear that this is not so. The athletes are perhaps in some sense the guests of the god, certainly they are under his protection and in all probability he was held to enjoy the exhibition of their strength and skill, but in themselves their contests are quite normal performances, the natural amusements of a crowd of Greeks, who were always very fond of sports, met together on a holiday occasion. This was true of the Athenian festivals also; but the interest of the god to whom the festival belonged was shown in the nature of the prizes offered. At the Panathenaia, these were jars of olive oil from the sacred olives which abounded in Attica; the jars themselves, of which a number survive, bore a figure of Athena. At Eleusis, the prize was barley from the Rarian Plain, a district closely associated with Demeter and her gift of bread-corn to mankind.

The next month is Boedromion, the month of the Feast of the Helpers (Boedromia), again connected with Apollo and probably on his day, the seventh. But far more important than this, or than the commemorations at various times within the same month of the victories at Plataiai and Marathon, was the most widely known and discussed ceremony of classical Greece, the Eleusinian Mysteries, which lasted, with their preliminaries, from the 15th to the 22nd. It is well to rid ourselves of sundry misconceptions before discussing them. They did not and could not teach a secret doctrine, unfit to be revealed to the profane. Not only have we already seen that Greek religion had no creeds and no theology in our sense of the word, but the many allusions to what went on in the Hall of Initiation (Telesterion) at Eleusis speak of things done, or shown, never of things taught. Initiates were vowed to secrecy, and almost always kept their vow, but we know that on the occasions when the vow was broken and the Mysteries profaned, what took place was not telling others of any doctrine that had been learned but the performance in public of some of the ritual, or of a parody or imitation of it. Indeed, one of the phrases for this kind of impiety signifies literally "to dance out the Mysteries," implying that at the ceremony itself something like a sacred, probably dramatic, dance took place. We may perhaps compare an elaborate Christian ceremonial such as a pontifical Mass, at which nothing is done or said which comes as a revelation to those present of a doctrine with which they were unfamiliar, but their religious emotions may be profoundly stirred. But the parallel is imperfect, for underlying the words and actions of the celebrant of the Mass is the highly metaphysical doctrine of Transubstantiation, while behind the Mysteries there lay nothing more than a picturesque myth, which ran as follows. Hades was amorous of Kore, daughter of Demeter, and carried her off to the underworld. Her mother, in wild grief, sought her throughout the world. During her wanderings, which went on day and night, the goddess carrying a torch to show her the way in the dark, the world suffered from famine, for the earth, deprived of the kindly activities of the Corn-mother, produced no food. At last she came to Eleusis, and there, in the outward semblance of an old woman, was kindly treated by the king and his household, and made nurse to the infant son of his queen, Metaneira. In return for this hospitality, she planned to make the child immortal, and every night she burned away his mortality in the hearth-fire. Anointed with ambrosia, the food of gods, he took no hurt from this magical process, but one night Metaneira saw her baby lying in the fire, and screamed with terror. Demeter therefore broke off her relations with the royal family, revealed herself in her true form, and proclaimed that the child would now be mortal like other men. However, she still showed favour to the people of Eleusis, bade them build her a temple and taught her rites to them. Meanwhile an agreement had been reached between her and the other gods; if Kore had eaten no food in the world of the dead, she was to return to her mother, but if she had, she must still be the wife of Hades-Pluton. Hades had contrived that she should eat a few seeds of a pomegranate, which was enough to bind her to him and his realm, but a compromise was struck between him and Demeter; Kore should stay with him for part of the year, but spend the rest above ground with her mother. As we have the legend, which is certainly very old, there is a certain amount of confusion between two classes of gods, both belonging to the earth, Hades (the Unseen One), lord of the dead, and Pluton, the giver of the riches of the soil (cf. p. 13), and consequently between Persephone, queen-consort of Hades, and Kore, the Corn-Maiden. This is important, for it explains the interpretation which pious minds from an early date put upon the Eleusinian rites.

The whole myth is apparently the statement in words of what was shown in action, by means of a dramatic dance or simple and primitive play, at Eleusis. Words and actions alike set forth what actually happens year by year, for the Corn-maiden does indeed go underground in a Greek summer. The harvest is much earlier than with us (we have seen that there was a harvest festival in Hekatombaion, which is very roughly equivalent to July), and once it is reaped the fields lie bare and desolate under the blaze of the summer sun until the autumn rains begin and it is time to start ploughing. The corn was commonly stowed in underground silos. The main crops are those which ripen during the mild winter, a time of green fields, and have grown well above ground in early spring. Hence in Anthesterion, which is about February–March, there was another festival of Demeter and Kore at Agrai, which, after Eleusis had been annexed by Athens as part of the consolidation of Attic territory under one government, became a necessary preliminary to initiation at Eleusis and was commonly known as the Lesser Mysteries, those of Eleusis being the Greater. It is highly likely that this ceremony celebrated the return of Kore, but we have no details concerning it.

But of what went on in the Telesterion at Eleusis we have a few glimpses. Some minor details were apparently pretty well known and, not being essential parts of the holy revelations, they might be spoken of or shown in art. Some Christian converts in later days were initiates, and some of them mentioned a little of what they had seen. Furthermore, there was nothing secret about the names and persons of the Eleusinian clergy. We know that there was a hierophant ("shower of holy things") and a daduchos (torch-bearer), also a whole priestly family, or clan, the Kerykes (heralds). We know that the deities worshipped included, besides the mother and daughter, a god called Iakchos (probably "he of the loud cry"; he was identified with Dionysos-Bakchos, but had nothing originally to do with him), also a nameless pair referred to simply as "the god" and "the goddess." We have reason to believe that some ritual jesting of a broad kind went on during part of the ceremony, and was supposed to commemorate the antics of a girl who had made Demeter smile in the midst of her grief and anxiety. We have something like proof that there was a scene of pretended kidnapping, no doubt representing the carrying off of Kore. We know that the initiand's head was veiled at one point in the proceedings, and that he handled or tasted sundry sacred things. We are informed that at the climax of the ceremony an ear of reaped corn was shown amid silence. There seems to have been a kind of pass-words which initiates used among themselves; there was proclamation made of the birth of a holy child, Brimos, from someone called Brimo. But we are very far from being able to reconstruct the *drómena* (things done), as they were called. Of the words used, we have information that a short and simple prayer, consisting of the two words "rain" and "conceive," was addressed to, presumably, the sky and the earth. It is perhaps worth mentioning that the notorious formula *konx ompax*, of which some of the older books about Eleusis made much, simply did not exist. It is the fruit of a misunderstanding of a passage, already miswritten and certainly having nothing to do with Eleusis or any other religious rite, in the lexicon of classical Greek compiled by the Byzantine scholar Hesychios.

Putting all we know together, it seems that the rite, which is certainly very old, for there was a holy place at Eleusis even in Mycenæan times, grew out of a ceremonial, as much magical as religious,[1] intended to increase and continue the fertility of the fields. In this, we may reasonably guess, some kind of pantomime was gone through showing what happened year by year to the corn, and also ritual was performed intended to bring the participants in the ceremony, themselves farmers of the district about Eleusis, into close touch with the powers concerned, so that they too might possess something of their *mana*, and therefore all that they did when tilling the earth might prosper with more than mortal certainty and speed. But, as already mentioned, confusion is apt to occur between those chthonian powers who send up the plants and those who have the dead in their charge, and Demeter is not exempt from this confusion, still less Kore. Consequently, as initiates were brought into close relation with these goddesses and the other deities worshipped at Eleusis, an idea grew up early that to be initiated made for happiness in the next world, through the

[1]The difference between magic and religion is essentially that the former is supposed to be effective in itself, the words, actions and so forth of the magician having power to compel, if necessary, both nature and the gods governing it to obey him. The religious attitude is more dependent, involving petitions to whatever beings are believed in to do what the worshipper wants, and not trying to force them to agree. The distinction is emphasized by the late Sir J. G. Frazer throughout his works.

favour of the powers there. This is as ancient as the hymn to
Demeter traditionally ascribed to Homer (which, in this case
as in many others, means simply that it was old and no one
knew who had composed it; it may date from the seventh
century B.C.). It was, nevertheless, certainly no part of the
ceremonies themselves, but the reading into them of the aspirations of later generations. It won wide favour, and was doubtless
one of the reasons why the Athenians threw the Mysteries
open to everyone who could understand Greek and was not
polluted by blood-guilt or some other serious impurity, offensive to even the least moral of the gods.

A question not yet finally answered is why the rites were
secret at all. It was already noticed in antiquity that similar
ceremonies were gone through in Crete publicly, with no pretence of concealment. It is unlikely that the worship at Eleusis
or anywhere else had ever had to face persecution from practitioners of another religion during the shifts of population which
in time built up the historic Greek people. As already stated
(p. 18), polytheism is tolerant, and the normal instinct of
ancient peoples was to get on as good terms as possible with the
gods of any country which they entered, peacefully or otherwise. It is more probable that the Eleusinians set great value
on their rites and were therefore jealous of any outsider getting
to know the true names of their deities and the proper way to
invoke them and win their favour and co-operation, lest he
tempt them away or perhaps work counter-magic to benefit
his own community instead of Eleusis. We have plentiful
ancient examples of such things as prayer-formulæ and charms
being kept secret and of the exclusion of foreigners from a rite
held to be very efficacious.

Be that as it may, there was no secrecy whatever about the
preliminary ceremonies which the *mystai*, as candidates for
initiation were called, had to go through. On Boedromion 15,
all who wished to be initiated, or re-initiated (there was a
higher grade, the recipient of which was called an *epóptes*,
literally a beholder) assembled, together with their conductors,
persons already initiated who went with them to help them
through the complicated ceremonial. On the 16th, known as
"Seaward, ye *mystai*," all went down to the coast and there

purified themselves and the pigs which each had to present as a sacrifice to Demeter, by a bath in the sea. The next day, an offering was made to Demeter and Kore, and on the 19th the procession started for Eleusis. It was a merry journey, traditionally made in old clothes and accompanied with singing, dancing and joking. We need not suppose that everything which was done then had a ritual significance; it was a holiday crowd, despite the solemnity of the rites in which it was to take part. These began on the 20th, that is, by our reckoning, after sunset on the 19th, for initiations always took place at night, by torchlight. They lasted till the 22nd, perhaps simply because there were generally more candidates for initiation than could be dealt with at once in the not very large building available.

The next month, Pyanopsion, was named from the Pyanopsia, again a festival of Apollo and certainly known to have taken place on the seventh day of the month. Its central feature was the presentation to Apollo, at a solemn meal, of a sort of porridge made of various kinds of pulse boiled together, hence its name, literally "the boiling of beans." Doubtless the intention was, by presenting some of this kind of food for the god to eat, to get his blessing on the whole of the corresponding crops. Another old and popular rite took place on the same day and probably had had originally nothing whatever to do with Apollo, perhaps not with any god. It was the carrying of the *eiresióne*, a kind of small maypole, consisting of a branch of olive or laurel hung with fruit, bread, cakes, and little bottles of honey, wine and oil. The bearers of it were children, who went about collecting contributions from private houses, a very widespread custom attaching to several seasonal festivals up and down Europe. We still have an old song (ascribed, as usual, to Homer) which they sang on this occasion in Samos; it is a series of praises and good wishes for the householder and his family, followed by a request for a gift. The Athenian children sang,

"Eiresione brings figs and fat loaves, honey in a jar and oil to scrape off her, and a cup of strong wine to drink herself to sleep on."

The bough was hung up over the house door and kept there till next year; but (by a custom which the Athenians declared

Theseus, their great legendary king, had originated) at the Pyanopsia one was brought to Apollo's temple, by a boy who had both parents living, and hung up there. The god, evidently, took his part in the luck-bringing rite, like his worshippers. This was naturally desirable; the whole performance was intended to bring success to the people's activities in producing food, and the strong *mana* of Apollo, working through the magical object which decorated his door, would react on all that it stood for.

Earlier in the month, on the 5th, came the Proerosia, literally the previous ploughing. It was one of three holy ploughings, as Plutarch calls them, which took place at various spots in Attic territory, and undoubtedly its object was to bring a blessing on the work of the husbandmen, who about that time of year would be getting their fields ready for the autumn sowing. An old hymn of which a scrap is preserved calls on Kore to be present. Still more interesting was the Thesmophoria, the festival of Demeter Thesmophoros (Bringer of precious things), celebrated at Athens itself on three days, the 11th–13th inclusive, known respectively as the Day of Ascent (or "ascent and descent"), Fast-day and Day of Fair Increase. The celebrants were women, men being rigidly excluded from the holy spot, the Thesmophoreion, where the women gathered. A like rule was observed in other places, for the rite was old and widespread. Probably the ceremonies did not differ essentially, but the date was not always the same. Thus, at Halimus in Attica, the festival was held a day before the Athenian one began, and lasted one day only. To understand what is signified by "ascent and descent" we must look more than half-way across the Athenian year. In the last month of the twelve, Skirophorion, occurred the festival from which the month took its name, the "carrying of the *skira*." What these were we happen to know, thanks to a nameless scholar of late antiquity who wrote some explanatory notes on the works of Lucian. They were sucking-pigs and cakes made in the shape of serpents and of the male organ of generation, and they were thrown into certain hollows in the ground known as *mégara*, where they remained and were for the most part devoured by the serpents who lived there. Now at the Thesmophoria, women

who had purified themselves for three days in advance went
down into these *mégara*, making a noise to frighten away the
snakes, and brought up any remains of the pigs' bones and
rotted flesh that might still be left. These they solemnly laid on
altars, and afterwards they were mixed with the seed-corn.
The object of all this is not hard to make out. Skirophorion
would come, at least nominally, a little before harvest, when the
earth might well be supposed exhausted by the effort of producing the crops. Therefore young and fresh specimens of the
most fertile of domestic animals, a creature sacred to Demeter,
were given her, together with representations of things productive of increase and of the mysterious creatures belonging
to the underground world. These, it was hoped, would supply
fresh *mana*, which would be needed for the next year. But when
they had remained so long in contact with the underworld, the
remnants of such an offering must themselves be very full of
the magic of fertility; therefore, the now vigorous earth
could spare them to give a higher rate of increase to the
seed-corn. Of the second day of the Thesmophoria we know
little, except the obvious fact that the women fasted, a common
rite enough in connexion with both religious and magical
ceremonies; it was a preparation for what was to come on the
third day, and it was reinforced by the women living, not in
any building, but in little booths made of leafy branches, that
is to say, in close contact with the earth and what it bears. The
"fair increase" of the third day, on which sundry sacrifices
were offered, may refer to the blessing of abundant harvests,
or of children, or of both; the celebrants were married women of
respectable families, which did not prevent them keeping up
the old ritual custom of making rather broad fun of each other
during the ceremony.

For the rest of this month and the whole of the next, Mai-
makterion, there is little of interest. The latter was named from
the festival called Maimakteria, held in honour of Zeus
Maimaktes, an old title which apparently means "stormy."
It may have been meant to keep off damage from autumn
storms. The winter month Poseideon, named from Poseidon's
festival (Poseidea) on its eighth day, contained yet another
festival of Demeter, the Haloa, on the 26th. The name seems

derived from an ancient word for arable land; the ritual included a good deal of fertility-magic, some of it to our modern taste indecent, and also, a characteristic feature of festivals occurring at that dark and cold time of year, a joyous feast, one might almost say a Christmas dinner, or rather, it appears, two, for the women who were the sole officiants in the rites feasted on Demeter's holy ground at Eleusis, but a meal was served to the citizens generally, on 'a less sacred spot. Several details of the ceremony are noteworthy. The women's feast might not include certain fruits, several kinds of fish, poultry nor eggs. Part of the ceremonial was the ritual tasting of the new wine, just beginning to be drinkable. Poseidon had his part in the rites, for a procession was held in his honour; being the husband, as we have seen (p. 56), of the earth-goddess, he is not seldom associated with the Corn-mother also. The tabus, the uncouth rites, and the appearance of the god in what must be one of his oldest functions, before he became a deity of the sea, all indicate that we have here to do with a very old feast, possibly brought by the Achaians from a region where winter is a colder and more lifeless time than it is in the comparatively mild Greek climate.

We have now reached the second half of the Attic year with the month Gamelion. Of the festival which gave it its name we know practically nothing. Presumably it was called Gamelia, and there is some reason for supposing that it celebrated the marriage of Zeus and Hera, that is, once more, of Father Sky and Mother Earth. This was not a mere commemoration of a mythological event in the dim past; festivals, at least in their origin and in the earlier religions, have no such object. Year by year, Sky weds Earth, or how can she be fruitful and bring forth her children, the harvest, after the spring sowings? This is a deep-rooted idea, and there are accounts of Greek peasants of to-day to whom Christian festivals such as Easter, which really are commemorative in official theology, seem to deal with contemporary, not past happenings.

However, we know more of a very interesting feast which was held on the 12th, 13th and 14th of this month. It was called Lenaia, that is to say, the festival of the Lenaion, the place of the Lenai, one of the several words meaning female devotees of Dionysos, and it was indubitably his festival. The god had already been honoured the month before, not, however, by any ceremony in Athens itself, but at a number of places in the country, which celebrated what we call the Rural Dionysia. Now the city performed his rites, of which, unfortunately, we know but little, save for the fact, more important to literature than to religion, that plays were performed then, as they were at the Great Dionysia, of which we shall have to speak later. The glimpses we catch of the proceedings make us curious to learn more. The presiding official was that archon, or yearly magistrate, who bore the title of King (Basileus; hence moderns, but no ancient, often call him the Archon Basileus, or King-Archon). This in itself indicates that it was of no small importance. Those very usual features of a classical Greek holy day, a procession and a sacrifice, were organized by him on this occasion. But, as Apollo at Delphoi had recognized the younger god, his half-brother, and given him a share in his sanctuary, so, it would seem, the great powers of fertility whose holy place was at Eleusis extended a welcome to this newer deity of fertility whose title, Bakchos, sounded a little like the name of their own Iakchos. The welcome took the form of declaring that Bakchos and Iakchos were one and the same. Consequently, the Daduchos (see p. 72), carrying his sacred torch, cried at some part of the ceremony, "Invoke the god!" and the faithful replied, "Son of Semele, Iakchos, bestower of riches!" Greeks, who were apt to assume that all peoples really worshipped the same gods, although the names might differ, often made identifications on slighter grounds than that. The god returned the courtesy, it would appear, for at the Lenaia an offering was made to Demeter, Kore and Pluton. Beyond this, however, nearly everything about the Lenaia is uncertain; this is not the place to describe, much less try to settle, controversies which have arisen between able specialists as to the interpretation of some data from ancient art which, if we were really sure what they represented, might tell us rather more.

In the fluctuating Athenian calendar, Gamelion might include part of February, and the Greek spring is much earlier than ours. Hence it is not surprising that the next month has a name derived from the flowers which made their appearance then. It is Anthesterion, and the festival after which it is named took place on three successive days, the 11th, 12th and 13th, and was called Anthesteria, the Feast of Flowers. Despite its name, it was not entirely a joyous occasion. Spring is a somewhat unchancy time, for the awakening earth and the farming activities which accompany its revival let loose forces which may be dangerous. These included unburied or untended and therefore hungry and resentful ghosts, who apparently were admitted to Athenian houses at the Anthesteria, presumably given some kind of nourishment, and finally dismissed with the formula "Out of doors, ye harmful spirits (*Keres*)!" But Dionysos had his part, and a very important one, in the proceedings, and for once the date of a ceremony in his honour can be connected with a fact concerning wine and wine-making, quite a rare phenomenon in classical Greece, which did not worship the god at such dates as vintage time, as no doubt would have happened had he been a wine-god originally, like the Italian Liber. By spring, the fermentation of the grape-juice pressed and stored the previous autumn would be fairly complete, and more than one Greek community set aside a day in a spring month for a formal and ritual opening of its store-jars. Boiotia, for example, did so on the sixth of the spring month Prostaterios, but apparently said nothing of Dionysos, but invoked the Agathos Diamon, the kindly power who, among other characteristics, likes to see people enjoying themselves. Such a rite of beginnings is not peculiar to Greece or to any country; there is a world-wide opinion that the first time of doing anything is rather risky, and should be safeguarded with measures likely to secure divine favour, or magical good luck, or both. Athens, then, called the first day of the Anthesteria Pithoigia, the festival of opening store-jars. The first wine taken from these receptacles (the ancients did not use casks) was poured out in libation, and the people, or the officiant priest, we do not know which, prayed that the use of the wine might bring no harm but preserve the drinkers. They did not, it appears, call it wine on that occasion, but *phármakon*, a word which in Greek medicine means a drug, but in popular speech had a wider significance and included magical substances. However familiar, a drink which starts by being simple grape-juice and later alters into a something which may trouble a man's wits is to be treated with

a certain respect, as plainly containing *mana*. So it was brought
into contact with powers known to be friendly, Dionysos or the
Agathos Daimon according to local usage, that its potency
might have a good effect only. The second day was the Choes,
plural of *chus*, a large vessel holding something like two English
quarts; the word refers to a peculiar feast which was held on
that day, by representatives of the State and certain persons
who were invited, in a public building, and no doubt by private
individuals in their own houses also. The peculiarity was that
each guest was given his own *chus*, instead of all being served
from a common mixing-bowl. Thus everyone had the same
amount of wine, and there was a contest in drinking, the prize
going to him who finished his wine first. Yet it was not so
frivolous an affair as it might seem, for everything was done in
silence. Each guest had not only his own wine, but his own
table, unlike the ordinary social meal where the Greeks, like
us, had one large table for all the guests. It was so unusual that
the Athenians sought a reason for it and decided it was in
commemoration of the visit to Athens of Orestes when he came
to be judged and purified after the killing of his mother, and
those who received him had to find a compromise between
refusing him hospitality altogether and talking, eating and
drinking with one still polluted by blood-guilt. Precisely what
it all meant is still none too certain, but the silence indicates
that the spiritual atmosphere was electrical and every slightest
danger of ill-omened words, or perhaps noise of any kind,
must be avoided. As likely a suggestion as any seems to be that
ghosts were about, and it was well to get the whole ceremonial
over quickly (hence the drinking-race) and quietly. We may
remember that the Passover, also a spring festival, is to be
eaten "in haste," with a show of being anxious to start at once
on a journey. However this may be, Dionysos made himself
felt in the ceremonies of the day by no less a rite than his own
marriage. On that occasion, the wife of the Basileus (cf. p. 79)
was brought to the Bukoleion, her husband's official residence,
attended by a group of women carefully chosen and sworn to
purity and to observance of certain Dionysiac rites. She herself
must be living in a first marriage. The "queen" and her attendants made certain sacrifices, the nature of which was kept

secret; exactly how the sacred marriage was carried out we do not know, but it seems probable that Dionysos, whether represented by an image or, as is quite possible, by the Basileus himself, was brought to the building on a carriage shaped like a ship (he was a foreigner and had come from overseas), and there was introduced to his bride. Yet all this while, the ghosts were about the houses, and everyone chewed whitethorn (it is a laxative and therefore good for keeping off or getting rid of evil things in general) and smeared his doorposts with pitch, whether to catch the ghosts like flies in fly-paper or drive them off by its smell. The day was accounted unlucky for this reason, despite its impressive ceremonies and despite the fact that it seems to have been a joyous time for the children who, if we may trust numerous vase-paintings, had their own imitations of the ceremonial of their elders.

Last came the Chytroi, a name which means simply "pots." It was definitely a day of the dead, for the "pots" in question contained an offering to Hermes, consisting of a kind of porridge made of all manner of edible seeds. The expressed intention was to win his grace for the dead, whose guide he was (cf. p. 62), and a quaint explanation was offered by antiquaries, to the effect that in the days of the Flood (Deukalion's, not Noah's, for this is a Greek tale) the survivors had done this for the first time, on behalf of the souls of the drowned. But a significant fact is that the cooking was not done in the ghosts' time, but by day. No priest might taste of the grains, and apparently each family prepared its own. We may safely conclude that the meal was to be shared by the family dead, who were thus summoned to come back for a little while and once more eat with their living kin. That Hermes was thought to be present also we may well believe.

Later in the month came another festival of high antiquity, the greatest, said Athenian tradition, of the feasts of Zeus. It was called the Diasia and fell on the 23rd. The first thing to notice is that the god in whose honour it was held is Zeus Meilichios, who is not Zeus the weather-god at all, but a chthonian, often shown accompanied by a snake or even in snake-form himself. How he came by the name of Zeus is a point on which opinions differ. Hence it is not surprising

to learn from our authorities that the festival was marked by
"a certain gloom" and that the sacrifice was a holocaust, that
is, entirely burned, none of it being eaten by those present. The
usual offering, from one of the general public, was not a beast
but a cake shaped like one; such beasts as were sacrificed were,
at least usually, swine. However, the day was a holiday for
Athenians, on which guests were invited and gifts given to
children. The god's title, which means something like "easily
entreated," may not have been simply due to politeness or
euphemism; he was one from whom pious people hoped for
benefits. Since, then, the proper rites were being conducted,
there was no reason why the rest of the population should not
enjoy themselves, in secure confidence that Zeus Meilichios
would not hurt them and might bless them.

Elaphebolion, the next month, took its name from the festival of Artemis, the Elaphebolia ("shooting of stags"). The
divine Huntress was given "stags," but not real ones, for the
name was used of a kind of sweet cake, presumably in the shape
of a deer. Far more interesting was the great feast of Dionysos,
which lasted from the 9th, or, counting its preliminaries, the
8th to the 13th. It was known as the Great or the Urban
Dionysia, and popularly as "new tragedians," for it was then
that plays were principally staged. It is fairly certain that
drama in Greece, as in several other parts of the world, began
as a religious or magical rite, though we cannot trace the intervening steps. Whatever ritual mummeries or guisings may have
preceded it, Tragedy first appeared as a literary form in the sixth
century B.C., and was encouraged by that great and enlightened
tyrant, Peisistratos. Its first known author was Thespis of
Ikaria, a district of Attica connected in other ways with Dionysos. Tradition has it that the subject of the first plays was always
the god's own adventures, and it was not till later that other
myths than his were drawn upon. Comedy also seems to have
begun in some kind of rustic merry-making which had a ritual
value, a sort of feast of misrule, in which customary restraints
were at least slackened, and the *komos*, or party of revellers,
after whom the drama itself was named, for "comedy" means
"revel-song," had full licence to use the most outrageous
language and gestures to the most respectable and important

people in their community, including its gods, and not least the god they were honouring. Aristophanes and Kratinos, the greatest masters of Comedy in its earlier form, were but following tradition and pleasing the god of the festival when they portrayed him a coward and a fool, with a gift for getting into absurd and humiliating scrapes. It was not to be expected that politicians, literary men, artists, and ordinary people who had or could be said to have some weakness or peculiarity, should escape comic abuse, which was sometimes pure fun-making, sometimes half or wholly serious criticism. But Comedy became an organized, State-supported performance later than Tragedy, which showed its greater importance by the larger number of productions, twelve plays as against three comedies during the festival, at which other exhibitions also took place, including performances of Dionysos' own variety of hymn, the dithyramb. But the details of the organization, and still more the story of how the plays departed from their original forms and became more literary and less religious, belong to a history of Greek literature, not to a work on Greek religion. The nominal connexion, at least, between the god and the drama was kept up till a late date, for professional actors styled themselves the craftsmen of Dionysos. It may be mentioned in passing that the association of two of the Muses, Melpomene and Thaleia, with Tragedy and Comedy respectively, is the fancy of a few late pedants. It perhaps arose from the fashion of setting up statues of the nine Muses (their number goes back to Hesiod, as do their names), forming a group, in which it was natural to give each Muse some one emblem of the arts, such as a scroll, a lyre or an actor's mask. In cult and in normal imagination, all the Muses, or any of them, might vouchsafe to inspire an artist in any branch; thus, a pretty story is told of how all nine were seen leaving the house of Philemon, the comic poet, on the day he died. Their name means the Reminders, they are, in Hesiod's system, the daughters of Mnemosyne, i.e., Memory, and their function is to call to the mind of anyone they favour the story he is to tell, or the best way to set about a work of art of any kind.

We thus see how the cult of the wild Thraco-Phrygian god of the overflowing vitality of nature was transformed, by Greek moderation and artistic sense, into a decorous festival at which some of the finest products of Greek poetry, and doubtless also of their music, were displayed to a public which seems to have been, on the whole, the most critical and discriminating that ever filled a theatre. In the age of the great dramatists, the fifth century, and for some time afterwards, there were no theatrical performances except at Dionysos' festivals, and the idea of producing plays simply for the amusement of those who liked to pay for seats and for the profit of a manager and his company was quite unheard-of. However secularized in content, the drama continued to be part of a religious ceremony, popular and interesting no doubt, as many ceremonies were, but not to be detached from its context of worship.

In the next month, Munichion, there occurred little of religious interest. It was named after the Munichia, which took place on the 16th, at the same time as an annual commemoration of the victory at Salamis in 480 B.C. This had apparently been attracted to the existing feast-day, for the battle actually was fought later in the year, and a naval display was part of the proceedings. But of the Munichia itself, except that it was a festival of Artemis, we know next to nothing. A better-known rite of hers, though its date is not recorded, was the Brauronia, named after the little town of Brauron on the Attic coast. At this besides the sacrifice of a goat, her most usual victim, there took place a dance of "bears." These were little girls, about ten years old, dressed in robes dyed with saffron, whether to imitate the beast's tawny hide or merely because that was the usual dye for a girl's or woman's holiday frock we do not know. But it gives us a glimpse into something much more primitive than normal Attic cult, suitable for a festival not belonging to the capital itself. The goddess, being lady of wild places and wild things, herself appeared on occasion in bestial shape, and that of a she-bear was one of her manifestations. By a very common tendency of all manner of religions, her worshippers were attracted into their deity's outward form; the bear-goddess is attended by bear-virgins. Another remnant of Artemis' ancient and savage past was preserved at Halai, where the Tauropolia was annually celebrated in her honour. This included a vigil, the women who worshipped the goddess filling the night hours with songs and dances in her honour, but it also contained a last trace of something much grimmer, human sacrifice. A man was led up to the altar and a slight cut, just enough to draw a few drops of blood, made in his throat. It can hardly be doubted that there had been a time when the knife was driven deeper. The Athenians themselves saw that this was the original meaning and, with their usual dislike of savagery, declared that the rite was not Greek, but brought from the land of a barbarian people, the Tauroi, in ancient days. They were right in a way, for the ceremony had no doubt descended to them from an age earlier than the Achaians' arrival in Greece. Whether it was they or the "Pelasgians" who substituted this milder form of bloodshed for the original, we cannot tell. Unlike Dionysos, Artemis never was at home in a city, and consequently showed, in normal Greek cult, clearer traces of her earlier days.

Thargelion, the last month but one of the year, takes its name from the Thargelia, celebrated on the sixth and seventh days in honour of Apollo. The frequent occurrence of this god in the Athenian calendar is probably due to a political reason. Athens claimed to be the mother-city of all Ionians, and Ionians are descended, says the legend, from Ion, son of Apollo, who therefore is the *theòs patrôos* (cf. p. 34) of that whole section of the Greek peoples. Such claims were taken seriously in antiquity. It has been wittily said that the modern equivalent is the concept of race, which is about as historical. At least Apollo, with his loves and his half-divine children, is a more picturesque figure than an abstraction like Nordic Man. So Athens, in secular affairs, more than once appeared as a champion of Ionia against Persian domination, while in religious matters she worshipped Apollo with, apparently, no little fervour until his partisanship for the Spartans and their allies during the Peloponnesian War cost him his popularity, though the city never went the length of abolishing his official honours. On the sixth of the month took place a curious rite of purification, the Athenian form of a custom fairly widespread and used especially in Ionia and one or two cities culturally connected with it, either for an annual expulsion of ill-luck or on extraordinary occasions such as a plague. It is essentially the same as the Hebrew rite of the scapegoat, for it consisted in loading the accumulated ill-luck, or sin, on to living beings and then getting rid of them and their burden together. Two wretched and ugly men were chosen, one for the men and one for the women of Athens. For some reason which is not easy to find, they were then adorned with strings of dried figs, black for the men's representative, white for the other. Finally they were driven out of the city; possibly, though this is not directly testified, they were stoned out. How they were chosen, if they were natives or foreigners, bond or free, whether they were compensated for their uncongenial duties or forced to accomplish them, and precisely how the ill-fortune of the inhabitants of Athens was transferred to them are points on which we lack information, but the general purport of the rite is clear. Also, the word used to describe them, *phármakoi*, i.e., men acting as a *phármakon* (cf. p. 80), was the reverse of complimentary; when Aristophanes is abusing the politicians of the day, he says that in old times Athens would not even have used such people as *phármakoi*. The next day saw the now purified city performing the ceremony from which the whole festival had its name. Grain from the ripening crops was cooked in pots and formally presented to Apollo. These first-fruits were called *thargélia*, and no doubt the point of the offering was to secure, by bringing the god into contact with the cereals, his good influence for the coming harvest.

Later in the month, on the 24th and 25th, probably, though the exact days are not certain, fell two ceremonies which go back to the ancient and naïve conception of the statues of the gods as being themselves divine and living in the temples which sheltered them. Athena, like all good housewives, must have her times of housecleaning and clothes-washing, and that is what is meant by the names of the days, Kallynteria and Plynteria. Of the former, we know only what the name tells us; *kallýnein* means to tidy a room or house, to sweep and dust it, therefore that was what happened on that day to Athena's official abode. As to the latter, we are better informed. We know that two girls, called "bath-women" or "laundresses," took Athena, that is to say, her ancient statue, for that was the really sacred cult-object, not the magnificent figure which Pheidias wrought for the Parthenon, down to the sea at

Phaleron, the old harbour which was in use before the Peiraieus. Superintending their activities and the procession which attended the goddess were members of an old family, the Praxiergidai, whose duties further included undressing the goddess and wrapping her in a cloth before the procession started, and dressing her again that evening, when the return to the temple was made by torchlight. This was not the only statue of Athena which was so treated, for we know that a similar rite went on at Argos, the chief difference being that the bath took place in a river, not the sea. It need surprise no one that the two days so occupied were ill-omened; the goddess was too busy to attend to her usual functions.

We have seen that the last month, Skirophorion, got its name from the *skira* (see p. 76). It had another interesting and ancient festival, the Dipolieia, that is to say, the feast of Zeus Polieus, or god of the city and its citadel (*polis* means both in Attic use). Its date is the 14th, that is to say, at full moon, an appropriate time for the rites of a sky-god; in like manner the Romans honoured their Juppiter at the Ides, the middle day of the lunar month. But the most striking and puzzling ceremony of this holy day was the Buphonia, literally the murder (*phónos* in Greek law means homicide) of the ox. Usually, in a Greek sacrifice, the beast was killed with due observance of ritual, its flesh was disposed of with or without a sacrificial feast, and that ended the matter. Apart from certain vegetarian sectaries and some few philosophers, all of comparatively late date, no one seemed ever to feel that there was anything wrong in killing the creature to furnish a meal for the god, with or without his worshippers. But in this instance a most extraordinary mummery was gone through, the details of which are obscured by contradictory ancient accounts of what happened. Keeping to the simplest and most credible description, that of Pausanias, we find that, to begin with, grain was laid upon the altar of Zeus, which would consecrate it to the god; cereal offerings were very common and could be made without any animal sacrifice. They were left unguarded, and an ox allowed to come up and eat of them. A priest, technically known as the ox-slayer (*buphónos*), then killed the ox, threw down the axe he had used, and ran away. By Attic law, inanimate objects which had caused anyone's death could be formally tried for murder, and this was solemnly done to the axe, which apparently was found guilty and thrown away, probably into the sea. Why such tenderness should be shown in the case of this one ox, when hundreds of others were killed every year, up and down Greece, in the service of Zeus and other deities, is a question which has been answered in a variety of ways by students both ancient and modern, without any explanation as yet finding general acceptance. Perhaps as likely a suggestion as any is that the animal, having eaten the holy food of Zeus, itself became sacred and could not be killed without danger, like a common beast. Yet sacrificed it must be, for the god in whose honour the festival was held could not miss his promised gift. Therefore it was killed, but with precautions; the weapon which had struck it down, and so had become charged with highly dangerous *mana*, was as perilous as if it had killed a man and had the pollution of death and blood-guilt upon it, and therefore was got rid of in due form. The priest who had handled the axe had not, presumably, actually touched the ox, and therefore, separating himself as he did from the *mana*-laden implement as soon as possible, and avoiding the equally dangerous neighbourhood, he was not affected.

The month and the year closed with a sacrifice to Zeus and Athena, both of whom bore the title of Saviour (Soter, Soteira).

This, in outline and with omission of a number of festivals which were merely commemorative of events in Athenian history, or were brought in by foreigners with the permission of the Athenian government, or finally are so obscure and difficult that the proper place for the discussion of them is a full technical description of the religion of Athens, was the ecclesiastical year of that Greek community which we know best, or rather of which we are, in this and other respects, least ignorant. A few general remarks may conclude this chapter.

It is not only in the titles of this or that god but in countless passages in the surviving literature which speak of their relations to mankind that we find Greek deities described as saviours. The salvation they brought was of a purely material kind, protection of communities, and, to a somewhat lesser degree, of individuals, from the physical dangers of political or individual life. Some gods specialized in warding off a particular kind of danger from those who appealed to them; for instance, the Dioskuroi (cf. p. 60) rescued mariners in distress, by calming the storm; the phenomenon known as St. Elmo's fire was associated with them, and if it appeared at two points on the rigging was held to be a good sign. But generally, any god might and, in the belief of the average man and the average community, did save from anything that might threaten. Thus it was especially the task of the principal deity of a city, say of Hera at Argos or Athena at Athens, to save that city from enemies, though other gods might help.

How, then, did the gods of a city fare if the city was taken and destroyed? The usual answer was that they left it. Sometimes it was said that they turned against its inhabitants and, in punishment for some offence, helped to destroy it. Although, in a way, the deities of any state were a kind of very superior citizens, yet they were immortal and all-powerful, consequently they could not be killed or enslaved. But certainly the faithful expected that they would not let things come to the last extremity. Hence the cults of the classical age had two weaknesses. The objects of communal worship were in a sense on trial, and if they could not protect their adorers, these might no longer trust them, but either turn to other gods or cease to believe in divine protection altogether. Secondly, the individual, who normally had trusted in the general justice and kindliness of his gods, was liable, sooner or later, either to feel wants which were not physical and so lay outside the normal range of divine blessings, or to be confronted with the problem why the good, who presumably are well-pleasing to the gods, do not always prosper. Philosophy supplied reasoned and elaborate answers to both difficulties; but this is not a history of ancient philosophy, and the following chapters will discuss rather the solutions which occurred to the unphilosophical when, from either of the causes mentioned, the established system of worship became unsatisfactory. For between unintelligent and uncritical acceptance of traditional ways, or equally unintelligent rejection of them *en masse*, and the thoroughgoing attempts of really superior minds to explain the world and its governance by logical deduction from first principles which are or seem too certain to be questioned, there lie a multitude of stages, some more, some less intellectual, of modification, variation, elaboration of the beliefs with which the dissatisfied enquirer starts, and, perhaps still more important, a great variety of emotional reactions, which induce correspondingly varied tendencies to this or that type of religious, or irreligious, conduct.

Finally, the democratization of parts of Greece accompanied the growth of ethical feeling, first among the more philosophic minds and then, working down from them, among the multitude. The old acceptance of the gods as having laws of conduct peculiarly their own grew less and less general. If there were principles of good and evil action binding on all men alike, why not on men and gods as well? Alternatively, if some things were right for men and others for gods, was there any real moral difference between actions at all?

Thus the three assumptions, that gods exist, are beneficent and regard righteousness, which underlay normal Greek cult became less axiomatic as time went on. Not only the philosopher but the tolerably intelligent ordinary man felt something of the resulting difficulties. Some of the better-known solutions will be dealt with in the next chapter.

CHAPTER V

THE GODS ON TRIAL

THAT the gods hate evil, at least some kinds of evil, and punish it is an assumption as old as Homer, who represents Zeus as saying that it is men's own frowardness which brings upon them troubles beyond the allotted portion which everyone must endure. That Zeus is lord of the universe and is just is insisted upon by Hesiod, whose zeal for righteousness is as marked as that of Amos, his probable contemporary. Hesiod also gives us that normal, moderately optimistic Greek picture of the results of righteousness and unrighteousness. The former means a community with enough to eat, protection against enemies, and so forth, in fact the degree of prosperity which a small free cultivator like himself might hope for, a condition of things under which the hard-working man made enough to live on in decent comfort, though no more. The latter results in defeat, plague and other such disasters which would quickly bring at least the poorer classes down to the starvation-line. Obviously, then, to anyone who accepted Hesiod's universe, a time of great economic and political upset, resulting in widespread hardship and ruin to many, would be a time of unrighteousness, deservedly incurring the wrath of heaven.

Now the centuries just preceding the rise of the great cities of the classical epoch were an age of turmoil. Revolution, economic and political, was a commonplace. The old forms of government were often violently overset and replaced by tyrannies, in other words the irresponsible rule of men carried into power by force or guile, generally as heads of a successful faction. New forms of wealth arose, owing to the increase of trade and the introduction of the Lydian invention of coined money. At the same time, military tactics altered; the old-fashioned Homeric warrior, dashing about in his chariot and alighting to fight, protected by his elaborate armour, against a foe equipped like himself, gave place to the pikeman (*hoplites*), who, in close order with his comrades, made a wall of points which only another body of pikemen could break. Thus the man of such moderate means as would enable him to procure shield, spear and the rest of the infantry-man's armament had become of military importance, if not individually, at least as a class, and since that class often proved too much for the traditional nobility, there was always a possibility that in times of discontent some of them might also tamper with the traditional hierarchy of the gods. It is not, then, surprising that by about the sixth century or earlier we hear of religious innovations.

Of these, one of the most remarkable was expressed in a considerable amount of literature, in verse, ascribed to Orpheus, a legendary musician and prophet of Thrace, or to some one closely connected with him, such as Musaios, his kinsman or pupil. It is convenient to call this Orphism, though we have no right to claim that there ever was a single and self-consistent body of Orphic doctrine, still less that there existed anything like an Orphic church. What did exist, however, in some of this literature at least, and apparently at a fairly early date, was a strange other-worldly religion, remarkably unlike the normal Greek beliefs as shown in their ritual and customs. Yet it is the sort of religion which one could imagine springing up among individuals and classes of society which combined lively faith in gods of some sort with bewilderment at the hardships which fell to the lot of themselves and others in those troublous times, while at the same time their intellectual development was not so advanced as to make them be repelled by crudities and absurdities in their own or their teachers' portrayal of divinities. The new doctrine, once accepted, accounted satisfactorily enough for the misfortunes of the good in this life, and held out hopes of compensation in another. It was nothing less than a doctrine of original sin and regeneration, of heaven, purgatory and hell.

The myth which embodied these teachings has come down to us only in writers very much later than the time of which we are speaking, but there is evidence that its kernel at least is really old. Zeus, according to these authors, had a son, Zagreus, by his daughter Persephone, and intended to make the infant lord of the universe. But the Titans, incited by Hera, contrived to murder the child, whom they devoured. Zeus killed the Titans with his thunderbolts and from their ashes sprang men, who thus have in them a little of the divine nature of Zagreus and a great deal also of the Titanic wickedness. Zeus swallowed Zagreus' heart, which Athena had saved, and then proceeded to beget Dionysos, who is therefore a second Zagreus. The chief end of man is to rid himself of the Titanic and preserve the divine element in his complex being. He has before him a long series of lives, in this world and the next, during each of which he may be rewarded and punished for the good and evil deeds in the preceding existence. In the end, if he perseveres, it would seem that he may attain something like deity and eternal happiness. The method he is to use is the Orphic life, a mixture of ceremonies and abstinences (some Orphics at least were vegetarians, for example) with some modicum at any rate of ethical conduct.

Given any such belief as this, it is evident that a sort of explanation and no small degree of comfort in his misfortunes was afforded the devotee of this religion. If he seemed to suffer undeserved misfortunes, it was because he had offended in some way the last time he was in the other world, or at all events had not yet advanced so far that Persephone was reconciled to him and had forgiven him his share of ancestral guilt. If he persevered, he might hope at least for a much happier existence when next he changed this life for one in her realm, at best for elevation to very exalted rank indeed, perhaps returning to earth as a king or a sage and winning his way in time to superhuman status. If his unjust neighbour prospered, he might console himself by the thought that such injustice would be severely punished in another life. Meantime, if he seemed insignificant to his fellows, at least a god, and a great one, was interested in him and would see that he got his just reward in the end. Incidentally, and this was probably no small matter in an age in which the superstitions of certain strata of the populace, which Homeric tradition had quite neglected in favour of the comparatively rational beliefs of the feudal gentry, were making their way to the surface and becoming articulate, there were to be found schools of thought which provided a justification for some at least of his traditional or acquired religious practices. Pythagoreanism, which at its best was a highly intellectual system, had on its fringes a most extraordinary mass of tabus, in their origin showing a mentality no better than that of a savage, which seem to have been taken up by some members at least of the school and given a justification, probably by methods of interpretation not unlike those in use at a much later date, which found in them allegorical precepts of morality and religion. In this strange region of thought, a man might observe such precepts as, never to leave the impress of his body on the bed-clothes in which he had slept, not to eat certain unlucky kinds of fish, not to use a knife to stir his fire, and hundreds more of the same kind, with the satisfaction of knowing that he was, by doing so, brought into a kind of fellowship with men whose learning and wisdom were renowned throughout those districts (Southern Italy and Eastern Sicily especially) where Pythagoras' followers were active. In Pythagoreanism also, or in its popular off-shoots, he might find justification for a belief which has left its traces here and there in the Greek region, namely, reincarnation. Although, as already said, there was nothing like an organized religious body teaching Orphic doctrine, the ideas themselves were abroad and showed their influence in many quarters during the greatest ages of Greek culture, the sixth, fifth and fourth centuries B.C. Peisistratos, tyrant of Athens, who looked to popular support for his enlightened and mild despotism, would appear to have encouraged Orphic literature; certainly we hear that Onomakritos, a celebrated diviner of that age, was banished for interpolating some prophecies of his own forging into a collection of the oracles ascribed to Musaios. The culprit was caught in the act by Lasos of Hermione, a poet of great technical skill who is said to have taught the great Pindar, and the sentence pronounced by Peisistratos' son Hipparchos, who himself acquired a reputation for teaching popular morality to his subjects, or his father's, by inscribing wise laws on the monuments he erected. At Delphoi there was set up a picture of the underworld, very different from that given in the Homeric poems, where the bulk of the dead continue to lead a life which faintly shadows their earthly activities, and no one is tormented save a few direct offenders against the gods, such as Tantalos, who stole their divine food, and the giant Tityos, who tried to rape Leto. The picture, which was executed by

Polygnotos, a contemporary of Sokrates, and so cannot be much later than the end of the fifth century, purported to represent a Homeric scene, the visit of Odysseus to the other world in search of advice from the ghost of Teiresias, the Theban seer. But it is a world very different from Homer's realm of the dead. Conspicuous on the banks of the infernal river Acheron were an undutiful son being strangled by the father he had wronged and a temple-robber also in torment. Elsewhere, the daughters of Pandareos, who according to Homer were mysteriously snatched away by whirlwinds, were revealed in a state suitable to their innocent youth; they were crowned with flowers and merrily playing. Orpheus himself was seen there, standing in a grove and attended by musicians of the past. In another section of the great painting, two women were trying to carry water in broken pitchers, and an inscription told the spectators that they had neglected to be initiated. Their punishment, apparently, was to strive endlessly and fruitlessly to get water for the lustral bath which was part of most ceremonies. A legend condemns to a like fate the daughters of Danaos, who sinned grievously against the sanctity of marriage by murdering their husbands. But it was not only the painters who took hints from the other-worldly doctrines that were taught around them; so great a poet as Pindar, who for his own part was a most pious and enlightened worshipper of the established gods and especially of Apollo, was attracted by such teaching and introduced it more than once into poems which were to bring comfort to the sick or bereaved. We still have from him descriptions of a blessed existence in which there is abundance of activity such as a Greek of the upper classes loved, but no toil and no want. Later, Plato himself introduced myths of what may be called Orphic colour into his works, when he would find appropriate imagery for his intuitions concerning the lot of the soul.

As might be expected, there was a reverse side to this picture. In Greece, as in other countries, there were rascals who traded on the fear of what might happen after death which not a few Greeks by this time began to entertain, some it may be vividly and continually, more, like old Kephalos in Plato's *Republic*, when weakened by age or infirmity. We know, also from Plato, that there were to be found pushful sellers of indulgences, so to call them, who knocked at the doors of the rich, produced whole libraries of books by Orpheus and Musaios, and professed themselves ready, at very reasonable fees, either to secure divine forgiveness for any sins of their patrons, including ancestral guilt, or, if preferred, to put a curse on those patrons' enemies. Needless to say, such impostors knew better than to prescribe a life of asceticism, but advised sacrifices, with their attendant feasts, which would procure for those who performed them both success in this life and freedom from all pains and penalties in the next. There was no scripture universally regarded as inspired for these men to quote, but a text of Homer was nearly as authoritative, and they did not fail to cite, out of its context, the remark of old Phoinix in the *Iliad* that the gods have mercy on sinners who approach them with prayers and offerings. This sort of thing was apparently quite common in the fourth century, the wane of the classical period, when Greece, weakened by the series of intestine wars, contained many anxious people, the more likely to turn their hopes in what was, for Greeks generally, an abnormal direction. Other hedge-priests of a like type were plentiful, not only for wealthy men, but for those of moderate means, when they needed something more exciting than the sober State cults. Theophrastos' pietist, of whom we have already made the acquaintance, was one of the customers of the *Orpheotelestai*, or performers of rites laid down by Orpheus, to whom he would resort once a month, taking his children and his wife, if she was not too busy, in which case he would bring the nurse with him.

To the average man, there were two sources for a knowledge of what the gods were like, art and the traditional myths concerning them. Neither of these constituted articles of faith, but they were generally received. Few would doubt, for instance, that Zeus, if he appeared in his true shape and human eyes could bear the sight, would have the outward form of a majestic and stalwart man in the prime of life, Athena that of a strongly-built and sternly beautiful woman in the armour of a Greek foot-soldier, while Aphrodite's beauty would be of a softer and more voluptuous type, and Hermes would show himself as a graceful young man with intelligent and kindly features. Yet there were dissenting voices. Near the beginning of the fifth century lived an eccentric rhapsode, or professional reciter of epic, named Xenophanes, who spent some part of his time in contradicting, even reviling, the very poets by whose works he gained his livelihood, and the artists whose carvings and paintings adorned the public buildings near or in which his audiences gathered. If cattle and horses, one of his poems stated, could and would make pictures or statues of the gods, they would show them in bestial form. Ethiopian gods are black and flat-nosed, Thracian deities have blue eyes and red hair. The greatest god of all neither looks nor thinks like a man, but is all sight, all hearing and all mind, governing everything by his intellect, without effort, and never changing. So much for art. As to myths, Homer, all men's teacher from the beginning, and Hesiod likewise, had attributed to gods the very acts most disgraceful in human beings, such as theft, adultery and deceit. Few, perhaps, at that date went so far as Xenophanes, who was on the borderline between poetry and philosophy (later ages classed him as a philosopher), but many, no doubt, would have agreed with part of what he said.

For we find, even at a date much earlier than his, a tendency to correct the existing myths in the interests of morality or theology. It is Hesiod who tells the story (cf. p. 38) of how Prometheus befooled Zeus; it is Hesiod also who spoils it by saying that Zeus was not really deceived at all, but only pretended to be. Hesiod's fellow-countryman, Pindar, can be very critical of myths. A story was told how Tantalos, to test the gods' omniscience, served up to them the flesh of his own son Pelops. One of them ate a little of it without recognizing it, and ever afterwards Pelops had, though miraculously restored to life, one shoulder of ivory and not of flesh. To Pindar this is both incredible and impious. Pelops was snatched up alive to heaven by Poseidon, who loved him for his beauty, and the tale that he had been murdered by his father was nothing but slander. As to his ivory shoulder, he had had that from his birth. When Apollo loved Koronis, mother of Asklepios, and she played him false, no bird warned him of her misdoings; his own divine omniscience told him. Tales of the battles between gods are best left untold; Pindar dares not handle them. Years later, Euripides, who was a radical in religious matters as in many others, put into the mouth of one of his characters the bold statement, "If the gods do aught base, they are no gods." Pindar would have said rather that they are gods, therefore they do nothing base, whatever lying fables men tell of them. Nor was it only poets and philosophers who thus corrected mythology. It seems to have been believed for a while in Athens that Peisistratos was raised to power by Athena in person. But this was offensive to the moral sense of the republic which succeeded the fall of his house; how could a goddess so debase herself as to favour a tyrant, even an intelligent and mild one like Peisistratos? By the time Herodotos, about two generations after the establishment of democracy, heard the story, it was all a trick of the wily adventurer, who dressed up a tall, fine-looking woman in appropriate costume and took her with him into the city. Herodotos is a little doubtful, for it is strange to him that the sharp-witted Athenians should have been imposed upon by so transparent a fraud. But others had a lower opinion of the intelligence of the common people, and a few, who seem not to have won much assent, went so far as to class all mythology and all religion with Peisistratos' alleged ruse. When government was new, so Kritias the oligarch, who was a friend of Sokrates, taught in a tragedy he composed, it was soon discovered that while the laws could check overt wrong-doing, it still went on in secret. Therefore, some subtle man invented the gods, and told the public that they lived for ever, knew everything, and so could not be deceived, also that their dwelling was in the sky and they had the thunder and other formidable phenomena at their disposal. Thus religion is a salutary check on the vicious vulgar. Whether this doctrine was put into the mouth of a sympathetic character or of the mythical rascal Sisyphos who gave the play its title, we do not know, for no more of it is preserved; but it found a certain amount of acceptance here and there. So also, but mostly in later times, and among Romans or Christian apologists rather than normal Greeks, did the strange romance of Euhemeros, who lived about the end of the fourth century B.C. In his rather stupid work, an inscription had been discovered on a conveniently distant island, in which it was shown clearly that the conventional gods were real and the stories about them largely true, but with this difference, that they were ancient kings and other noteworthy persons, deified after death by the gratitude or flattery of their people. But Euhemeros did not deny that there were such beings as gods at all, for he mentioned certain celestial ones, perhaps the heavenly bodies. Still less did Epicurus, who was his contemporary, for his system involved supposing the conventional figures of the gods really to exist. But their abode was out in space, between the innumerable universes which Epicurus postulated; they were perfectly happy, and therefore they had no such toilsome duties as looking after the world or mankind. They had created nothing and would harm nothing and no one.

"That which is blessed and imperishable," he wrote, "has no troubles itself and makes none for another; therefore it is not bound by fits of anger or feelings of good-will, for all that belongs to weakness."

Such beings it was very proper to admire, but neither to fear injuries nor to expect blessings from them. Earlier than either of these men, the great sophist Protagoras had said that he could not tell whether there were gods or not. But downright atheism was a very rare phenomenon in antiquity; those who were called atheists for the most part turn out, on examination, to have been deniers simply of the current religious opinions. It is interesting to note that in late times the word is applied to Christians, who of course denied the divinity of all the pagan deities, but certainly did not hold that there was no God at all.

The generality of Greek mankind, therefore, continued to believe that there were gods of some sort, and usually that the traditional ones existed. But as the political situation worsened for the Greek city-states, there were many who doubted if the gods deserved their title of Saviours. Solon had proclaimed that Athens was sheltered under the mighty hands of its tutelary goddess. In the Macedonian period, Athens changed hands more than once and was often under foreign domination. What had become of Athena's power to save? And, if she and her like could not preserve their worshippers, to whom should men look? One answer, though never very popular in Greece itself, gained currency and at least official recognition in many Greek-speaking cities, such as Alexandria, where the population was largely non-European in origin, the fruit of Alexander the Great's spread of Hellenic culture to the mainland of Asia and to Egypt. It was, that a new kind of saviour-god was manifest in the persons of the great kings who succeeded him, and whose alliance and friendship was certainly worth having. If these men could save, which the gods were supposed to do, why not draw the logical consequence and call them gods? It was not pure flattery, though it disgusted many Athenians, when an Athenian poet addressed these words to that brilliant but unstable prince, Demetrios Poliorketes, on his visit to their city:

> "For other gods live far, so far, away,
> Or, belike, are earless,
> Or are not, or care nothing how we fare.
> Thee we see before us,
> Not bronze nor marble, but thy very self,
> Therefore thus we pray thee:
> Before all else, beloved, grant us peace,
> For 'tis thine to give it."

This was no isolated freak of a verse-writer, for the whole city had turned out to meet the exalted visitor, garlanded, burning incense and pouring libations. Nor was it confined to Athens, for temples to Demetrios' mother and his mistresses sprang up in several places, and he himself was credited with being the son of Poseidon and Aphrodite. He had, despite his ambition and erratic life, too much common sense to relish this sort of thing, unlike that extraordinary person, Menekrates the physician, who insisted on being called Zeus and gave the names of lesser gods to his attendants, patients cured, as was alleged, of epilepsy (the "holy disease" in Greek, because it was commonly thought to be a supernatural visitation). This oddity, who seems really to have been a man of considerable skill in his profession, was a native of Syracuse, corresponded with kings on the footing of one potentate addressing another (a tone which Philip II of Macedon, father of Alexander, did not relish), and dressed in a costume copied from statues of deities, especially, of course, Zeus. But even such freaks of individuals of probably unsound mind were not so offensive to the general religious consciousness, nor so markedly blasphemous in tone, as the similar insanities which occur to-day and as a rule are promptly subjected to proper treatment in madhouses. There was indeed a great gap between men and gods to the ordinary Greek mind; they are children of the same mother, says Pindar, although man is as naught and the gods have their heaven which abides firm forever. But the gap is not infinite, nor quite unbridgeable. In popular estimation, several of the existing gods had once been men, notably Herakles, whom indeed more than one of the later philosophies took as their prime example of the way in which transcendent virtue can raise a man above humanity. As regards kings especially, from at least the time of Plato, when the failure of Greek democracy was becoming plain to the more intelligent and opinion was moving towards monarchy of some kind, a very high standard was set for the man of truly royal temperament, that is to say, fitted to govern a state, whether he had the title of king or not. When Alexander and his successors revolutionized the political situation in Greek-speaking lands and beyond them, substituting great monarchies everywhere for the smaller political units, the question of what constituted an ideal king and how the aspirant for so exalted a post should be trained was obviously of more than theoretical interest, and hundreds of essays were written on the subject, whereof considerable fragments have come down to us. In these, and not merely in court poetry, we find it stated often enough that a king is, if not exactly a god, at least parallel to one, corresponding on earth to deity in heaven, and that his is a rare type, much excelling ordinary humanity, an imitator of Zeus himself, not inferior to him in moral worth, and so forth. It was therefore not illogical that when an able king died he should be deified, as several of the Ptolemies were in Egypt, for example. However, this reverence for monarchy, together with its theoretical basis, developed chiefly outside of Greece proper and her older colonies, and to discuss it belongs more to an account of Roman, or rather Græco-Roman, than purely Greek religion. Let us return to those developments which were more normal in Greece.

Apart from the treatments of mythology which have been dealt with, there were two others at least which found considerable favour among those who had some tincture of philosophy and therefore were open to new doctrines originating among the philosophical schools or their predecessors, the lectures of the fifth-century sophists. One was, to regard the myths as dealing with personified natural forces. Poetical language, familiar to everyone from the many writers in verse whose works formed the basis of education in all Greek schools, helped this assumption. For instance, it had been common since Homer's day to speak of Hephaistos when nothing more than fire was meant. Also, some at least of the minor deities really were a sort of personification, in the sense that they arose out of the animistic outlook on nature (cf. p. 21). Thus the same word, Boreas, was the name of the north wind and of the legendary being supposed to govern it. Hence it needed no great ingenuity (as Plato shows when he ironically pretends to admire the cleverness of the theory) to say that an Attic story, how Boreas had carried off the daughter of one of the kings of Athens and married her, was nothing but a poetical record of her death by an unfortunate accident. She had been blown off a hill-top by a strong blast of wind, and thus killed. Many explanations were far more elaborate than this, and not a few of them depended upon etymologies, which, in the infancy of grammatical science, were generally nothing more than bad puns. Zeus was the subject of some of the worst. His name, a very old one, is declined in more than one way, and among the resulting forms are an accusative, *Dia*, and a by-form of the nominative, *Zen* or *Zan*. These happen to sound like the Greek words for "through" and "live" respectively, hence it was often assumed, in one form or another, that he was thus named because he was the power through whom things happen, or who gives life. His consort was the subject of like speculations. Her name, Hera, easily transposed into *aër*, for the aspirate, always lightly pronounced in Greek, tended strongly to be dropped altogether in some dialects and was not always written as a separate letter in the current alphabets. Once this was accepted, obviously all the objections to her legends vanished. A jealous and ill-tempered goddess might be an unworthy object of worship, but if the myths were nothing but a figurative way of speaking of atmospheric disturbances, they at once became harmless poetical ornaments. Their father, Kronos, yielded even more easily to such pious word-play, for it needed only to aspirate the first letter of his name to make him Chronos, Time. A very ancient story told how the god, fearing to be overthrown by his own children, swallowed them, or at least the males, as fast as they were born. To believe such things of a veritable god shocked the feelings of those who took the myths at all seriously, but what harm was there in setting forth in an allegory the observed fact that Time, which brings everything to pass, also brings everything to an end? Ingenuity, coupled with a great reverence for the wisdom and piety of their forefathers, led Greeks to indulge in most extraordinary explanations of their literary heritage. Plutarch, whose writings are a storehouse of interesting speculations, picked up from his wide reading and augmented by his own meditations, for he was a man of thoughtful and deeply religious temperament, has left us an essay on how to benefit from studying the poets. It contains some most remarkable distortions of their plain meaning, especially of Homer's, in the interests of morality and theology. For instance, Homer says that the gods spin a life of woe for "wretched mortals", the epithet being a recurrent one in Epic. But the gods, being beneficent, assuredly do no such thing. We must therefore, according to Plutarch, understand the adjective to be used pityingly of foolish persons, to whom life is indeed woeful, because their own stupidity and ill-doing make it so. Hesiod says that Prometheus advised his duller brother Epimetheus to accept no gift from Zeus. But certainly Prometheus gave no such irreligious advice to anyone. Clearly, then, "Zeus" is used by poetic licence for "fortune," and Epimetheus was warned not to put his trust in the deceits of worldly wealth, which comes by luck and not by desert. Those readers who are acquainted with the older interpreters of the Bible will recognize something familiar in this exegesis, and rightly, for the strange meanings which a number of ancient critics, such as Philon of Alexandria and above all Origen, got out of Scriptural texts are the direct descendant of this moral exposition of classical authors.

If myths, which at least make definite statements, and poets, who give their own form to myths, were subject to such strange treatment, it was not to be expected that ritual would be left without comment. As Aristotle well says in a famous passage, those undergoing an initiatory rite are not to learn anything, but to experience something and get into a certain frame of mind. And, as already stated (p. 73), not a few who underwent such ceremonies as those of Eleusis came out profoundly impressed. Cicero, whose philosophical works preserve many Greek ideas of his own and earlier times, seems at first glance to contradict Aristotle in speaking of Eleusis, at which, he says, "we not only learn with gladness the way of living, but with it a better hope in dying." But, as so often, Plutarch gives us the key to the puzzle. Cicero, as he recommends, had evidently brought with him to his own initiation "a doctrine from philosophy to be his guide." He had read into what he saw in the Hall of Initiation ideas which he had learned in a philosopher's lecture-room or from private study. But he was far from being the only man to do the like, and Eleusis by no means the only ritual to furnish material for edification to those who came with at least the beginnings of a religion of their own. For example, in Greek cult as in all other, purity was an essential prerequisite for those who would take part in worship, whether at a shrine or elsewhere. To begin with, this was a formal affair. The would-be worshipper washed; he put on clean clothing of the prescribed colour (for instance, an inscription tells us that women who wished to be initiated into the rites of Despoina, a goddess adored at Lykosura in the Peloponnesos, must have on no jewellery, be barefooted, and dress neither in purple, black, nor any embroidered fabric). He also observed various ritual abstinences. Some of these were from certain foods; thus, at Lindos in Rhodes, anyone who had eaten cheese must wait a day before entering the temple, and if he had eaten goat's flesh or beans, three days were required. But one of the most important requirements was sexual continence; generally speaking, the sexual act disqualified from worship for a longer or shorter period, as did also contact with the two ends of life, i.e., with a woman in childbirth or with a corpse. But here, moral ideas began to intrude. At Pergamon, for instance, if a man had been with his own wife or a woman with her own husband, either was welcomed at the temple of Athena that same day. If the indulgence had been illicit, two days and a lustral bath were needed. This is no great distinction, but Theano, wife of Pythagoras, is credited with a complete transference of the ancient tabu into the ethical sphere. Someone asked her, as an authority on sacral matters, how long a woman must wait to be ritually pure after contact with a man. She replied, "If it was her own husband, she is pure at once; if any other man, she never can be." Theano is a misty figure, like most early Pythagoreans, but the sentiment was not peculiar to her. Apollo, renowned for his advocacy of purificatory rites, was not untouched by such moralizing of them, if we may believe some of the pious legends told concerning Delphoi, one of the most famous being that of the three travellers. They were attacked by brigands on the way to the shrine; one ran away, the other two defended themselves, and in the scuffle one of them wounded the other accidentally, so that he died. The robbers, however, were beaten off, and the survivor, thus polluted by the blood of his dead friend, hurried to ask the oracle how he might be purified. The god answered by the mouth of his priestess,

"Thou hast slain thy comrade in trying to defend him; this blood hath not polluted thee, but thou art cleaner than before."

but when the pilgrim who ran away arrived at the temple, he was bidden to leave it, as being no better than a murderer. Someone put about a pretty little poem which he alleged was an oracle given at Delphoi. It bade the worshipper to come in a state of purity, but it is purity of soul. The good are sufficiently cleansed by the usual lustration in running water, but all the stream of Ocean will not suffice for the wicked. Another poet made the god say that the good needed no purification at all, and the temple-doors stood open to them, whereas the bad were none the cleaner in soul for all their bodily washings. Whether Apollo's official clergy ever put forth such sayings as these or not, it is fairly to be assumed that they are the kind of sentiments which many thought appropriate to the god. Thus, as the moral conscience of the more enlightened Greeks developed, they put a corresponding interpretation on the every-day religious acts and credited their deities with the principles which they themselves professed and often followed. If we once more take Plutarch for our guide, as being one of the most amiable pietists of whom we know anything, and also the one whose works have come down to us most nearly complete, we find in him curious examples of this tendency. He was very much interested in ritual, both Greek and foreign, and he found in it his own gentle intellectualism and his own kindness of heart. Being convinced that such is its meaning, he does not shrink from the boldest allegorizing. For instance, he knows that permanent trophies are new things in Greece, and that it was the older Roman custom not to repair or renew them. A trophy (*trópaion*) was erected at the spot where the rout (*tropé*) of the enemy had taken place. It consisted normally of a suit of armour taken from them and set up on a rough wooden mount, often a tree-trunk with two short boughs projecting cross-wise from it. It probably was in origin a piece of war-magic, the hostile armour being exposed to the weather until it fell to pieces, in hopes of affecting in like manner the equipment the enemy still had and their power of waging war. But Plutarch is of opinion that the authors of the custom either wanted their citizens not to dwell too long on memorials of their former valour and success, but win new renown by fresh deeds, or else intended enmity not to be too lasting, and so provided for the quick decay of everything which might remind them of it. He knew also that white is occasionally a mourning colour, that the dead are mostly clothed in white and that they are taken to burial with garlands on their heads. This, to him, indicates the prudence and optimism in face of death of the ancients who began this practice. The dead man is free from the body, which stained or dyed his soul as colouring matters dye wool. Also, he has emerged victorious from the struggle of life. Is it not, then, most fitting that he should be dressed in a white fabric, signifying the simplicity of the soul's true nature, and at the same time brightness and cleanness? The wreath others certainly, Plutarch it may be, assimilated to that which a victorious athlete wore.

Plutarch's gods are kindly and free from jealousy; to think otherwise is base superstition, and more displeasing to them than any atheism could be. As he teaches in a famous passage of his essay *On Superstition*, he himself had far rather someone denied that any such person as Plutarch ever existed than have it said of him that he was a man capable of mean anger and cruel revenges. So it is, no doubt, with the gods. But there is one blessing above all which he seeks from them, and that is wisdom, especially that wisdom which leads to knowledge of the divine nature. This, he tells his friend Klea, a lady of tastes like his own, is something which the gods share with us, while their other blessings are merely things which they give at our need. Their greatness lies in their wisdom, not in their power, and if they had not such wisdom, their everlasting life would be nothing but empty time. The goal of true worship is knowledge, *gnosis*, a word of which we shall hear more later. It is to be found in the mysteries, if they are understood rightly, and it sometimes includes strange details.

"That Osiris is the same as Dionysos, who should know better than you, Klea, seeing that you are a leader of the Thyiads [female worshippers of Dionysos] at Delphoi, and consecrated to the rites of Osiris as your father and mother were before you? But if we must have evidence for the benefit of others, let us leave these secret things alone. . . ."

And he goes on to argue for the identification of the two from certain Egyptian ceremonials. This, incidentally, is a sign of the times. From about the age of Alexander the Great onwards a growing tendency existed to combine various gods, native or foreign. This is clumsily known in modern times as syncretism, and sometimes manifests itself in strange art-forms, one deity being shown with the attributes of another, or of several others. Naturally enough, it flourished in regions where Greek religion and culture met those of other lands, and not least at Alexandria, the home of the cult of Sarapis, which was the creation of Ptolemy I, helped by the advice of an expert, Timotheos of

Eleusis. It united Greek, Egyptian, and apparently also Babylonian elements, and was plainly intended to be a worship in
which all could join, regardless of nationality and local prefer-
ences. But that is merely an extreme example of what meets
us on every hand if we examine at all closely the phenomena of
later Greek religion, throughout the age known as Hellenistic,
i.e., after Alexander and before the Roman conquest of Egypt.
As we have seen, such things occurred earlier, as when Artemis
and Ortheia (p. 19), Apollo and the Sun (p. 59) were taken
to be the same goddess and god respectively, but the later ages
pushed it to fantastic extremes, running together deities who
had originally borne not the least resemblance to one another
and complicating matters by introducing elements completely
foreign to Greek cult and thought.

But to return to Plutarch, and those who thought with him;
they probably were many. Despite his optimistic view concerning the gods generally, he could not but see that there were not
only myths representing some of them as behaving in a way
quite inconsistent with any developed ideas of deity, but rites
which seemed to aim at propitiating unfriendly powers and
inducing them, not to do any good, but simply to refrain from
doing harm. He, and many others, found a solution for this
difficulty in the conception of *daímones*. This word, which to
begin with seems to have been merely a vaguer equivalent of
"gods", had tended from Hesiod onwards to signify superhuman beings of something less than divine rank, and by the
time Plato was an old man, i.e., about the middle of the fourth
century B.C., it was taking on a quite definite meaning. Plato
perhaps, his immediate followers and successors certainly,
elaborated a new doctrine concerning these beings. Their proper
abode is neither heaven, which belongs to the gods, nor earth,
which is the home of men and the lower animals, but the air,
which lies between heaven and earth. Corresponding to this
intermediate dwelling-place is their intermediate nature. They
are superior to men, inferior to gods. A god is morally perfect,
but a *daímon* is not necessarily so; he may be good or bad, and
in any case he is subject to passions, somewhat as men are,
and therefore capable of doing unreasonable things, of departing
from strict justice to serve some personal end, of being angry

or amorous, and so forth. According to some at least of the elaborators of this theory, a *daímon* is not, or not always, an immortal being, nor is he bodiless. Once such a belief gained credence, as it seems to have done early, and not only in philosophic circles, it inevitably grew and ramified, all manner of further complications being introduced, until it passed into the angelology and demonology of Christian speculators, such as the ingenious author who wrote under the assumed name and personality of Dionysios the Areiopagite, St. Paul's Athenian convert. But long before that, or before Christianity began, it served the pious by providing a way out of many difficulties. If a myth, authoritative through its age or its association with venerable rites, was morally unpleasing, it might still be accepted and the believer's conscience rest undisturbed, by the simple assumption that it referred to *daímones*, not to gods proper. The former might indeed, being ethically imperfect, fight one another, make love to mortal women, be banished from the society of their kind for their offences, or even die, none of which things is becoming to divine majesty. The Apollo who killed the Kyklopes because they had made the thunderbolts which slew his son Asklepios was not a true god, but a *daímon* bearing the god's name. If his oracles ceased, as for a while they showed signs of doing, the reason was entirely to his credit, for he was becoming so exalted that contact with matter was no longer possible for him. If rites of aversion existed (we have seen what some of them were like, see p. 42), they were aimed at *daímones* of an inferior order, who had yielded, as a man might do, to their own baser impulses, and so did harm or must be bribed into going away. Magic, also, became explicable. The sorcerer did not really influence gods by his charms, but it might be that he was powerful enough to press *daímones* into his service and make them help him in his not always worthy purposes. So convenient a theory was almost universally accepted, and when the long controversies between Christian apologists and the supporter of the old religions arose, both sides made use of it, the Christians maintaining that all *daímones* were evil and thirsted to destroy and mislead men; hence the meaning of "demon" in modern languages.

Amid this concourse of supernatural beings, great and small, there was no lack of someone for the ordinary, uncritical men and women to appeal to, and about the time when confidence in the power of the traditional deities to protect whole communities was weakening, several new figures appear on the religious horizon of antiquity, or at least, if known before, take on a new aspect and greater importance. One of the most outstanding of these was the healer Asklepios. Until late in the fifth century B.C., not much is heard of him. To Homer, he is the father of two minor heroes, Machaon and Podaleirios, who served in Agamemnon's army before Troy and distinguished themselves for their skill in curing wounds. There is nothing to indicate that he was himself divine, or indeed that he differed from a normal Homeric baron in anything except his abilities in medicine and surgery. Whether he was originally a man, possibly real, or a minor god is a point on which modern opinions differ, but his usual legend made him the son of Apollo by a mortal woman, Koronis. Like his divine father, he was a most potent healer, and he came to his end by taking his skill too far and using it to raise the dead, whereupon Zeus, troubled it would seem for the order of the universe, by which only gods live forever and men all die, killed him with a thunderbolt. By some process which we cannot follow, he was singled out from among the many heroes who performed miracles of healing to become the patron of physicians. He was associated in cult with several vague figures, such as Iaso (Healing) and Hygieia (Health), and both he and they found their place, together with Apollo, in the physicians' oath. Quite suddenly, during the concluding decades of the fifth century, his cult spread to several places in Greece, the most noteworthy being Epidauros in the neighbourhood of Argos. Here an elaborate precinct was constructed, containing among other buildings a dormitory for patients who desired to consult Asklepios for his advice about their health. The regular, though not the invariable, method was for the god to send a dream, either recommending some remedy or restoring the sick man or woman immediately. A long list of cures was recorded on stone in the holy place, and many of these inscriptions have survived to be discovered and commented on in modern times. They present the usual difficulties of records of healing shrines, Christian or non-Christian. There is no solid ground for supposing deceit on the part of the temple clergy, such as disguising an earthly doctor as Asklepios or one of his family. There are some stories which are perfectly incredible, always assuming that the diagnosis of the ailment was correct; for instance, some totally blind persons are said to have been cured, which, if it really happened, points to hysterical simulation of blindness. There are cures easily enough accounted for by supposing that a not very serious disease happened to have run its course about the time of the patient's visit. There are manifestly true relations of fantastic dreams. There are records of the visitor having been told to follow some quite intelligible regimen. When all these have been subtracted, there is the usual residue of inexplicable cases, which may become less so as our knowledge of the effect of mind upon body, the psychology of faith-healing, increases. But apart from all this, there is the clearest evidence that Asklepios became the god of all classes of society, worshipped by bond and free, rich and poor, and continued to be zealously worshipped, both in Greece and elsewhere (his shrine at Rome was highly popular, and its site is now occupied by an old and famous hospital), until the triumph of Christianity, which indeed was itself obliged to produce a counter-attraction in the shape of its miracles of healing, whether by the prayers and exorcisms of living men or at the tombs of martyrs and saints. To-day, SS. Kosmas and Damian, popularly known as the Haghioi Anárghyroi (the Holy Ones who take no fees), largely supply the place of the ancient god, at all events in the Greek world. Greek residents abroad identified Asklepios with native gods of healing (for instance, with Im-Hotep in Egypt), while in Greece itself, his great name obscured those of local powers reputed to be able to cure, as the almost unknown Heros Iatros (Physician) in Attica.

However great the intellectual difference between a man like Plutarch and the pilgrim to the shrine of Asklepios who believed every miracle recorded in the temple-inscriptions and firmly expected the god to come to him in person during the night and heal him by some marvellous operation or magically effective drug, there was a resemblance which extended to much of the religion of the age after Alexander. It had become decidedly more personal than formerly. The State cults did not stop;

indeed, many of the newer cities, such as Alexandria and Pergamon, celebrated the feasts of their official gods with enormous elaboration and splendour and built them temples and altars which were triumphs of the art and architecture of that day. But they seem to have lost in reality as they gained in magnificence. Certainly the impression given by Alexandrian literature is that to the educated classes the Olympians meant hardly more than they do to us; they were very picturesque figures still, excellent subjects for poetry and interesting topics for learned discussions, but the life had gone or was rapidly going out of them. Even when they were imaginatively handled, what is stressed is not their superhuman features, but their resemblance to ordinary humanity. They are often humorously drawn, and humour is not the best companion to reverence. When Kallimachos, for instance, the most influential poet of the Ptolemaic age, writes a hymn to Zeus, although his expressed sentiments are perfectly orthodox, it is clear that his real interest in the god is of two kinds. The legends concerning Zeus give good material for displaying antiquarian learning in the neatest of verse, and the acknowledgment of his supreme power as king among the gods leads up, through an account of his dealings with earthly monarchs, to a great deal of clever indirect flattery of Ptolemy II. No doubt Kallimachos joined decorously in the ritual of Alexandria; but what his personal beliefs were, or if he had any, we simply do not know. That he professed in verse reverence for the gods he mentioned, horror at impiety and abhorrence for the views of Euhemeros proves nothing at all; those were the correct things for a poet to say, and therefore he said them. Myths, for example, which represent gods as cruel or revengeful are told without comment or criticism, as a modern might tell a story about a wicked fairy; they are literary material, no more. Apollo is the source of the poet's inspiration, and well pleased with his performance; in other words, Kallimachos has his literary principles and takes credit to himself for not departing from them. The god is rather a personification of good criticism, or of the judgment of readers gifted with good taste, than the deity who, in Homer, strode dark as night to bring plague to the Achaian camp, or who inspired his prophetess to comfort the involuntary slayer of his comrade. Even his manly beauty has degenerated, and his figure is rather that of a young dandy with scented hair than of the old protector of herdsmen.

Yet, while poets of the Royal College of Literature in Alexandria (for that was what the Museion, or Temple of the Muses, amounted to) were writing in this style, or ransacking the accumulated treasures of the great library for curious facts about local customs and rites, to be embodied in scientific treatises or used for erudite allusions in literature, a vigorous religious life was going on around them, taking many forms, some higher and some lower, but mostly influenced either by theological ideas evolved by Greek philosophers, or by beliefs and practices imported from the Near East, or, commonly and characteristically from Alexander's generation on, by some combination of the two. To outline some of the creeds which resulted from these tendencies will be the business of the next chapter; before beginning it, however, it is well to dispose of one belief which was almost a negation of belief, and was widespread.

This is the immense popularity of the cult of Fortune or Chance (Tyche). Men have always and everywhere believed in luck, good or bad, but in the Hellenistic age the belief took definite shape, and the goddess Tyche, who in the classical period is mostly a literary personification, took artistic shape and found worshippers everywhere in the Greek world. In Euripides, Talthybios the herald of Agamemnon, musing upon the reversals of fortune, wonders whether Zeus really governs the world or it is in the hands of Chance. In later times, Chance (Tyche) is actually worshipped alongside of Zeus, besides her associations with many other deities. Her statues, which sometimes showed her standing on a globe or a rolling stone, to signify her instability, often holding a steering-oar, perhaps a reminiscence of a much older period when she was a very minor sea-goddess, were familiar sights. Coins of innumerable cities were stamped with the figure of the community's Tyche, so that it is not always easy to say whether she or a mere personification of the city itself (which often had a feminine name) is meant. Philosophical discussions and less technical works dealing with the question of what exactly chance might be and how much influence it had in human affairs were among the commonest productions of literary men. The reason for all this was plain enough. By chance, we mean something whose causes we can neither control, predict nor understand. The Hellenistic age had seen many events which came unexpectedly and were revolutionary in their effects. Old powers had sunk to impotence, new ones had grown up rapidly and often fallen again with no less speed. The individual Greek, who under the old system of city-states had been generally, in some small measure at least, the arbiter of his own destiny, and tolerably well acquainted with the forces which made for or against the prosperity of his city, now was the prey of movements, political and economic, which he did not understand and over which he had not the smallest influence. He must often have been in doubt whether the next month or year would see him still nominally a free citizen, and if so, what new name it would be proper to hail as that of the "benefactor" or "saviour" of his state, or of all mankind. If involved in one of the frequent wars of the time, he was fighting, or watching others fight, not on behalf of a cause which he could know and sympathize with, but on account of a quarrel between two potentates whom he had never seen. Under the circumstances, it was no great wonder if very many gave up trying to find a rational cause for the happenings which influenced their public and private lives, and resorted to a belief in a blind and capricious power and a vague hope that they might be able to induce that power to favour them.

We now pass to less negative attempts to deal with the problems of human life and the world men live in.

CHAPTER VI

THE GODS OF THE WISE

FROM early times there existed in Greece a tendency towards monotheism. Zeus, already the strongest of the gods in Homer and Hesiod, has by the time of Æschylus reached such supremacy, both in power and in righteousness, that it is not unfair to say that other deities have become something not unlike angels who are his ministers. The exception to this statement apparently presented by one extremely puzzling play, the *Prometheus Bound*, may for our purposes be neglected. Of the great philosophies, the systems of Plato and Aristotle alike culminate in a single supreme deity, immaterial and transcendent, while the immanent and material god of the Stoics is still single, being the only survivor of the periodical destruction of the universe by fire, which is the element whereof he himself consists. With those philosophies which tended towards a denial either of the existence of gods or of their interest in the affairs of the world we are not concerned, as they had no influence on the development of religion, but only of a non-religious attitude. But the monotheism of the Greeks was of a different sort from that of those Semitic-speaking peoples who developed one. Theirs was exclusive, expressed by the familiar Islamic formula "There is no god but Allah." Greeks of all ages were willing to allow the possibility that other divine beings besides the one supreme god existed, and to use the same name for them as for him. Aristotle furnishes an interesting example of this. Having given, in his *Metaphysics*, a famous and subtle account of the nature of God, as an eternally active intellectual being, whose activity has himself for object, he goes on to consider, on the basis of contemporary astronomical theory, how many divine beings we may suppose to exist, although he insists that the ultimate deity is one. Seeing that the thoughts and theories of the greater minds influenced the lesser, in Greece as all over the world, the systems worked out by such first-rate philosophers as these came down in simplified and popularized forms to lesser intellects. Of all the schools, the most widely influential was that of Plato, and among those whose private religions were based on doctrines of his there must have been many who had read little or nothing of what he wrote; for his dialogues are not easy for any but a tolerably alert mind to follow at any point, while, like all thinkers of high rank, he often discusses themes too abstruse for any but the philosophically trained to comprehend him. But compendia of his chief doctrines and other such derivative works were common, and with these in their hands many could either understand or think they understood some portion of his results. So in our own times, standard works, for instance on political economy, influence many who know them only at second or third hand. Such second-hand and often very uncritical study of him naturally led also to modifications of what he had taught and blending of it with ideas from other philosophers, even those of totally different schools. Two chief blends came into being in the last decades of the pre-Christian era and afterwards. Poseidonios, who lived about 135—60 or a little later B.C., made Stoicism, as he understood it, into a mixed philosophy containing strongly Platonic elements, and thus provided his school, which originally seems to have held that the human soul was material and mortal, with a doctrine of the Last Things holding out hopes of a blissful eternity to the virtuous. During his lifetime also, Pythagoreanism, or what was understood to be Pythagoreanism, revived and produced a new literature alleged to be written by early followers of Pythagoras. It also borrowed largely from Plato, who in his turn had been influenced by real Pythagoreans of his own day, and came out to a doctrine in which high metaphysical conceptions were combined with curious mystic juggleries with numbers and a fair amount of sheer magic and superstition. Platonism itself, as the Christian era went on, was blended with new subtleties and so became what is known as Neoplatonism, a school which produced one first-rate metaphysician, Plotinos, and several minor thinkers of interest. All these systems agreed on one principal point at least. The world was divided into the material or phenomenal, which we can perceive with our bodily senses, and the intellectual, which can be grasped by the mind only, being quite imperceptible to any sense. In Platonism and the allied schools it is immaterial; in orthodox Stoicism it is not, but consists of very rare and fine matter, while the coarser elements constitute the greater part of the world we live in. It is the intellectual world which alone is real and permanent; the material is subject to constant change. The grosser the matter, the less perfect its obedience to the divine laws by which nature is governed. Hence phenomena on the surface of the earth itself are subject to fluctuation, whereas the movements of the stars are exact and never vary. This is because the heavier elements, earth, water and the grosser and less pure strata of the air, tend towards the centre of the universe, but the lighter and purer, especially fire, tend upwards. Generally, the sphere of the moon is the boundary between the two regions in the physical world; the abode of the true gods, as opposed to the *daímones*, is all above this, and the ultimate divine powers live outside the solar system altogether, beyond even the fixed stars which move only with the continual revolutions of the empyrean, the outer heavens. The whole universe is immense, making our earth look little bigger than the point which is the centre of a geometer's circle.

To this system, by which all matter is one great sphere with the earth for its centre and an imaginary line drawn through the earth's centre for its axis, cruder and more primitive cosmologies making their way in from the East conformed more or less, although originally some at least of them, notably those of the Semitic-speaking nations, thought of the universe as a kind of many-storied building, with the "deep" or "waters under the earth" at the bottom and the successive heavens at the top. However, to make this fit the more scientific Greek ideas, it was necessary only to think of the planes as hollow spheres.

In Mesopotamia, owing partly no doubt to the clear air and the long seasons in which there is no rain, an extended series of astronomical observations had for ages been going on. The reason for them was not disinterested zeal for natural science, but a conviction that the heavenly bodies were divine beings and their apparent movements significant to mankind. An elaborate astral theology grew up, in which the conventional gods of Babylonia were identified with stars, Ishtar, for example, becoming the planet Venus, which still, in modern parlance, is called after that Italian goddess who became identified with Ishtar. It was observed, for the accuracy of these Mesopotamians was most praiseworthy, considering that they were wholly without instruments, that all the apparent movements of the sun, moon and planets take place within that part of the heavens which we, adapting one of its Greek names, call the Zodiac (*zodiakòs kýklos*, figured belt), i.e., from the point of view of an observer on earth, they are always in line with some part of those constellations which form the Zodiac. By the time this system and the beliefs attached to it reached Greece, i.e., about the generation after Alexander the Great, the Zodiac was usually divided into twelve constellations, or signs, corresponding to the twelve months of the solar year. In each of these groups, a lively and pictorial fancy caught a resemblance to some familiar figure. Thus, the first group, roughly one-twelfth of the whole, was thought to be a ram, the second a bull, the third two human figures standing side by side, and so throughout. Now, by a series of fanciful analogies, each of these was associated with something of interest to human beings, for instance, the twelfth sign, supposed to be two fishes, with the industry of fishing, the bull with farming, and so forth. The planets also, among which sun and moon were included (it was not, of course, recognized that the earth is itself a planet, and Neptune and Uranus had not been discovered), were credited with similar associations. Mars, for instance, as we call it—a Greek would say "the star of Ares," if he did not use its older name, Pyroeis (Fiery)—influenced war and all things connected with it, including violent death. Now obviously, at the moment of anyone's birth, the planets must be in some of the signs, and the influences which they were credited with sending out centripetally towards the earth as they circled around it would affect the new-born child then and afterwards. As time went on, and doubtless also as many of the older and simpler predictions were falsified by experience, a prodigiously complicated system of divination, which took account of a large number of celestial phenomena at once, was evolved, and went generally under the name of *mathesis*, *the* science. We call it astrology, which in antiquity means more nearly what we term astronomy.

About the time this began to attract the serious attention of Greeks, who were ready enough to believe the stars divine, though, as we have seen (p. 13), they did not worship them, the

Stoic doctrine of Fate or Necessity was making headway. According to this, all things that befall the universe and its inhabitants are minutely predetermined. All that is left in our power is our attitude towards events; we may accept them willingly, knowing that to do so is to be in accord with the divine plan, or foolishly to try to oppose what is inevitable. To a good Stoic, this was a very comforting doctrine, for Fate is nothing but the purpose of an entirely wise and beneficent God. To many, it must have seemed terrible, for the Stoic contention that there is nothing good or evil except that which is morally so, and that such things as riches and poverty, free or servile status, sickness or good health, are really indifferent, was too high a teaching for the average man to accept. Indeed, most Stoics went so far as to allow that health, for example, was "preferable" to illness, i.e., to be chosen if no moral issue was involved, and so on. Now this fatalistic teaching was reinforced by astrology. The Chaldæans, as astrologers were generally called, after the region where their pseudo-science had originated, regardless of their own nationality, produced evidence that, if a man was poor, weak in body, unstable in mind, unlucky in business or in love, or otherwise afflicted, it was due to the position of the stars the instant he was born, or at the very first moment of his starting on the enterprise which turned out a failure. At most, he could avoid some of the consequences of his position by choosing, say for his wedding, a moment when the heavenly bodies were sending down favourable influences. Thus many more were added to the already long list of lucky and unlucky times for every kind of action, and there must have been not a few who, like the female astrologer in Juvenal, would not so much as rub salve on an itching eye without looking in their scheme of nativity, or diagram showing the aspect of the heavens at their birth, nor go a journey of a mile without consulting an astrological almanac.

Thus the average person, if he took these doctrines at all seriously, found himself, in addition to his political insignificance, a helpless victim of supernatural powers. To many, this must have seemed an intolerable slavery. There had always been a tendency among some Greeks in some moods to find fault with life; Theognis in the sixth century B.C., echoed by

Sophokles in the fifth, declares that the best thing is not to be born at all, the next best to die as soon as possible. This sort of sentiment, the much-talked-of "melancholy of the Greeks," is prominent in Alexandrian literature, and in that age also, many utterances suggest an acquiescence in, even a welcome of, the thought that this life ends all. A common epitaph, for instance, is, "I was not; I came to be; I am not; I care not." It is not, therefore, surprising that there were many who grasped eagerly at any way out of their position of bondage which was suggested to them.

The chief solutions, apart from an attitude of unbelief or cynical indifference, depended upon the distinction between the higher and lower strata of the universe already mentioned. Fate worked, in popular belief, through the stars, or at any rate between their spheres and the earth. Therefore, if contact could be made with the powers who are above the stars, Fate might yet be thwarted. Now the gods live beyond the planetary influences. To get them on one's side, by whatsoever means, is, as it were, to take Fate in rear and oppose to its inexorable decrees a force even more potent.

A very old attempt on the part of man to grapple with the difficulties of his environment is magic. Everywhere in the world, it has been held at one time or another that the performance of certain acts and the recitation of certain words would give the operator control over some part of nature, or over the thoughts and actions of his fellows. For the most part, in Greece, this had been a fairly simple business, comparable to the customs which still linger among European peoples and are either half-believed or kept up from mere force of habit and tradition, such as touching wood, saying "bless you" when someone sneezes, avoiding a dinner-table which has thirteen guests, feeling a vague uneasiness if a mirror is broken, and the like. In classical Greece, however, they were much more prominent, at any rate among the simpler people, and also more alive, less in a state of nearly fossilized survival. Instead of some few carrying "mascots," either always or when about some dangerous business, many, especially many women, commonly wore amulets. There are some people now who avoid Friday as a day for commencing anything of importance, because it is unlucky; there were multitudes in antiquity who believed firmly in lucky and unlucky days and recorded them in official calendars. Charms are not unknown now; they were part of ordinary medical practice then, except among the best and most strong-minded of the profession. Therefore there were many ready to listen to the claims of magicians who worked with an elaborate system.

According to these practitioners, of whom we must suppose many to have been perfectly sincere, though doubtless that age, like others, had its charlatans, there exist in nature certain forces, "powers" or "activities" (in Greek, *dynámeis, enérgeiai*), understood in a way partly reminiscent of the employment of like words by modern scientists, partly of the ancient and savage conception of *mana* with which we began (p. 20). These it was possible, if one had the right technique, to direct in the desired way. That way was usually to be found through following a supposed natural law (for much of this magic was pseudo-scientific), the law of sympathy and antipathy. "Sympathy" is not purely a magician's word, but found in ancient scientists. Thus Theophrastos (third century B.C.) speaks of plants developing because they are "in sympathy" with certain conditions of the atmosphere at certain seasons, although he elsewhere says that they "follow" the season and "are symmetrical" to it. In medicine, again, the word is quite common, Galen, for instance, speaking of the effect on one part of the body resulting from some affection of another as taking place "by sympathy." But the magicians, and the philosophers who found a theoretical justification for their practices, went much further than this, and bound the whole universe together by a chain of sympathies. The Stoics, who were generally favourable to magic, in accordance with their general principle that anything which is widely believed must be in some way true, applied the medical terminology to the universe, conceived as a vast living creature, and the Neoplatonists preached a very similar doctrine. Examples seeming to support the thesis were not wanting, among the commonest being the alleged tendency of certain animals and plants to grow larger or smaller as the moon waxed and waned, and the real fact of the tides being due to the position of the moon. The laws of gravity being then totally unknown, the latter phenomenon had no simple mechanical explanation, and therefore the temptation to attribute it to a "sympathy" between what was regularly held to be a watery planet and the element of water on earth was very strong. But innumerable "sympathies" were deduced on far less plausible grounds than this. In many cases, indeed, we are quite at a loss to know what produced the belief in a particular sympathy, or an antipathy between two disparate objects. Why, for example, was it ever supposed that an elephant when *musth* grew calm at the sight of a ram, that a bull, however wild, became tame and manageable if tied to a fig-tree, that a lion which stepped on the leaves of a kermes-oak was numbed, and that a hyena produced the same effect upon a man if it approached him from his right side, but not if it came from his left? Bad observation might result in the notion that a snake could be put out of action if struck once with a cane, but revived if struck several times, but one would think that a very little experience would have taught that it did not relieve the pain of a scorpion-sting to whisper into the ear of an ass "a scorpion has stung me." Nevertheless, this and other equally fantastic beliefs survived, and, from about the year 200 B.C. on, it became extraordinarily common for dabblers in science to take such ideas at their face value and find reasons for them, instead of refuting them by experiment. Among the many things to which the doctrine applied was the gathering of herbs. These, because many of them really have an effect on the human body and many more were supposed to, always formed a great part of the *materia medica* of antiquity. Now they were brought into close relation with the heavenly bodies, whose influence, still in accordance with the general theory of sympathies, could pass into them if the proper precautions were taken. There survive not a few directions of astrological type, telling the practitioner to gather this plant when the sun is in Virgo, that one in the hour of Venus, and so forth. The collector must himself observe sundry rules regarding his person, such as sleeping beside the herb he means to gather in the morning, wearing loose clothing with no belt or other constricting part, abstaining from sexual indulgence, and other tabus, all tending to prevent him bringing a hostile influence to bear on the plant he means to use. Logically, for once the grotesque alleged facts are conceded, the whole pseudo-science is logical, the stars had likewise their relations to the animal and mineral kingdoms. Thus it was possible to get a chain of influences, comprising star, beast, herb and stone, all working in the same direction and all dirigible by an operator who knew his art. It was only to be expected that the ubiquitous *daímones* would have a share in all this, the more so as the progress of magical theory gladly accepted an elaborate doctrine of their classification under the presidency of the various gods. Thus, there were *daímones* of the class of Apollo, of Ares, of all manner of deities native and foreign. So it was possible, if one had the right plant, mineral or other material object, and knew how to make use of it, to come into potent contact with a series of influences which led, say, from a flower astrologically connected with the planet Venus up through a long line of *daímones* subordinate to Aphrodite to the veritable goddess herself, the divine power which lies behind and governs the visible star. The importance of this for securing the magician's ends, good or bad, was obvious. Suppose a love-charm was wanted, how could the lover be more certain of attaining his desires than by enlisting the help of the goddess of love herself? Nay, it was possible to get a deity more directly under the expert's influence, at least by adopting Egyptian methods. In that country, as in Greece (cf. p. 68), it was an old custom to clothe the statues of gods in their temples with garments of various sorts, generally made of linen. According to a doctrine widespread in the later ages of antiquity, these statues were no mere portraits or symbols of the gods in question, but veritably their dwelling-places, certain rites of invocation having brought the deities themselves into them. Therefore, the clothes put on such a statue had been worn by the god himself. Now, in the magic of practically every people in the world, a person's clothes are a part of himself, and to perform magic on a piece of them is to affect the person himself. If, then, a really potent charm was needed, a fragment of one of these holy garments was secured and employed as what the magicians' jargon called an *usia*, literally a substance, exactly as a piece of clothing once worn by a human being whom it was desired to harm or otherwise influence might have been. True, a god was too mighty to be so utterly in the power of the operator as a human being or an ordinary ghost; but even a god found himself unable to smite the daring sorcerer who, protected by one of these bits of sacred cloth, ventured to summon him to give advice or help. Those whose ambitions did not soar so high as this had plenty of ways to charm lesser powers. For instance, anyone having an enemy whom he wished to harm, or a too coy sweetheart, would use some such method as the following. Having first obtained an *usia* of the person to be affected, he would, if it was a love-charm, make a magical figure of potter's clay and attach the *usia* to it. Then he would go to the grave of someone who had died untimely by violence, this being one of the most restless and potent of the dead, and, with sundry invocations of chthonian powers to help the ghost, leave the apparatus in its keeping, with instructions to go and find the woman in question and give her no rest till she visited the magician. If hate, not love, was the motive, a curse might be written (regularly on lead, Saturn's metal) and put into the grave of a suitable person, for instance an executed criminal. It would contain an adjuration of the ghost, by all manner of potent names, Greek and foreign (Yahweh and Jesus, the latter after Christianity had begun to make itself felt, are not uncommon), including names of deities who never had any sort of existence, but are put together from a variety of uncouth sounds, to trouble the offender. In simple forms, this kind of magic is quite early, being found in Attic graves before the Hellenistic period, and it lasts late, Christian examples occurring to show that the new faith had not done away with the old desires and their attendant superstitions. Generally, however, the milder doctrines seem to have brought with them sufficient change of heart to make the wizards rather perform spells for the healing of diseases, or protection against enemies, fleshly or ghostly, than for positively harmful ends.

But there were magicians whose aims seem to have been higher than the satisfaction of everyday lusts and hates. All magic professed—it is one of the commonest assertions, even of the most vulgar practitioners—to be a divine revelation. It was a form of the *gnosis* which we saw Plutarch seeking from the gods (p. 108). Its name was derived from the Magoi, or Zoroastrian priests, of Persia, whose reputation stood high, from at least the days of Plato onwards, for wisdom and sanctity. It was practised in some of its most elaborate forms in Babylonia and Egypt, lands which had in reality a very ancient religion, by no means without its higher side, and whose wisdom was more and more impressing the later Greeks as confidence in their own culture began to wane. That is a recurrent phenomenon, though in our days it is rather India (not without its admirers in late antiquity), or China than the nearer East that makes proselytes among Westerners, when the incidence of a more than usually damaging war or of other economic and political disturbances results in pessimism. And, as among ourselves some of the better sort of intelligences, instead of retelling old wives' tales of Tibetan or Yoga magic, endeavour to deduce some sort of a religious philosophy from Oriental traditions and practices, so it was in antiquity also. There were higher as well as lower magicians. The ancients themselves recognized this quite clearly, and had technical terms for the two kinds. The lower magic, the mere making of petty spells meant to affect the result of a horse-race, cure a headache, get influence with the local potentate or win success in a sordid love-affair, was *goëteía*, conjuring or sorcery. The higher sort was *theurgía*, literally "god-working." It sought, by magical processes sometimes grotesque and superstitious in the extreme, but at least not base in intention, to get into intimate relations with the higher deities, to know them and win their grace and friendship. We can trace more than one stage of *theurgía*. For instance, one of our principal documents, that known as the great Paris Papyrus, has an extraordinary piece of magic ritual, so different from the usual procedure of magicians that it has been held by some, wrongly but excusably, to be a liturgy of the worshippers of the Persian sun-god Mithra. The expert who uses it is allowed to communicate it to another, if he wishes, but only on condition that he tests the would-be learner and makes sure that he is of sufficiently good moral character, for the initiator will be responsible for him. The ritual itself is not revealed to him, but murmured over his head when he has been anointed with a magic oil; he is taught only the prayer with which it begins. So far, this might be but one more of the many prohibitions against revealing magical lore save under strict precautions which often accompany quite trifling matters and ultimately go back to a tendency to keep all magic secret which is very widespread,

But something higher is to be found when we come to analyse this particular ritual. It begins with the following address to the deity invoked, presumably Mithra, who is said to have sent it to the expert "by his archangel."

"First origin of my origin, first beginning of my beginning, breath of breath, first of the breath that is in me, fire, god-given for my blending of the blendings in me, first of the fire in me, water of water, first of the water in me, earthly substance, first of the earthly substance in me, perfect body of me [here the officiant names himself, adding, in the usual magical fashion, the name of his mother], shaped by a glorious arm and an immortal right hand in a world which is not lit but shines throughout, a world which has no soul but is animate, if it be your good pleasure to restore me to eternal birth, according to the nature which underlies me . . . since it is beyond my power, being but mortal, to meet the golden beams of the everlasting light, be still, mortal nature, and take me again safely when the unavoidable need which now presses on me is past."

This, in the first place, shows clear signs of a philosophical origin. The god is a celestial counterpart of the four elements which, in the opinion of most schools of thought in Greece since the fifth century B.C., go to make up all material things, including the living bodies of man and the lower animals. Then, like the Orphics, the officiant claims something more than an earthly origin; it is his "underlying nature" which makes him capable of the rebirth he ardently desires. He is still in the body, and therefore his experience of supernatural life will be but for a little while; still, he is capable of it. On the other hand, his methods are definitely magical. Not only does he use a fixed form of words, which in itself might be part of a non-magical religious service, but he mixes them with a number of meaningless sounds, recitations of the vowels of the Greek alphabet arranged in various orders, whistlings and hissings and strings of magical names, which have been omitted in the above translation. Having recited the opening prayer, he is directed to breathe deeply three times "from the rays of light"—apparently he is facing the sun as he performs his ritual. He will then feel a lightness and seem to be lifted high up, "so that you will think you are in the midst of the air." Rising higher and higher, and passing the lesser astral gods, whom he addresses in certain formulæ, he will at last behold the disk of the sun opening and the god appearing to him, surrounded by attendant deities and in human shape, dressed like the Persian he is. Having uttered another and very elaborate address to Mithra, the officiant receives a revelation from him, which, in his exalted condition, he is able to remember exactly, "although the oracle be ten thousand verses long."

What we are to believe concerning such procedures is hard to say. Undoubtedly, trickery was rife, and we have fairly full descriptions in several late authors of devices like those of modern stage conjurors, whereby the simple were grossly deceived by unscrupulous exploiters of their credulity. But there is no need to doubt that some practitioners of *theurgia* were perfectly sincere. It seems probable that a slightly abnormal man, with his head full of mystical doctrines and a firm belief in the efficacy of the higher magic, could work himself up into a condition of self-hypnotism in which he honestly supposed that he had the experience outlined above. It is not hard to find parallels to the subjective sensation of being lifted up into the air, and if he imagined that to be real and not a trick of his own excited nerves, some at least of the rest would follow; he would think he saw what his rather fantastic cosmography assured him was to be seen, if only the observer could get far enough away from the surface of the earth. There are many instances of persons who, in a trance-state, have visions of the other world, and it is a commonplace that the heavens and hells they then see are those they have been led to expect by whatever theology they have been taught. Something of the kind may well have happened to more than one experimenter with the ritual just mentioned. As to the lower forms of magic, it is well known that many credulous people, if they hear that spells are being used against them, are badly frightened, even to the point of becoming seriously ill, or in extreme cases dying, with no physical cause for either. On the other hand, one really ill, if he believed in magic, no doubt would be much cheered by the recital of powerful charms or the administration of some concoction of herbs or the like which he supposed to be a supernatural cure for his ailment. Thus his confidence would be increased and his chances of recovery proportionately bettered; most of the traditional magical cures appear to have been quite harmless, though few of them had any real therapeutic effect whatever.

But by no means all seekers after *gnosis* were magicians, even of the lofty "theurgic" type. Not a few found satisfaction in mysteries, of which many existed in the Hellenistic world, for not only did Eleusis continue to initiate people of all nations, but several new cults of a similar kind sprang up or were revived. A famous example is the mysteries at Andania in the Peloponnesos, which Pausanias reckons the holiest, next to Eleusis itself. We have not only his account of them, but a long inscription, much earlier than his time, which prescribes minutely for their organization, though naturally it does not tell us what the secret rites were. The cult, which concerned deities known as the Great Goddesses, had ceased to be celebrated when Sparta conquered Messenia, but long after, when Thebes broke the power of Sparta in the fourth century B.C., it revived. A picturesque legend told how Epameinondas, the great Theban statesman and general, had been warned in a dream to restore Messenia, while at the same time his ally, Epiteles, the commander of the forces of Argos, was miraculously instructed where to find the records which contained directions for the conduct of the festival. We can well suppose that these venerable, or supposedly venerable, ceremonies had read into them whatever doctrines the initiates believed in, exactly as happened at Eleusis and doubtless in many other, less-known centres. Private cults, founded in obedience to warnings in dreams or visions, are often attested by surviving inscriptions, and it is to be regretted that we do not know more concerning their ritual. Foreign mysteries, on the other hand, such as those of Isis and Osiris, which flourished in Ptolemaic Egypt and spread throughout the Roman empire, were not so popular with Greeks as in other nations. We have indeed seen (p. 108) that Plutarch's friend Klea was an initiate of the Egyptian gods, and she was not unique or even very exceptional in this respect; but local patriotism remained fairly strong in religious matters, and it is worth noting that Klea accepted the theory that Osiris is merely another name for that Dionysos whom she worshipped in her own country. But to treat of Egyptian, Persian and other foreign mystery-cults is the business rather of a history of late Roman, or Græco-Roman, religion than of a book like this.

Religiosity continued to be an outstanding phenomenon among these later Greeks, whether in Greece proper or in the many other lands of Hellenic speech. One symptom of it was the decline of the scientific spirit. Men like the great Galen, whose system of medicine is purely rational, its defects being due to incomplete knowledge of the relevant facts and not to any lack of desire to learn them or confidence in observation and reason, seem to have been increasingly in the minority, and largely confined to the medical profession, at least in the centuries between the beginning of the Christian era and the end of antiquity. Most, even among the educated, were willing to believe wonders at which a contemporary of Aristotle would have laughed, and to accept as supernatural quite trifling things, such as a curious dream or a passing hallucination. Confidence in purely human means of getting knowledge was lessened, partly by the conflicting views of the different philosophers, as made known to the general public by little epitomes and doxographies, i.e., books in which the "opinions" (*doxai*) of famous thinkers of the past on everything in heaven and earth were listed, without criticism and with nothing to show how they were arrived at, modified or superseded. Even the one great philosopher of late paganism, Plotinos, attributed his surest knowledge of ultimate reality not to his subtle metaphysical reasoning, but to the mystical experience of union with the Absolute which he claimed to have had several times.

But it was an age not without its saints and prophets, even if we neglect the great names of late Judaism and early Christianity. An outstanding example is the leading neo-Pythagorean, or at least the most famous, Apollonios of Tyana. Our knowledge of this man's life and actions comes through an obscure and distorting medium. Philostratos, a rhetorician of the third century, wrote his life at the behest of the then Empress, Julia Domna, wife of Septimius Severus, who had literary and philosophical interests and entertained men of learning at her court. He professes to use the memoirs of a disciple of Apollonios himself, one Damis of Assyria, whose work, if it ever existed outside Philostratos' imagination, must have been as full of inventions as the most unreliable of the lives of Christian saints. According to the wordy romance which Philostratos concocted, Apollonios was marked from his birth for something more than the general run of mankind; he rebuked sinners, went about uttering short, dogmatic sayings full of pith and force, travelled over a great part of the world, including India, to converse with sages of various nationalities and languages, performed a number of miracles, overcame all manner of evil powers both temporal and spiritual, including the Emperor Domitian, whom he impressed by suddenly vanishing from before him and whose assassination he saw in a clairvoyant vision, and finally, after living to a great age, disappeared from among men without anyone being sure whether he had died or not. Subtracting this fanciful ornament, we may gather from this and other sources that he was a man of ascetic life, impressive in manner and doubtless perfectly sincere, who lived through a great part of the first century A.D. and made a name for himself as a sort of combination of philosopher and prophet. He seems to have been interested in ritual, at all events a work on sacrifices was ascribed to him, and may quite possibly have dabbled in magic of the higher sort. That he gave instruction in philosophy as he understood it is credible enough, but his abiding reputation as either a supernaturally gifted man or a wizard, according as the testimony is friendly to him or not, suggests that he was in some way abnormal, perhaps subject to trances and visions, whether natural to his constitution or artificially induced. In other words, he was what is now sometimes called "mediumistic".

So much for one remarkable individual; it should not be forgotten that there were whole sects and conventicles of mystics having more or less tincture of philosophy, and their literature has come down to us in sufficient quantity for us to judge of their doctrines. The Egyptian Thot, identified by the Greeks with Hermes, was credited with the authorship of a great number of works on various subjects, including alchemy, astrology and other forms of divination. Among these is a collection known as the Hermetic corpus, which we can supplement by remains of similar documents from other sources, including a Latin work, *Asclepius*, manifestly a translation from a Greek original, which has come to us under the name of

Apuleius of Madaura, a rhetorician of mystical tendencies whose life falls within the second Christian century. Whether he had anything to do with it or not, the dates of the Hermetic literature seem to range from about his time onwards for a century or more. They are not the scriptures of any one well-defined sect, any more than are the Orphic writings, but they are all the more interesting for that very reason, since they represent a fairly widespread tendency of at least the Græco-Egyptian population, and show the lines along which not a few pious minds were working. Underlying the thought of these mystics, whether they were grouped in small bodies of co-religionists or were individual seekers, is a doctrine which developed out of the teaching of Plato. The distinction between the real world, which is immaterial and to be grasped only by the mind, or even by something superior to the ordinary intellect, and the material or phenomenal universe was more and more accented in the thought of that day. The problem thus arose, how God, Who is wholly of the world of reality, could come into contact with anything so base (or, in some forms of their thought, positively evil) as matter at all. The answer regularly was, that He made use of some kind of intermediary, or intermediaries, lower than Himself but still much loftier than matter, because they were directly or indirectly His emanations. The most familiar form of this is the doctrine of the Logos (inadequately and misleadingly rendered "Word" in the Authorized Version), used by the writer of the Fourth Gospel. *Logos* has two main significations in this context, "speech" (thought expressed in language) and "ratiocination," "reasoning" (thought as an activity of the mind). As a man can reason or plan and afterwards put into words what he has thought or contrived, so the Divine intellect can put forth something corresponding to our mental activities and their embodiment in speech. This something, the Divine Logos, plays a great part in several philosophies and religions of the early Christian era, and not least in the Hermetic writings. We may illustrate from the first item of the Hermetic corpus, the treatise *Poimandres*. The writer says that after long contemplation of reality, he fell into a deep and heavy trance, in which there appeared to him a being who introduced himself as Poimandres (Shepherd of

Men), "the Mind of Authority". Poimandres then shows the mystic a vision, in which he sees a great light and a great darkness, respectively reality and matter. From the light comes "a holy Logos," which attracts to itself the fiery part of matter, followed by the air; earth and water remain below, but are stirred by the Logos, which blows upon them like a wind and makes them ready to listen. This Logos is asserted to be the "shining Son of God," who proceeds from Mind itself; and Mind and the mystic's God are expressly identified.

So far, this might be a Stoic cosmogony. The arrangement of the lighter and heavier elements agrees with their ideas, and indeed with those of all schools; they are based on the observed facts that flames tend to rise and that air or gas will bubble up from water. The Logos also might be Stoic, for they made great play with *lógoi spermatikoí*, "generative principles," as active forces in the universe, while their deity was of the nature of fire or light, and not wholly immaterial. But the work goes on to describe a further process of creation, which involves several emanations of the Mind and results in the appearance of the material universe. It is therefore plain enough that the first vision showed the formation of the Platonic Form or Idea of ordered matter, the concept of it, thought of as a separate reality of which the visible embodiment, the material universe, is but an imitation or reflexion. We have therefore a mixture of the thought of different schools, not uncommon after the time of Poseidonios (see p. 117). But one of the chief lessons which Poimandres teaches his disciple is that, as a result of this long and complicated process of world-making, the Logos itself dwells in man; its father is the Mind itself, they cannot really be separated, and their union is life.

All this doctrine, which besides the Greek elements already mentioned shows clear traces of influence from non-Greek sources, including apparently Zoroastrianism, is represented, not as the result of thought, however eclectic, but as a revelation; Poimandres shows his pupil visions and afterwards explains them, briefly and dogmatically. It is a *gnosis*, to be won by those sufficiently prepared for it, not a conclusion to be attained by metaphysical reasoning. Indeed, the obscure style of the work and a certain confusion in the terminology are enough to show that the author, though not without imagination, was no dialectician. Other works of the same kind introduce us to theological lectures from divine or semi-divine persons, long prayers, often eloquent and impressive, and other such expressions of a temperament not philosophical in any proper sense, certainly not critical, but profoundly religious. Many passages prove likewise that the Hermetists, if we may call them so, believed firmly in the efficacy of ritual to establish communication between themselves and Deity, through the hierarchy of its emanations and subordinates. Theirs was a lofty, transcendental religion, much higher than the various processes by which the inferior representatives of a like tendency sought to attain their ends through alchemy, astrology and so forth, yet allied to it, in that these practitioners also had their *gnosis*, and both astrology and alchemy had a distinctly religious and mystical flavour. Manilius, for example, the one poet of any merit whom astrology produced, is convinced that his science is of divine origin; a much-quoted passage asks,

"Who can know heaven save by Heaven's gift, or find out God, if he be not part of the gods himself?"

and what he said neatly in Latin verse was felt, if not expressed, by many less vocal adepts. He also ascribes the discovery of astrology to no mortal, but to Hermes, thus once more connecting his ideas with those of the Hermetists.

Since such cults and such feelings as these were rife in the early Christian centuries, it is not to be wondered at that when Christianity itself grew to be better known, it found partial acceptance among upholders of such views as have just been sketched. The whole Gnostic movement, the sect of those to whom *gnosis* was the most important feature of their religion, is, so far as our actual records go, a Christian heresy, although it is extremely likely that it existed in pagan circles before it became partly Christianized. We have sketches of its tenets in the writings of Christian controversialists, and therefore unfriendly accounts of what such men as Basileides, Valentinian and others taught. However, some few specimens of the writings of the Gnostics themselves survive, principally the Coptic work known as the Pistis Sophia. In general, all these schools, for Gnosticism was not one doctrine but many, stressed the difference between the immaterial and material worlds far more even than the most idealistic of the Greek thinkers had done. Matter they regarded as entirely evil, and consequently seem to have prescribed a rigid asceticism, at least for those who aimed at perfection, although some, if we may believe their opponents, held all ordinary moral distinctions to be matters of indifference, or even encouraged the grossest vices, as being something which the incarnate soul was bound to fall into while in such a vile place as the body, and therefore best got through with as quickly as possible, since the inferior powers who rule the visible world would insist on reincarnating those who still had some sins left to commit. All alike interposed between Deity and matter a series of emanations, more and more elaborate as their doctrines developed, only the lowest of which were capable of having anything to do with matter. On blending this theory with Hebrew tradition, they reached the logical conclusion that the God of the Old Testament, since he created the visible world, was a very inferior being, many removes from the true Deity. The comparatively simple Christian dogma of the Incarnation was caught up into the meshes of the system and adorned with complicated subtleties. The least absurd of these was a distinction between Jesus, who was a man of unusually pure and strong soul, remarkably resistant to the evil influences of the lower creation, and Christ, an emanation of rather high grade who entered into Jesus at his baptism and left him again just before the Passion. Many more such details have been preserved for us by the shocked interest of orthodox Christian writers, to whom it was all most abominable blasphemy.

It thus becomes clear that when the new religion began to develop and spread, it did not come as a thing wholly unfamiliar. It was monotheistic; so, in effect, were the more philosophical of the existing cults. Its God was transcendent; so were those of Hermetism, Neoplatonism, and half a score of other systems. He was a creator, and therefore could come into some sort of contact with matter, though Himself immensely superior to it; no genuine Platonist would be surprised at that, for Plato himself describes an elaborate process of creation in one of

the most influential of his works, the *Timæus*. The gap between
Him and matter, furthermore, was early bridged by the inter-
position of the Logos (the fourth Gospel seems to date from
about the end of the first century). Christianity had a doctrine
of sin and redemption; these were familiar to many Greeks,
from Orphic and other literature. It insisted from the very
first on a high standard of moral conduct; the ethical side of
religion had received attention from the days of the fifth-century
sophists. As early as the time of St. Paul, it had begun to use
the religious and philosophic terminology of the existing systems,
while its Jewish vocabulary was not entirely unfamiliar, owing
to the vigorous activities of Jewish missionaries. It soon
developed a ceremonial, a thing familiar and welcome in itself
and, unlike many of the older cults, containing nothing offensive.
For instance, it did not sacrifice beasts, a rite against which
some schools of thought were inclined to protest, for reasons
connected with their doctrine of reincarnation; it was said that
Pythagoras in his day and Apollonios of Tyana in his had refused
to conform to the prevailing practice in this particular, substituting bloodless offerings. As negative advantages, it had no
mass of savage or immoral myths to explain away; its writings
were, with few exceptions, the work of their alleged authors;
indeed, when its canon came to be formed, the framers of it
were unusually successful, for the uncritical age in which they
lived, in including only books which might, so far at least as
date went, have been written by the actual Apostles. Not least
important, its Founder was a historical person, of recent date,
biographies of whom began to be written within about a generation of the Passion. It is therefore not at all surprising that a
large number of persons who were not only pious but highly
intelligent took an interest in the new faith. It is still less to be
wondered at that not a few of its adherents, being of acute
intellect and trained in philosophy, set about explaining what
they conceived to be the doctrines implicit in their religion,
evolving, after some centuries of discussion and reflexion, the
theology of the Nicene Creed, besides the numerous heresies,
Gnostic and other, which represent experiments which did not
commend themselves to the main body of Christian opinion.
The resulting theology was Greek in form and largely also in

content. In particular, its eschatology and its conception of the nature of supernatural beings below Divine rank owed nearly everything to Greek speculations. The *daímones* divided into angels and devils; Hell, Purgatory and Paradise had long been current ideas in Greece; that the souls of the righteous should attain to more than mortal condition was a familiar enough conception, for it had long been taught that the soul of a good man might become a "hero", a hero a *daímon*, and a *daímon* ultimately a god. Even the location of the places of reward and punishment were in accordance with existing ideas, Heaven being the natural abode of the soul in Platonic and other philosophies, while Hell is the descendant of Tartaros, the traditional prison of rebels against the classical gods. Even the visions of the other world which are to be found in early Christian literature, such as the so-called Apocalypse of Peter, have at least as much Greek as foreign imagery in them. It is significant that someone such as Clement of Alexandria, who was far from unsympathetic to Greek thought as he understood it, claimed that it was one of the forms of providential preparation for the perfect doctrine, and that Christianity was the true *gnosis*.

But what has been discussed in this chapter must not be taken as a description of every Greek, or the average Greek, of the later ages of antiquity. The pious and saintly are rare in every country and at every time; the normally respectable, whc usually conform to any religious usages which may be prevalent are many. It is not to be forgotten that the religions which for a time rivalled Christianity were of the cities, and that Christianity itself spread mainly in the larger communities. The countryside mostly remained as it always had been, so far as its sacral observances were concerned. Since the succession of the seasons was unchanged and the peasants' labours likewise, it was but natural that they should remain interested chiefly in the rites which traditionally aided them in their seedtime and harvest. It may well be doubted if many converts to any of the more developed systems, with their elaborate theologies and wire-drawn controversies, lived outside the towns. Demeter and her daughter, or their local equivalents, the Nymphs and other minor deities, had a strong hold on rustic affections.

Consequently, when the official conversion of the whole civilized world to the new faith did at last take place, the countryside was less ready for it than the townsfolk. Names changed, churches replaced temples, not seldom by converting the latter into the former, old rites were forbidden under severe penalties, but untutored minds, brought up in polytheism, did not alter so much as outward semblances indicated. It is a commonplace that saints have very often taken over the functions of gods and heroes, thus replacing the little local cults whose lack was felt when the official ceremonies of the churches satisfied the needs of the cities. It is no less a fact, though the details are harder to make out, that many survivals of the old beliefs and ways remained, thinly disguised. To sketch them will be the business of the concluding chapter.

CHAPTER VII

SURVIVALS

FEW subjects require more delicate and skilled handling than
that of the survival of ancient in modern Greece. Resemblances
between the customs, legends and beliefs of the present-day
country people and the myths and ceremonies of antiquity are
numerous and well known; but to assume, as investigators were
once apt to do, that the former descend directly from the latter
is rash, for similar resemblances can be found in countries
which have no historical connexion with classical Greece at
all. Also, Greece has been invaded several times since the close
of the latest classical epoch (for convenience, we may take the
reign of Justinian, A.D. 527–565, as the dividing boundary),
and a proportion of her present population, how large is matter
of dispute, is not of Greek descent. Her culture also has been
much affected by foreign contact and domination, witness the
numerous Italian and Turkish words which, along with a few
that are Slavonic and a sprinkling from other sources, including
English and French, mark the modern vocabulary. Hence,
if we find something in a Greek village which reminds us of a
description in some classical author, we must examine it closely
to make sure that we are not faced with a story or a practice
brought in by Slavs, Albanians, Italians or Turks sometime
in the troubled centuries which have elapsed since Justinian
died. The question has been further obscured by the natural
and excusable zeal of some Greek antiquarians who, properly
proud of the glorious history of their ancestors, have tried to
prove everything in Greece to be Greek. Yet, when all modifications and subtractions have been made, there is a solid residue
of modern material whose descent from the classical period is
either quite certain or so strongly attested as to be practically
beyond dispute. This chapter will confine itself to a few examples
belonging to this category, omitting many interesting speculations and much that is attractive to any folklorist for its own
intrinsic value, regardless of its origin.

As is to be expected, we find but few survivals of the great

gods, apart from bits of antiquarian learning which have made
their way down to the people. For instance, there is a little
trace of Zeus in Crete, several mentions occurring of his tomb,
not only in learned documents but in local traditions. Needless
to say, his name has been somewhat corrupted (it is now Ziás)
and the tomb is not always in the same place; but the tradition
goes back to late mediæval times, at all events. But we must
remember that it is the "Zeus" of Crete (cf. p. 48), one of the
favourite examples among Christian apologists of the thesis
that the pagan gods, if not devils, were dead men, and that
Byzantine scholars were perfectly well acquainted with this
argument. It is therefore more than likely that such popular
accounts as now exist have filtered down from more lettered
circles; for Greece has never lacked scholars since early in the
classical period, and these have one and all been interested in
the history of their country and its written traditions. Artemis
is in rather better case, for we have reliable accounts from the
eleventh century onwards of belief in a being called the Good
(or Beautiful)[1] One of the Mountains, whose identification with
Artemis is at least plausible. Generally, however, the cult of
the major deities was successfully stamped out by Christian
reformers, and scarcely even a name is left, save of a few who
have survived in literary tradition now popularized; folk-poetry
to-day will on occasion call a beautiful woman Aphrodite or
speak of a lover's pains being inflicted by "Erotas," i.e., Eros,
which name can also be applied to a pretty child.

More important are some of the minor powers. Charon, who
in classical mythology is a subordinate figure, the ferryman who
transports the dead across to the realm of Hades, has not only
remained prominent (with a slight change of name; he is now
Charos or Chárondas) but become a popular death-god.
Indeed, his name is a synonym for death, Hades being now,
as in the later stages of classical Greek, a place, not a person.
But he seldom plies his ferry. Instead, he rides a black horse,
and innumerable folksongs describe him carrying off young and
old pitilessly to his gloomy abode. At times he has a wife,
Charóntissa, and a recurrent theme is that of his wrestling with
some heroic youth, whom he invariably overcomes. Occasion-

[1] *Kalé*, which means " beautiful " in ancient, "good" in modern Greek.

ally, instead of a wrestling-match, he engages in a contest of
jumping, which he wins with a prodigious leap, securing the
agreed stake, which is the person of the vanquished competitor.
Despite all the efforts of Christian teachers, the popular imagination still has the same attitude towards death and the other
world as it had in the days of Homer; Charos' abode is devoid
of all attractions, dark, gloomy and full of decay, with none of
the cheerful occupations of the life on earth. This picture
exists side by side with that derived from the teaching of the
Orthodox Church, with which, of course, it is completely
inconsistent. Such self-contradiction, however, is characteristic
of the popular eschatologies of all peoples. As in antiquity, so
to-day, the average Greek is desirous of life as he understands
it, that is to say, in the body and under the familiar sun. He
may be intellectually persuaded of the immortality of the soul
and future rewards and punishments, but not imaginatively
much interested in them. This may reasonably be taken as
indicating that none of the other-worldly religions, even that
which finally won universal acceptance, penetrated deep into
popular feeling. One or two examples may be given. In a
song from Chios, the speaker, climbing a cliff to get at an apple-
tree, comes to a burial ground and accidentally treads on a
grave. A voice comes from it:

"Was I not also young, was I not also a champion? Did I not
walk by night when the moon was shining? Did not I carry a forty-
cubit sword and a sixty-cubit lance? And now do you trample over
my head?"

Some such imaginative picture of the dead man protesting
against the disrespect to his buried body might have been
composed any time in the last three thousand years or so. It
has nothing specifically Christian about it, and owes nothing to
any eschatology. The following, from Kephalonia, actually
combines a Hades of Homeric dreariness with a fragment of
Christian terminology:

"I would be a merchant, to go down to Hades, to take clothes
for the young girls and weapons for the young men, also fezzes from
Tunis for the handsome bachelors. I clasped my hands, I besought
Charos to lend me the keys, the keys of Paradise, that I might see

how the young men fare, how the young women pass the time. I found the girls without fine clothes, the men without weapons and the poor little children with never a shirt."

Mention has already been made (p. 57) of the ancient Nereids and the modern Neraïdhes. The latter are the fairies of the Greek countryside and have all the characteristics of their kind. They are beautiful and accomplished; they sometimes carry off human children; they have been known to become the mistresses of mortal men; they are capricious and easily offended, wherefore it is well to address them in complimentary terms. They may be seen now and again, conspicuous by their white clothing (indeed "wearers of white," *asprophóres*, is one of their popular names). The widespread story of the human midwife summoned to help a fairy mother is told of some of them; in one version, the midwife (a real woman, personally known to some who were alive at the end of last century) was called up in the middle of the night, performed her office, and was paid in a sort of reversed fairy gold, for she was handed two bits of onion-peel, but on reaching home, found that they were Turkish gold coins. That they are fond of their own offspring, though these, by human standards, may be singularly hideous, is indicated by a story of the encounter of a priest with one of the Milighánes, as the Neraïdhes are sometimes called. She came up to him as he was riding his mule, and asked him to let her baby ride, which he did. Thereupon the mule bolted; the priest, very prudently, protected himself with the sign of the Cross, and made straight for his church, into which the Milighána dared not follow him. A compromise was then reached; the baby was returned to its mother on condition of the Milighánes digging a well and planting a vineyard, and the agreement was honestly kept by both parties.

In this tale, which is or was told at Mestà in Chios, we have the old and the new powers in conflict, after a fashion familiar to anyone who has read the earlier Christian literature concerning the powers of darkness ("those outside" as colloquial modern Greek styles them). It remains to ask whether the Neraïdhes, Milighánes, or whatever one of the popular names we prefer, are purely ancient Greek in their origin, i.e., survivals, not merely of the Nereids but of the Nymphs. It must not be forgotten that similar figures exist in the folklore of more than one Balkan people, but the case for the Hellenic origin of the Neraïdhes is strong. Practically everything they are said to do and be can be paralleled from antiquity. Nymphs on occasion play the part of fairy brides to mortals (Daphnis, the half-divine shepherd of Sicilian Greek tradition, was beloved by one of them, who blinded him when he proved unfaithful to her); they are very beautiful, they sometimes carry off mortals, though they do not seem to kidnap babies and leave changelings in their place, as Neraïdhes sometimes do. They can drive people mad, but also they can heal diseases, if properly approached, and similar activities are reported of the modern spirits. In the latter case, it is proper to make them an offering of honey-cakes or some similar delicacy, which, incidentally, was a common sacrifice in antiquity. Also, the Neraïdhes are very apt to haunt wells, in other words, to behave like ancient Naiads, or water-nymphs.

Another survival is a purely evil being, the Ghelloú, in ancient Greek Gelló, a formidable ghost who haunted Greek nurseries as far back as the seventh century B.C. and was supposed to cause untimely deaths of children. It was her revenge for her own early death. Nowadays Ghelloú, or the Ghelloúdhes, for like most vague figures of this kind she is now one and now many, seems especially to attack young mothers if she can get admission to the house by any wile.

More important are the Moires. In antiquity, these were spirits of birth, who were also powers of fate; we hear of them visiting the birth-room and there determining the destiny of a new-born child. It is the same to-day; they visit houses where there has been a birth—in Aigina, they come on the third day and an entertainment is prepared for them, to put them in good humour—generally after dark, but sometimes earlier, if the mother is asleep and no one else is in the room. Popular descriptions of them vary, often being influenced by ancient myths or representations in art of the three traditional spinners, but sometimes showing independence of such learned sources, as they probably are. In some places there are signs by which it can be known whether the fate they have assigned the child is good or bad. In later life, they may be invoked. There is, for instance, a story of a pretty servant-maid who envied her ugly but rich mistress. The mistress took her up to the roof at night, and there said "Moires of the Moires, let my own Moira come to me." The Moira appeared, in the form of a beautiful girl, richly dressed. The maid was then instructed to use the same formula, and her Moira appeared in the shape of a ragged and loathly hag. She thus saw the reason for her own inferior station and was content. There are other stories of a similar kind, and in some of them it is not the Moira but the Fortune (Tyche) of the individual which is concerned.

Here we have something more than the mere survival of a belief or a legend. The Moires have some remains of ritual and there is a kind of prayer which may be used in dealing with them, for the words maid and mistress alike speak are a quite well-known metrical formula. Tyche also has not lost all her ancient importance, however insistent official theology may be that there is no such power and everything depends on the will of a personal God. Another interesting fact is that there are individual Moires and Tyches. Their ancestry is easily traced to ancient demonology, which often taught that everyone has a personal *daimon* watching over him. This has left its deposit also in official Christian angelology, for guardian angels are part of Orthodox teaching and the people firmly believe in them. Thus a philosophical theory, which had made its way into fairly general belief in ancient times, has arrived by two different routes, one official, the other popular, into the minds of the peasants of to-day.

Still more important are large sections of the pattern of life which can be traced with more or less certainty to antiquity. Of birth and its ritual something has already been said; it is worth looking at the other great crises, marriage and death, for resemblances to ancient ways which may fairly be deemed survivals. As regards the former, it must be noted that, with the modern Greeks as with other Europeans, the religious service of their Church is intrusive, no real part of the ceremony of marriage, but an elaborate way of calling down a blessing on the ceremonial, or what is left of it, which constitutes the real wedding. This in turn has been so overlaid with a great

growth of customs unconnected, so far as we know, with anything ancient that it is an almost hopeless task to pick out
fragments of the old ways from the mass of newer ones; although
much of the traditional popular ritual which attends a Greek
village wedding is certainly not of yesterday, and much more
of it than we know of is perhaps ancient, for we are but ill-
informed about the details of the classical ceremonial, even in
Athens, to say nothing of less-known places. For instance,
music is a regular feature of weddings in modern times; it is
produced by local singers and instrumentalists, it includes
elaborate traditional compliments to all concerned, especially,
of course, the young couple themselves, and it occurs both
before and after the actual day and night of the wedding. But
it would be rather a large assumption that it descends directly
from the wedding-songs of antiquity, the most famous of
which, the *epithalamion*, made its way into literature, so that
we know from Sappho and Theokritos something of its contents; it complimented bride and groom and was sung outside
their apartment. The wedding-songs of to-day are indeed
largely traditional, but their metre, poetical technique and
formulæ are all distinctively modern, showing no trace of
anything derived from ancient or even early mediæval sources.
We can, therefore, only say that it is quite possible that the
custom has been continuous, changing its outward form little
by little as language and ideas as to what constituted metre
and poetical diction altered. Perhaps more to the point is that
rice, small coins and sweetmeats are often flung over bride and
groom, a possible remnant of the ancient *katachẏsmata*, though
the practice of flinging something of the kind over or at the
parties to a wedding is so widespread that it may have reached
Greece from any one of a number of sources. In all customs of
this kind, which imply ideas common to a large part of humanity (here, probably, a wish that the married couple may be
fertile as the grains are, and their life prosperous and pleasant,
as typified by the coins and sweetmeats) there is always a
possibility that we are not dealing with a true survival, but
rather an unconscious revival. Perhaps more significant is the
occasional presence at a modern Greek marriage of a little boy
who accompanies the bride. Anciently, on Keos, he used to

sleep with her the night before the wedding; he must be, as is still the case, one who has both parents still alive, that is who savours, so to speak, of fertility and normal family life, not in any way of death, but to-day the only example I happen to have come across (from Olýmpoi in Chios) shows him going about with both bride and bridegroom. Another detail suggests, not a piece of ancient ritual, but a familiar ancient metaphor, which may very well have ritual behind it. The wedding festivities in several places include a piece of traditional mumming, in which a grotesque pretence of ploughing and sowing is gone through. But ploughing, in classical Greek, is a very well-known periphrasis for performing the sexual act. Yet another feature of modern ceremonial is the formal and regular weeping by the bride, whether while she is being dressed by girls who are her relatives or friends or at some other moment, for the usage varies, but at all events, the ostentatious crying is part of the proper conduct of a girl on or just before her wedding day. This was so common in ancient times that "to cry like a bride" seems to have been a proverbial saying; its ultimate reason was in all probability part of the show of reluctance which it is suitable for anyone to make when leaving his or her original family. The household gods, or ancestral spirits, must not feel that they are slighted and their protection abandoned lightly by any member of the household, certainly not by a daughter of the house, who is never to return. Yet another detail found here and there is a ceremonial showing of bride and bridegroom to each other, accompanied by a formal pretence of uncovering their bodies; at Pyrghoì in Chios, a part of the bride's skirt is lifted, and the same is done with the bridegroom's *podhiá*, a kind of apron which forms part of the old costume of men on that island. We know that in several regions of classical Greece part of the ceremonial was the formal "unveiling" of the bride, it being apparently the proper assumption that her young husband had not yet seen her face. There are also places where it is still the proper thing for the bridegroom and his attendants to visit the bride's house in the evening and bring her to his house with singing and other merrymaking. This, now a mere frolic, has a good claim to be a relic of the times when it was the central ceremony of the wedding. It is independent of, indeed precedes, the ceremony at the church which is now, of course, the binding one, recognized by law and public opinion.

It can therefore be seen that, lingering here and there, we can find at least probable survivals of the pre-Christian methods of conducting a wedding. But if such ceremonies are apt to be conservative, those connected with death are still more so, however much eschatological doctrine may alter. Therefore it is not at all surprising to learn that the soul is thought of as leaving the body by the mouth, much as breath does. There is, indeed, nothing specifically Greek in this, Greek being but one of many languages which use words for "soul" and "spirit" etymologically connected with those which signify wind and breath. However, it is safe to take it as Greek when it occurs in the Greek area. The general feeling concerning its fate when it arrives in the other world, although naturally affected by ecclesiastical teaching and also by some other elements not traceable to antiquity, yet has much in it which an ancient would recognize as familiar. The judges of the dead are no longer, as in classical (at least Athenian) mythology, Aiakos, the just king of Aigina, Minos king of Crete and Rhadamanthys his brother, but the tribunal is still in some places a triple one; the judges are God, the Virgin Mary and the Apostles. Nor is worldly wealth a factor entirely to be left out of the calculation. In Plato, old Kephalos explains to Sokrates why it is good to be comfortably off, if one has led an upright life. It means that the dying man has no unpaid debts of any kind; he has settled with his human creditors, and he has also given the gods their proper sacrifices. There has been no constraint of poverty to cheat either of them, and so he can depart cheerfully to the other world. To the modern peasant, this has taken a Christianized form; if the dead man was well-to-do, there will be no lack of means to given him a proper funeral and appropriate requiem masses (or their Orthodox equivalent), for the good of his soul. And the fewer one has wronged, the easier it is to die, for one of the principal causes of a prolonged death-agony is someone's refusal to forgive injuries done him. It need hardly be stressed that an unpaid debt is one of the commonest of injuries and not the least bitterly resented. The actual funeral has several things about it which we may well suppose have come down the ages unchanged; there is still the ceremonial closing of the eyes (it should be done by a kinswoman), the shrouding of the dead in white, and the carrying of him to the grave, as was sometimes done in Shakespere's England, "barefaced on his bier." But the oldest survival is also one of the most interesting and picturesque. In most country districts (the custom is dying out, at least here and there), exactly the same thing happens as took place at the funeral of Hektor at the end of the *Iliad*; mourners of both sexes, but more especially the women, praise and lament the dead, sometimes in extempore utterances, which may be in verse, if the speaker, or rather singer, has enough skill to compose them, on the spot or beforehand, sometimes in traditional verse-formulæ, generally consisting of from two to four lines, but occasionally of longer and more ambitious poems, often full of very picturesque imagery. The language is modern, with little or no archaizing, and the poetical phraseology is likewise that of modern popular tradition, owing nothing ascertainable to antiquity. The custom itself, however, is descended, apparently in an unbroken line, from the earliest times of which we have any knowledge. Not only this, but much of the material of the laments (*moirológhia*) is drawn from the same sources as those of Homer's mourning women, the virtues of the dead, the sorrow of the survivors, and other such natural topics.

Another funeral custom suggests an origin for an ancient belief. It is regular, and it was regular in antiquity, to make much use of water during a burial. The ultimate reason for this is probably the very ancient idea that death is something material, a sort of adhesive, harmful substance which is liable to stick to those who come too near a corpse, or even a dying person. The obvious, if primitive, counter-measure is to wash this off, from the persons of those whom duty or affection bring into such a perilous contact and from the surroundings. We know, for instance, that in the days of Euripides, and no doubt long before and after, it was customary to put a vessel of water at the door of the house where the death had taken place. Modern usages vary locally, from pouring out a vessel of water on the ground to sprinkling water, often perfumed, on the

corpse itself as it is taken to the grave, but agree essentially in
that water is used. It will be remembered (cf. p. 30) that the
ancient under-world is cut off from this one by water of some
kind, which the soul must pass to get to its final abode. That
such a belief sprang from the funeral use of water seems not
improbable. But be it so or not, the usage itself, being found
without essential change in both ancient and modern rites,
and having nothing to do with official Christian teaching, may
safely be supposed to have survived and not to be an innovation
or an importation.

Setting aside one or two beliefs which seem to derive, not
from any classical Greek idea, but from usages or doctrines
common to the whole or a great part of the Roman Empire,
we may note a close resemblance between the ancient and
modern days on which a rite of commemoration of the dead
takes place. Putting together data from sundry places in Greece,
we find that these are now the third, sixth, ninth and fortieth
days from the death, also the last days of the third, sixth and
ninth months, besides anniversaries. Of these, we know the
classic names of the first and third (*trita* and *enata* respectively)
and of one corresponding to the fourth ; the ancients used the
thirtieth, not the fortieth day. What has brought about the
change we do not know, but may conjecture that it is the importance of the number forty in Hebrew tradition, upon which a
considerable part of Christian usage is based. Monthly funeral
feasts sometimes took place in antiquity, and annual ones are
common; we have mentioned (p. 41) the *genesia* which were
held at Athens and elsewhere. Moreover, at the funeral itself,
when the body has been buried, a quite elaborate meal is,
or was, demanded by traditional custom, corresponding to the
funeral feasts which mark both Greek and Roman antiquity,
from the earliest times of which we have record onwards. At
this meal, an invariable dish, prominent in other ceremonies
relating to the dead, is *kóllyva*, an old word which in our days
signifies frumety, in other words boiled grain, generally with
some additions to improve the flavour, which, however, are not
essentials but only subsidiary things. This, one of the most
obvious and easy ways of preparing edible seeds, is probably
much older than the discovery of how to make any sort of

bread, and in one form or another it appears in simple popular rituals all over Europe; when we find it in Greece, both ancient and modern, there seems no need to seek another origin for it than inheritance from the ancestors of those who now make and ceremonially eat it.

We have thus seen that not a few fragments of certain or probable ancient ritual are embedded in modern life. But perhaps the most marked survival of antiquity, in Greece as in other Mediterranean lands, is seen in the popular (not the official) attitude towards the minor objects of Christian cult. The theology of the Greek Church is in all essentials identical with that of the Western Churches, i.e., it is a highly developed monotheism. There is but one Being to Whom adoration in the full sense of the word may be lawfully directed. But the Greek Church, like several others, allows of an attitude of deep respect towards a number of holy persons, noteworthy examples of Christian piety in the past, such as the Apostles, the Martyrs, and above all, the Virgin Mary. To have a devotion towards any of these and to ask for their intercession is perfectly allowable, and furthermore, it is supposed that many, if not all, of them can of the grace granted to them perform sundry miracles, for instance of healing. Therefore to address them in due form is part even of official cult. But it is much more so in popular usage, to judge by all that I have come across of prayers and hymns composed by the people and not belonging to ecclesiastical liturgies. These are regularly either to some saint, or else to the Virgin, oftener than not by some particular title; it is the Panaghia of this or that, perhaps obscure, country church who is asked to do whatever the suppliant wants. Like other widely popular objects of devotion, she becomes on occasion a war-goddess; there is no need to doubt that the stories of Greek soldiers who had visions of her leading them against the invading Italians in the late War are largely true. Other saints on occasion tend to specialize in particular functions, and to these their names sometimes serve as guides, with the help of etymologies as wild as any used in antiquity. St. Isidore, for example (Isídhoros), suggests "iron" (*sídheros*) to the popular ear, and so is asked to make an ailing person "strong as iron." St. Photios now and then becomes a female, Photiá, that being the common word now for "fire," and is credited with great powers of protecting against fire, including the rifles and cannon of the enemy. St. Eleutherios, or, as he is popularly called, Leftéris, can, as his name implies, "free" or "deliver," and especially, can aid the delivery of a woman in childbirth, a service which he is often enough asked to perform. We have already (p. 112) mentioned SS. Kosmas and Damian; they are far from being the only saints who have taken over the functions of Asklepios, and among their colleagues is one, popular at Mytilene, who bears the appropriate name of Therapon, "healer." Like Asklepios, these healing saints often encourage those seeking their help to sleep in their churches, when they are sent either visions of the celestial physicians or good advice as to treatment, and, like Asklepios again, they commonly receive votive offerings and other records of cures from grateful patients. These and many other facts remind us that, underlying the acceptance, often fervent and accompanied by most strict performance of the complicated religious duties attaching to the Orthodox communion, of a Christian theology, there is still more than a little, among the simpler folk, of the mentality belonging to polytheism.

We have thus traced, in very brief outline, the history of Greek pre-Christian religion from its earliest known forms to the traces which still linger at the present day or in recent times. Those who wish for a more complete knowledge are referred in the first instance to the works listed in the Bibliography.

BIBLIOGRAPHY

The literature on ancient Greek religion is very extensive. No attempt has been made at completeness here, but the following works, all in English, will be found useful.

(1) ORIGINS AND EARLY HISTORY

Harrison, Jane Ellen. *Prolegomena to the Study of Greek Religion.* 3rd edition, Cambridge, 1922.
Themis : a Study of the Social Origins of Greek Religion. 2nd edition, Cambridge, 1927.
Interesting material and ingenious, but often very hazardous attempts at explanation in the light of the customs of backward peoples.
Marett, R. R. (editor). *Anthropology and the Classics.* Oxford, 1908.
Essays by various hands on points of contact between known ancient beliefs and those of non-classical cultures.
Murray, G. G. A. *Five Stages of Greek Religion.* Oxford, 1925.
So far as it relates to the earliest period, this is somewhat on the lines of Miss Harrison's works.
Rose, H. J. *Primitive Culture in Greece.* London, 1925.

(2) THE CRETAN RELIGION AND ITS SURVIVALS

Nilsson, M. P., *The Minoan-Mycenæan Religion and its Survival in Greek Religion.* Ed. 2, Lund, 1950.
The standard work.

(3) CLASSICAL GREEK RELIGION

Farnell, L. R. *Cults of the Greek States,* 5 vols., Oxford, 1896–1909.
Same. *Greek Hero-Cults and Ideas of Immortality.* Oxford, 1921.
The above are the completest accounts in English and among the best in any language. Shorter works are :
Farnell, L. R. *Outline history of Greek Religion.* London, 1920.
A very good sketch. Its bibliography, which is well chosen, is now somewhat out of date.
Nilsson, M. P. *A History of Greek Religion,* trans. F. J. Fielden. Oxford, 1925.
Same. *Greek Popular Religion.* New York, 1940.
Same. *Greek Piety.* Oxford, 1948.

(4) PARTICULAR DEITIES

Such works are innumerable, as are also accounts of the cults of particular places, but two very valuable storehouses of material are:

Cook, A. B. *Zeus.* 3 vols., Cambridge, 1914–40.

Contains practically everything that is known or can be conjectured concerning the cult of Zeus and other known or supposed sky-gods. The present author is frequently out of agreement with the theoretical parts of the work, but the facts are gathered with meticulous accuracy and in vast quantity.

Edelstein, Emma J., and Ludwig. *Asclepius : a Collection and Interpretation of the Testimonies.* 2 vols., Baltimore, 1945.

(5) ORPHISM

Guthrie, W. K. C., *Orpheus and Greek Religion.* London, 1935.

The fullest work in English, well-informed and very sane, avoiding extravagances into which many writers on the subject have fallen.

Linforth, Ivan M. *The Arts of Orpheus.* Berkeley and Los Angeles, 1941.

Excellent critical study.

(6) CONTACTS WITH CHRISTIANITY

Halliday, W. R. *Pagan Background of early Christianity.* Liverpool, 1925.

Still one of the best sketches.

Nock, A. D. *Conversion.* Oxford, 1933.

In studying a single phenomenon, the passage from one religion to another, this work gives much information about the later periods of antiquity.

(7) CONTACTS WITH ETHICS, &C.

Farnell, L. R. *Higher Aspects of Greek Religion.* London, 1912.

Moore, Clifford Herschel. *The Religious Thought of the Greeks,* 2nd edition, Cambridge (Mass.), 1925.

Well-informed, pleasantly written sketch.

(8) SURVIVALS IN MODERN GREECE

Argenti, P. P., and Rose, H. J. *Folklore of Chios.* 2 vols., Cambridge (England) University Press, 1949.

Many of the examples in Chapter VII are taken from this work.

Lawson, John Cuthbert. *Modern Greek Folklore and ancient Greek Religion.* Cambridge, 1910.

Interesting, but often inaccurate.

It is to be regretted that no English work gives a reliable account of ancient magic, and no fully satisfactory book on Greek astrology exists in any language.

English translations of most Greek authors exist, some of them excellent. Only one need be mentioned by name here, viz., Frazer, (Sir) J. G., *Pausanias' Description of Greece*, 2nd edition, 6 vols., London, 1913, invaluable for its very full commentary. It also contains an admirable index.

ANCIENT
ROMAN RELIGION

CHAPTER I

NVMEN

In writing even a short account of the religion of ancient Rome an author is faced with a very different task from that which he must undertake if he would describe the pre-Christian cults of Greece.[1] In the latter case he must tell the story of a people who, at the earliest stage of which we have any documentary evidence, had gone a long way on the road which leads from a savage to a fully civilised conception of Deity and of man's place in the universe. The remnants of an earlier stage of thought have to be hunted for like fossils in the rocks and interpreted in the light of the manners and customs of populations that have remained very backward in their intellectual and spiritual development. The Greeks were keen, original thinkers, bold experimenters, capable of breaking with their past, if they thought it advisable, to a far greater degree than most nations. They had, moreover, a gift for abstract thought, and a remarkably high proportion of them had logical minds and were ready to follow their own ideas to the uttermost consequences. Hence they developed a highly abstract, largely monotheistic theology and read it into the traditional practices of their ancestral religion, and many of their conclusions, passing little changed into Christianity, have coloured the whole of European thought on such matters ever since. But the Romans were a much slower-witted people. Orderly and legalistic, willing to learn but at the same time extraordinarily tenacious of the past, at all events in form, they neither struck out any new lines for themselves nor ever quite abandoned the old, half-savage practices which they had inherited from simple ancestors, peasants and herdsmen of prehistoric days. Their theology and philosophy, when they had such things at all, were simplified adaptations of Greek

[1] These are briefly sketched in the author's *Ancient Greek Religion*, No. 5 of this series.

thought. Furthermore, the Greeks, the greatest artists of antiquity, had a vivid and pictorial imagination. The objects of their worship appeared to their mind's eye as clearly-defined figures, human in shape but glorious above the level of humanity, and as individual as any actual men or women. They had their peculiarities of dress and feature, their likes and dislikes, their loves and hates among themselves and towards men, and their relations of father and son, mother and daughter, sister and brother. The first attempts to systematise them were genealogies, and the beginning of history in Greece, so far as we know, was the setting down in verse, later in prose, of tales which chiefly concerned the gods and those mighty men, closely akin to the gods, who lived long ago, and were not an enfeebled race "such as mortals now are", to borrow Homer's recurrent phrase when he describes some prodigious feat of strength on the part of a Hektor or an Aias. But Rome had no mythology, or so little that it vanished before the brighter light of the Greek legends. The Greeks taught the Romans to write, in both senses of that phrase, for the Roman alphabet is derived from the Greek one, with few and trivial modifications, and all that the Romans ever knew of style was adapted from Greek models.

It follows that in dealing with Roman religion, the department in which that conservative people were most conservative, we can quite easily find, almost on the surface as it were, remnants of a very early and simple type of thought which, in Greece, we have to dig deep to recover. But, as Rome was never quite closed to foreign influences and at times received them eagerly, we have to add to these primitive remains a whole series of importations, adapted with the skill of born lawyers to the existing precedents and disguising their novelty under names and forms either of native origin or at least so modified as not to offend native feeling. These borrowings seem to have come, not so much from the nearest relatives of Rome, the other Italian peoples speaking languages akin to Latin and having apparently much the same historical origins as the dwellers by the Tiber, as from foreigners, first the Etruscans, then the Greeks (if indeed some of the earliest borrowings were not from Greek communities in Italy), then from Orientals, till at last the greatest of the eastern religions, Christianity, overcame all the rest, and, moulded by Roman organisers and systematisers, assumed its Western form, profoundly influenced by the Eastern Churches yet readily distinguishable from them.

In one respect the getting of facts about early and classical Roman cult is easier than the gathering of them for Greece. We are dealing with the religious history of one community, not of a multiplicity. We know, it is true, a fair amount concerning the rites and customs of other Italian cities in ancient times, but nothing like enough to write a complete account of any one of them. We may, therefore, for the purposes of the present short study, confine ourself to Roman evidence, perhaps taking an illustrative parallel now and then from some other place. In another way, the task is harder than for Greece. The Greeks were always a vocal people, not only interested in their own customs and thoughts, but given to speaking and, what is more to the point for a historian, writing about them at considerable length. Hence we have documents in fair abundance, though vastly more have been lost, for nearly all periods from early in the first millennium B.C. down to the end of antiquity. But early Rome wrote next to nothing, compared to early Greece, and what little there was not only is lost to us but had mostly perished when the authors who have come down to us were born. Cicero and Varro, Vergil and Livy, to say nothing of many others, were much interested from various points of view in the religion of their country ; but not only were they hampered by imperfect documents concerning at least the origins and early history of that subject, but what material they had they perforce interpreted in the light of what they had themselves been taught, the Greek methods of writing history and the Greek schools of philosophy. Most of the conclusions reached by the latter were quite false for native Roman beliefs, and the methods of the former, by no means perfectly adapted to the study of Greece herself, were still less so for dealing with Rome, or with Italy generally. Thus we find that the first care of a Roman political historian is to produce a tale of the origins of his native country modelled on Greek foundation-legends and crammed with fancies quite foreign to Italy ; while so able a man as Varro, for instance, when he tries to give an intelligible account of what his ancestors believed, is hampered at every turn by his own desire to find, what was never there, the expression of ideas which certain Greek thinkers conceived as fundamental to any religious system, these in their turn being handicapped by lack of knowledge of the way simple minds really work when they try to achieve right relations with the unknown powers, actual or imagined, on which their lives and prosperity depend, or are thought by them to depend. However, we can gather from such materials as are at our disposal many useful facts and interpret them in the light of our own broader knowledge, the harvest of investigations into the lives and thoughts of the more backward of mankind which have now been going on scientifically and with increasingly good method for some generations.

I said in discussing Greek religion that two ideas, whether or not they can be claimed as the first beginnings of religious beliefs and consequent practices, are certainly early and will serve to start from in dealing with the cults of a people who had risen above savagery when first we hear of them. One of these is animism, the conception of all manner of objects in the visible world as having in them something like the soul which, crudely enough pictured in most cases, is postulated as governing the bodies of men and beasts. The other is what has been called dynamism, the notion that there exists a kind of power, different from that power which is to be observed in ordinary muscular exertions and so forth, in which numerous favoured men and, still more, sundry non-human beings, varying from beasts to ghosts and gods, and also various processes, generally of a magical kind, are thought to share. This is most commonly called, in this country, by its Polynesian and Melanesian name of *mana*, which seems originally to signify no more than "force," or, for it can be an adjective as well as a substantive, "forceful, potent". The classical description of it was given in 1891 by Bishop Codrington in his fundamental work *The Melanesians*, the product of his own long residence among that people and his accurate study of their mental processes ; for, being a missionary of the best and most intelligent type, he conceived rightly that it was his duty to know the men and women whom he tried to bring to his own religious opinions. His account of *mana* is given on p. 118 of his book.

"The Melanesian mind", he says, "is entirely possessed by the belief in a supernatural power or influence, called almost universally *mana*. This is what works to effect everything which is beyond the ordinary power of men, outside the common processes of nature ; it is present in the atmosphere of life, attaches itself to persons and things, and is manifested by results which can only be ascribed to its operation. . . . But this power, though itself impersonal, is always connected with some person who directs it ; all spirits have it, ghosts generally, some men." A little later he adds : "The Melanesians believe in the existence of beings personal, intelligent, full of *mana*, with a certain bodily form which is visible but not fleshly like the bodies of men. These they think to be more or less actively concerned in the affairs of men, and they invoke and otherwise approach them." He goes on to explain that some of these beings are ghosts, others what he, perhaps a little rashly, styles "spirits".

A great deal of what the good Bishop says of his Melanesian parishioners could be taken over with little change when we speak of the earliest Roman ideas of which we can form any adequate conception. The Romans, like the Melanesians (and Polynesians) of modern times, believed in "a supernatural power or influence", which they called *numen*, plural *numina*. This word, which seems literally to signify a movement, perhaps especially a nod of the head (the verb *nuere*, with which it is connected, means to nod) would appear to have developed the sense of "result of action, sign of a force or power at work". Until the time of Augustus it never is used to mean any personal or individual god, and even then it is not often so misunderstood by good writers such as Vergil or Ovid. But it is something which gods possess. Juppiter the sky- and weather-god, in Horace, makes a crust of ice form over the snow *puro numine*, by his unmixed or unimpeded *numen*. In plain prose, it is a clear, frosty night.

Speaking of the great corn-goddess of Henna in Sicily, whom he calls Ceres but the Sicilian Greeks Demeter, Cicero informs his audience that abundant miracles make plain her power (*uis*, the ordinary word for force) and—here he adds the exactly right word—her *numen*. Verres, the scoundrely governor of Sicily whom he is impeaching, had possessed *uis*, as any man might, but the worst of his offence had been that he had set at naught the *numen* of the goddess and stolen one of the holiest adornments of her ancient shrine. Varro, explaining *numen* by the famous Homeric passage in which Zeus, by a mere nod of assent, makes the holy mountain Olympos shake, says it belongs to him whose authority is greatest, in other words to a supernatural being ; and Cicero again, speaking of the Stoic Supreme Being, says that all things obey his *numen*. But *numen* is not confined to gods. A single man does not seem to have it until we come to Imperial times, when it was the proper and loyal thing to say, or at least imply, that an Emperor was something more than mortal, and we hear quite often of the *numen* of the reigning one. But even under the Republic, a body of men sometimes possess it, for the Roman Senate, the most powerful assembly of human beings that existed anywhere in the civilised world for several generations, is said occasionally to have it ; it is true that the speaker is always using highly complimentary language when he talks in this strain, but clearly it is not felt that the compliment is out of all proportion to the facts and exceeds the limits of tasteful flattery. By the exercise of their authority, the senators collectively, though not individually, can do things "beyond the ordinary power of men". So can the sovran people of Rome, when they exercise the powers which are lawfully theirs, and therefore Cicero, addressing them in laudatory terms after they had decreed his recall from exile, tells them that he will reverence their *numen* no less than that of the gods themselves. A god can confer *numen* on a mortal. When one of the Imperial house was starting for the East, to secure what could be construed as at all events a diplomatic victory against Rome's one serious opponent, the Parthian Empire, Ovid, always decorously loyal, was ready with a prayer that Mars the war-god and Caesar (Augustus, the reigning emperor) would give him *numen* on his journey. Even inanimate things, if there is something holy or uncanny about them, may have, or even be *numen*. Hesiod, says Manilius the astrologer-poet, sang of "the gods of the woodland and the *numina* sacred to the Nymphs". I fail to see what he can mean save that the wild places which the Nymphs and their Italian equivalents were thought to frequent were themselves examples of a mysterious and superhuman activity, that the streams, caves, old forest trees and other such objects, which owed nothing to the hand of man and stood outside his fields and dwellings, were as weird and fairy-like as the divine or semi-divine creatures which the country folk of Manilius' day still supposed to haunt them. More commonly, it would be said or felt that there was *numen* in such places ; Ovid again tells us that there was in old days a grove of holm-oaks on the Aventine Hill at Rome, "at sight whereof you might say, 'There is *numen* here' ". A natural conclusion, but not inevitable, would be that some deity lived in the grove and the *numen* belonged to him. So in Vergil, Euander, the legendary leader of a band of Arkadian settlers supposed to have created the first settlement on the site of the future Rome, tells Aeneas, as he shows him the Capitoline Hill, where in later days the great temple of Juppiter, Juno and Minerva was to stand, that :

"what god it is we know not, but some god lives in this grove and on this tree-clad hilltop. My Arkadians believe that they have often seen Juppiter himself there" (being a Greek, he would of course call him Zeus) "shaking his dark mantle of goat-skin in his right hand as he marshalled his storm-clouds".

But more than this ; men themselves could on occasion confer *numen*, or at least persuade it to come where it was wanted, by performing the proper rites. A boundary-mark (*terminus*) was no trifling matter to Roman farmers, whose whole wealth consisted in the produce of their land and of such cattle, large and small, as they might possess. It was important to know exactly where Gaius' land ended and Seius' field began, and the Hebrew curse on him who removeth his neighbour's landmark would have been heartily echoed by any Italian of early days. Indeed something very like it occurred in their own formulae. There was an old law, so old that its origin was quite unknown, and therefore it was ascribed to Numa Pompilius, the second of the traditional line of kings, of whom we can say only that he bore a good Italian name and so may have been a real person before he was buried under a heap of edifying stories of Greek origin, such as any who will may read at large in Plutarch's *Life* of him. But whoever enacted it, this old statute laid down that if any man ploughed up a boundary-mark, both he and the oxen who drew his plough should be *sacri*, outlawed, a word we shall have to deal with later on, but for the present it is enough to remark that if a man was *sacer* he had no human rights whatever, and anyone who chose to kill him might do so with impunity. Later times had grisly tales to tell of the divine vengeance which would fall on the wrong-doer, ending in the complete destruction of him and all his house. Therefore, to set up a *terminus* was a business to be conducted decently and in order, with due observance of ritual, and we are so fortunate as to know how the Romans went about it.

Siculus Flaccus, a late but well-informed author on land-survey-ing, after mentioning with regret the abandonment of ancient custom, tells us how a boundary-mark was set in the old days. "They used to stand the stones themselves on the surface of the ground near the places where they meant to dig holes and fix them. The stones they would anoint, veil and garland. In the holes made for the stones to go into, when they had made sacrifice and burned the flesh of the slain victim on blazing sticks, they would, with their heads veiled, let some of the blood drip, and also throw in incense and grain. They would add honey-combs, wine and other materials customary for the ritual of boundary-stones. When all the offering was burned, they would set the stones on top of the hot ashes and then fix them carefully".

Now if, as our author assures us, the stones themselves were treated in this respectful fashion, and afterwards set into holes prepared by being used as the place of a sacrifice, the holy remnants of which were still there when the stone was lowered into place and fixed, clearly the boundary-mark was in close contact with things remote from the everyday world, the condition of non-holiness which the South Seas call *noa*, and thus transferred into the condition which that region of the globe knows as *tapu* or *tabu*, Latin as *sacer*. We are thus better enabled to understand Ovid when he says, addressing the boundary stone, or the god Terminus, for the two are one, "whether you are a stone or a stake fixed in the ground, you too have *numen*". Care had indeed been taken to give it a sufficiency of that desirable quality, by the farmers whose lands the mark bounded, as Siculus Flaccus explains later. Nor were they content with doing all this once, for every year the proprietors between whose lands the holy objects lay used to meet at or near them and offer sacrifice again. When such precautions were duly observed, neighbours might hope that no quarrels would arise between them, and presumably that the mere ordinary and unconsecrated sticks or stones which were put where necessary to mark out the rest of the boundary line would be kept in order and at their posts of duty by their "numinous" fellows. It is to be noticed that not a word of the descriptions that have come down to us suggests that a spirit or god was conjured into the stone ; it has *mana*, *numen*, and that is all. A Terminus was indeed worshipped on the Capitol, whether because it marked out some ancient precinct there or as a sort of representative of all boundary-marks in Roman territory, but Ovid's remark applies to any and every object of this kind which had been put into the ground with proper ceremony.

I have said that the sacrifice was annual, besides the original rite which made the stone once and for all holy. Sacrifice, to a Roman, was indeed an act of piety, but not gratuitous, for the sacrificer expected something in return, nor purely and simply a conventional way of showing what he would call *pietas*, dutiful affection, towards a celestial benefactor. There is very good evidence that the recipient, even if he was one of the greatest gods, was thought to be the better for it. While it was being performed, as the gift, regularly including food of some kind, was laid on the altar or otherwise conveyed to the recipient, the sacrificer would commonly say, "Be thou *macte* by this offering". *Macte* is an old word, apparently to begin with the vocative of a participle which signified "increased". It is hard to imagine in what the god was supposed to be "increased" if it was not in his store of *mana*. He had, no doubt, much *numen* of his own, but his activities would surely result in drawing on his capital of power. What if he spent it and had none left for the further benefits which would be needed by his worshippers ? Prudence, and the Romans were a very prudent people, not least so in business matters, suggested that if there was to be so much expenditure, there ought also to be a steady income, and, it would seem, this was supposed to be furnished by the sacrifices. Just how this was imagined to happen is not always clear ; we have neither complete accounts of all rituals in use among the ancients nor any authoritative exposition of the older ideas underlying or deduced from the ritual actions. But here and there a valuable piece of information enables us to make a good guess. One of the best examples is the festival known as the Fordicidia. The name means "the killing of the *forda*", and *forda* is a cow in calf. On April 15th of every year such a cow was slaughtered by each of the *curiae*, the very old divisions into which the citizen body originally fell, and another on the Capitol by the pontiffs, of whom we shall have more to say in another chapter. Parallels to such a sacrifice are to be found, for instance, in Greece, and the underlying idea is pretty plain. April is a warmer month in Italy than here, and much nearer harvest time. Earth is then manifestly busy preparing the crops which are growing on her surface, and Earth, Tellus Mater, is the goddess to whom the sacrifice is made. She is using a vast deal of *numen* in bestowing on the people who plough and sow her fields (for Tellus is no personification of the planet on which we live, but much more nearly the owner of the *numen* or *mana* of those portions of the surface which Latin-speaking farmers cultivated) the foodstuffs which they want, and it is well to renew her supplies, lest she become unfertile. Now the cows have shown that they possess fertility, in other words a certain amount of *numen*, for obviously *numen* is needed to produce offspring, else why are some women and some beasts barren, though they appear perfectly healthy ? Normally, they would use their *numen* in bringing forth living calves ; divert it, then, to the more immediately pressing needs of Tellus, and her lowered balance at the magical bank on which the gods draw is satisfactorily increased. All this does not mean that the Romans of any age which has left us a particle of evidence were too ignorant of agriculture to put barnyard manure on their fields or otherwise restore to the soil something at least of the chemical constituents it had lost in producing grain. Far from it ; we even hear of a godling called Sterculinus (*stercus* is the regular word for dung) who superintended the business of manuring, and much that their writers tell us indicates that they went about their task of raising cereals in a thoroughly business-like and practical manner. But to their ideas, which were substantially those of all farmers until quite late times, part of practical agriculture was the processes necessary to keep up the supply of *mana* which is needed if the ground is to perform its recurrent miracle of giving men many grains of corn for every one they have given it. Mysterious though *numen* may be, and much though its proper handling may need the guidance of experts, its use is a matter of every day, not of occasional festivals and high days.

Since, however, so much care was taken to keep the Roman earth well supplied with *mana*, or *numen*, there are signs that its power could be used for other purposes than growing corn. When early Rome had to deal with foreign nations (and foreigners' magic is dangerous the world over), it was done through certain officials called *fetiales*. These were formally directed by the king what they were to do, and one of them then asked the king for *sagmina*. The answer was, "Take them clean" (*pura tollito*) and the *fetialis* tore up some grass, with the earth sticking to its roots, from the holy ground of the Roman citadel. With this he proceeded to touch the head and hair of one of his colleagues, thus making him the chief and active member of the deputation, who would actually recite the terms of the treaty it was proposed to make and perform the necessary ritual to make them binding. Obviously, it is no light matter to engage the honour of one's state in this way, and is not made lighter by the ancient conception of it, not as primarily a matter of honour or international morality, but as a process which would bring down the immediate vengeance of the sky-god on Rome if the terms were not kept. Therefore the person entrusted with this delicate task needs all the *numen* he can get, and it would appear that some of the *numen* of his native soil was transferred to him for the occasion. The immediate source of it is the goddess Tellus, or perhaps the presiding deity of the citadel, Juno ; but human hands have performed the actual transfer. Man cannot, it would seem, originate *numen*, but he is capable of directing it, in this as in many other rites.

Mana in the Pacific region, *numen* in Rome, can attach itself to certain inanimate things ; Earth is not one of these, for she was not considered inanimate. To return for a moment to Bishop Codrington, he states that *mana* may be conveyed in such things as a stone amulet, a tuft of leaves or a tooth, all of which may be useful war-charms if properly used. A prosperous Melanesian cultivator owes his good fortune to "stones full of *mana* for pigs and yams". Hence it need not surprise us that in Rome there are distinct signs of *numen* about so holy a thing as an altar. It can be "increased" by putting some offering, even a trifling one, upon it ; but apart from such contact as this, it is too holy, or too dangerous, a thing to touch.   There is a well-known passage in Horace, a humorously kindly address to a simple and pious country-woman, in which he assures her that if she is guilty of such a sin (he implies that it is the only one at all likely in her case, and no doubt, since a domestic altar is meant, it is one which might occur while she was tidying her house) the simplest of offerings, a handful of salted grain, would be enough to recover the favour of the little household gods she has offended. In more serious cases, it was usual to touch an altar when taking an oath ; for an oath contains a conditional curse by the swearer, who calls for divine vengeance on himself if he is perjured. He is thus deliberately coming into contact with the power which will smite him if he deserves it.

However, an altar is regularly the altar of some deity, although instances occur in which the name of the god is unknown and the holy object dedicated "to whoever it is, god or goddess" (*si deus si dea*). There are material objects so very full of *numen* as actually to bear specific divine names. For example, in the Regia, the ancient palace of Roman kings, or the later constructions which occupied its site and bore its name, there were certain holy spears, with which war-magic was performed on occasion. This in itself is not very remarkable, but it sounds somewhat strange to modern notions that the spears themselves seem to have borne the name of the god Mars. It puzzled the later Romans, some of whom modified the name by speaking of the "spears *of* Mars" instead, but there is no real reason to doubt that to begin with Mars and the spears were one and the same. We know, from a bit of antiquarian learning preserved in the commentary on Vergil bearing the name of Servius, that when war was about to begin the Roman commander "went into Mars' shrine and first moved the sacred shields, next the spear carried by the image itself, saying, 'Mars, awake' ". But we also know that in old days there was no image of Mars or anyone else to hold a spear in its hand ; the earliest war-leaders, therefore, shook the *numen*-charged arms themselves, and in so doing aroused the *mana* of their god. The sanctuary no doubt was in the Regia, and the interesting and significant thing is that the arms *were* Mars. In like manner there is good proof, though details of the matter are not free from doubt, that a stone or stones, probably the latter, preserved on the Capitol, were Juppiter, distinguished from other manifestations of the great sky-god by their name, Juppiter the Stone (*Iuppiter Lapis*).

This brings us to a consideration of what a Roman of early days supposed a god to be. Since *numen* is found in sundry places and attached to various persons and things, it is not remarkable that its manifestations were sometimes less and sometimes more potent. If they were strong, and especially if they were regular in their occurrence, the natural conclusion would be that they were produced by a kind of person who had much *numen* and was ready to display it for the benefit of those who approached him in the proper manner. This person was a god or goddess, and concerning the nature of these beings the Roman, left to his own devices, seems to have had a great incuriosity. A god exercised his *numen* at certain times and places or under certain circumstances. Something generally, not always, indicated whether the power behind the action was male or female, a *deus* or a *dea*. Honorific titles were often bestowed on these powers, among the commonest being "father" and "mother", words, it is to be noted, which have no etymological connexion with begetting or bearing, whether applied to deities or to human beings. This point was made long ago by Fustel de Coulanges in his famous work *La cité antique ;* his words are still well worth quoting.

"The very name by which he (the head of a Roman household) is called, *pater*, contains some curious information. The word is the same in Greek, Latin and Sanskrit. . . . What did it mean and what idea did it evoke then in men's minds ? We can know, for it kept that meaning in formulae belonging to religious and legal language. When the ancients invoked Juppiter under the title of *pater* of gods and men, they did not mean that he was their [physical] father, for they never supposed he was, but on the contrary believed that the human race had existed before he did. The same title was given to Neptune, Apollo, Bacchus, Vulcan and Pluto, whom men certainly did not suppose to be their fathers, while the title of *mater* was applied to Minerva, Diana and Vesta, all three of whom were supposed to be virgin goddesses. Similarly, in legal language, the title of *paterfamilias* [literally, father of the household] could be given to a man who had no children, was not married, was not even old enough to enter upon a marriage".

Some of the examples from religious formulae confuse pure Latin with Latinised Greek usages, but the general conclusion is not to be upset ; *pater*, the Latin word cognate to "father" and closest akin to it in meaning, signifies not so much him who has begotten a younger person as him who has natural authority over one inferior in age or status, and, with a difference of sex, the same is true of *mater*, or mother. Therefore, when we find these titles applied to Roman gods, we need not ask what other beings, divine or human, were supposed to be their children, for the words do not imply any such relationship. One of the many indications of this is that in all native Italian cult there is but one doubtful instance of the natural correlative, to our notions, of the words "father" and "mother". Two inscriptions, of Praeneste, the modern Palestrina, not of Rome, call Fortuna the daughter of Juppiter. We have our choice between the misunderstanding of a formula still older than these ancient records and a rather early intrusion of Greek mythology, or personification, in which Tyche, or Chance, is sometimes the daughter of Zeus.

If the Romans therefore were so incurious about the persons of their deities as not even to try to arrange them in genealogies, it is not to be expected that they would invent many stories about their doings, other than their wonderful works towards men. Of these, indeed, there are a few. For instance, miracles of Vesta, the hearth-goddess, of whom more will be said later, seem now and then to have been told. It was said that once her holy fire went out, and Aemilia, one of the Vestal Virgins, was responsible, for she had left the tending of it to a novice. This was bad enough, but it began to be rumoured that some impious deed had profaned the holy place. Aemilia therefore prayed that, if she had served Vesta faithfully and in purity of body and mind, the goddess would manifest herself and save her priestess. With that she tore a strip from her dress and threw it upon the cold ashes, whereupon a great flame sprang up in testimony of the divine approval. Another Vestal, Tucca by name, was accused of the worst of offences for one in her office, unchastity. Called upon to defend herself, she replied that she would do so in deeds, not in words, and invoking Vesta, proceeded to the Tiber, where she drew water in a sieve, carried it to the Forum, and poured it out before the feet of the pontiffs assembled to try her. Another tale and a famous one concerned no well-known divinity but one whose very name was hidden from his worshippers. Before the Gaulish invasion of 390 B.C., a certain Marcus Caedicius was out of doors late one night when a voice, louder and clearer than any man's, bade him warn the magistrates that the Gauls were coming. He reported this prodigy, but no one paid any attention to it, and the Gauls, routing a Roman army, took the city and held it to ransom. When they were gone, it was felt that some measures should be taken to express a proper feeling towards the power which had done its best to make known the danger to them, but, no one having any idea what being had pronounced the mysterious words, a chapel was erected in honour of the Speaker who gave utterance (Aius Locutius). Certainly there had been *numen* at work, but where a Greek would have set about finding, to his own satisfaction at least, what god it was, and probably would have added a suitable title to the name of some existing deity, the Romans were content to describe him in terms of the one fact relating to him which they knew. Whether the story is true or false, the chapel was real, and was still there in Livy's days, for he gives its position (it was near Vesta's shrine, on the thoroughfare called New Street), as well as telling the legend.

It hardly needs to be pointed out how sharp a contrast all this makes to the rich mythology of Greece, to say nothing of other peoples, such as the Aryan Indians. Hardly a Greek god, however minor, was without his legends, telling of his birth, his relation to other deities, his loves and quarrels, and all that is necessary to make a clearly defined personality. Even so pale a figure as Hestia, the equivalent of Vesta in Greek cult, was humanised in this way, for at least it was known whose daughter she was ; her parents were Kronos and Rhea, and she remained virgin at her own request, having no taste for marriage, though more than one god proposed for her. Vesta, despite her miracles, can hardly be called a person, and Ovid was reflecting not only the facts of cult but the usual conception of the goddess when he bade his readers understand that she was "nothing other than living flame".

Indeed, some features of early Roman cult reveal not so much a polytheism as a polydaimonism, the worship, that is, of an indefinite number of quite small figures, defined as regards their functions but in other respects mere names. This tendency was greatly elaborated by the official regulation of the cult, for nothing was more eagerly sought than to address precisely the right power at the right time. In the official records of names, titles and functions of the deities, known as *indigitamenta*, there were contained long lists of gods and goddesses whose *numen* manifested itself in highly specialised ways. For instance, there were associated with Ceres the corn-goddess and Tellus, of whom we have already spoken, no fewer than twelve minor figures, every one of whom has a name significant of some part of the cycle of farm-work. They begin with Vervactor, whose *numen* extends no further than to enable the cultivator to plough fallow land (*ueruagere*), and they end with Promitor, whose function is simply the taking out of the corn from its store-place to make flour, or perhaps to sow. Highly artificial though these lists are, they rest upon a real tendency of the Romans, to recognise with scrupulous accuracy of detail every instance of *numen* they thought they had observed and give it its appropriate label, so that when it was needed, it might be induced to function again. Within this plurality of little powers were several groups, no doubt clearly enough defined to ancient experts, but often very obscure to us. Thus, we do not know the nature and functions of the classes called Novensides and Indigetes, though modern conjectures concerning them are plentiful. We do, however, understand the name of the Penates, for it signifies "dwellers in the store-room" (*penus*), and so clearly enough explains itself as containing the little household deities who watched over the food-supplies of the household. On the other hand, a second group of domestic gods, the Lares, who were of some importance, for their worship extended beyond the houses and land of individuals, are extremely vague to us, and in antiquity they were much obscured by identifications with certain Greek figures of origin probably quite other than theirs.

But even in early times, there were some manifestations of *numen* large and imposing enough in their nature and varied enough in their activity to be ascribed to someone greater than a Vervactor or one of the Penates. The sky, considered not as the place where the sun, moon and stars are to be seen, but rather as the region of the weather, including that very impressive kind of weather, a violent Italian thunderstorm, evidently had a vast deal of *numen* in it. And it is visibly one, with no natural differences to mark off one part of it from another. Therefore, like other speakers of the group of languages to which most European tongues belong, the Romans had one great sky-god, Juppiter, the last two syllables of whose name are simply the title "father", while the first is etymologically equivalent to the name of the Greek sky-god Zeus. Corn, again, is one kind of useful product of the earth, though there are different species of it, as wheat, barley and so forth, for they all alike serve for food, and indeed the principal food of the ancient Italian peasantry, who ate no great amount of meat as a rule. So not only the Romans but the Italians generally worshipped one great corn-deity, Ceres. They knew, of course, as well as we do that different soils will produce, or are best suited to produce, different sorts of edible plants, but the getting of food out of the ground was all the result of the same kind of *numen*, therefore one great source of *numen* was active. As to why they concluded that that source was female, even their sluggish imaginations seem to have been active enough to catch the resemblance between a fertile woman and a fertile field, which is so thorough a commonplace to the quicker-witted Greeks that it found its way into the formula with which an Athenian girl was betrothed. It is one of the few exceptions to the rule that they were quite incurious concerning the sort of persons their gods might be, provided always that their *numen* could be got to work for their worshippers when needed.

I say "when needed", because there is no evidence that Roman cult was ever the continuous thing which various types of Oriental worship, including some of the best-known forms of Christianity, are or have been. The gods lived in their holy places, and as time went on, it became the custom (it had not originally been so) to build them houses, albeit for the most part of foreign style ; there is no such thing as a Roman fashion of making what we call a temple, but they adopted first the Etruscan and then the Greek method of building and orienting one. The deities' presence was commonly made known to worshippers by signs or emblems of some sort, such as the Juppiter-stones of the Capitol and, even more curious, for the stones may well have been real or supposed meteorites, and therefore naturally connected with the *numen* of the sky-god, by the bundles of herbs which were known as "heads of gods" and used to represent them at certain old ceremonies. Later, again, the foreign fashion of having images in human shape in the temples was adopted, though not universally approved, for the dislike of images in worship is not a phenomenon confined to Protestant Christianity. But apparently all this divine apparatus remained unused for most of the time in the case of most deities ; Vesta is something of an exception, for her fire had to be continually kept going, and apparently a certain amount of other housework was performed in her shrine. But Mars, for example, or Quirinus, seems to have been left very much to himself in normal times between one festival and the next, provided no emergency occurred which called for a use of his particular kind of *numen* or for a general appeal to all the gods to avert or cure an evil, or again a general public thanksgiving to them all for some great benefit. In such cases, the shrines would be thrown open and citizens would visit them with humble prayers, the women, as with many peoples, being often the most zealous. The name of such an occasion itself means "a bowing down" (*supplicatio*).

What did go on daily was the domestic cult, kept up in all ages in every decent house throughout the Roman dominions. We do not know by any means all the details of this, but a fair amount of information has come down to us from a variety of sources, enabling us to patch together a picture not too untrue to ancient life. We may begin with the Lares. One of them came, how early we do not know, to be known as the Lar of the household (*Lar familiaris*), and we have what purports to be first-hand information as to how these deities felt the family should treat them. In the *Aulularia* of Plautus, the play from which Molière took, or rather adapted, the plot of *L'Avare* and the character of Harpagon, the prologue is spoken by the Lar. He informs the audience that for two generations he has been the guardian of a treasure buried under the hearth by the grandfather of the house's present owner, a miserly man called Euclio, the son and grandson of misers.

> "He has one daughter. Every day she prays,
> Bringing me incense, wine or other gift,
> And garlands ; so for this her piety,
> I have revealed the hoard to Euclio,
> To make a marriage-portion for the girl,
> Because a high-born youth has done her wrong."

Of the Penates something is said in that ode of Horace which was mentioned on p. 168. The good country-woman there garlands them with rosemary and myrtle ; at the first of every month she makes formal prayer, presumably to all the deities of her household, raising her hands palm upwards towards the sky, the regular ancient gesture on ordinary occasions. She also is dutiful towards the Lares, if indeed, for Horace is not an expert on religious matters and the two classes of godlings were often mixed, he does not mean the Penates, or the gods of the house generally, again. At all events, she gives them offerings of corn and wine and occasionally a pig, probably a sucking-pig. The great and expensive sacrifices of cows and bulls are not for her, nor for domestic cult generally, and from what we know of ancient sacrifices it is safe to say that the pig, after the proper portions had been given to the friendly little deities, formed the staple of the family dinner.

For gods and men shared the same meals in a Roman household. The table at which the human inhabitants of the house dined was in itself a holy thing, having, it would appear, its own share of *numen*. At all events, several acts of innocent native magic, or worship, for the line between the two was never very clearly defined, are connected with it. Plutarch, who was much interested in Roman ritual, tells us a little about this.

"Why," he asks in his *Roman Questions*, "did they not allow the table to be taken away empty, but insisted on something remaining upon it ?" and after some vague guesses as to amiable and moral reasons which might have originated this custom, but certainly did not, he finds very nearly the true one, "because no holy place should be left empty, and the table is holy".

Certainly the table is holy, as already stated. Therefore it is not well to leave it empty, for that is, or may easily be, a piece of sympathetic magic of quite the wrong kind, hunger-magic, tending to make it permanently empty, or at least bare of wholesome and satisfying food ; "when he takes food, may he not be able to eat it nor lessen his hunger" says an ancient curse in the Oscan dialect which someone's hatred has preserved to us, written on a piece of lead and deposited in or near a tomb for the ghosts and other uncanny powers to fulfil it. So it is best always to leave something, perhaps a loaf of bread or some *puls*, a sort of porridge which Roman country folk ate, standing upon it at all times, to let its *numen*, or that of the household gods, work useful, full-table magic, that the family may always have enough to eat. Those who wait or sit at it (the Greek fashion of reclining at meals on a sort of sofa is not native to Rome, though it was adopted later) should be clean people ; Juvenal waxes very indignant at persons of filthy life being allowed to come near it. When the family gathered for the principal meal of the day, a little of the food was set apart, in a small plate it would seem, for the gods, and at the end of the dinner a boy would get up, take it to the fire which burned upon the little family altar (or, doubtless, in older and simpler times, to the hearth which was kept alight under the smoke-hole in the roof), throw it in, and formally announce, amid the reverent silence of the rest, that the gods were favourable (*di propitii*). After that the dessert, or, as they called it, the "second tables" was brought in. This was rather an indulgence than a meal, and seems to have had no ritual attached. The table might also be the centre of a grave omen. For food to fall from a diner's hand onto the floor was always an unwelcome sign, but especially if a pontiff was taking a formal meal. The exact meaning of the sign was determined by what the person who let the food fall was saying or thinking of at the time, and strenuous measures were taken to avert ill consequences, for the floor under a table is the regular haunt of houseless and friendless ghosts, who have no one to provide the proper soul-feasts for them but, being miserable and hungry, are ill-tempered and apt to do mischief. So the food must be picked up and laid on the table again, without blowing the dust off it, thus pretending that it had not fallen, or bringing it once more into contact with the *numen* of the table, perhaps a little of both. Lastly, it was cast into the Lares' fire, thus leaving them to deal properly with it and remove it from the world of ghosts altogether. Pliny is our authority for this custom, which was obsolete or nearly so when he wrote (the principate of Vespasian, A.D. 69-79), as is shown by his use of past tenses in describing it. It belongs, then, to the old days, when the concept of *numen* was likely to be strong.

Vesta the hearth-goddess was herself one of the Penates in a way, at least very closely associated with them, but we know little of her private cult. It seems to have been the duty of the housewife to see that the hearth was clean every night before she went to bed, and to judge by the public cult, of which we shall have more to say later, the daughters of the house, if there were any, performed such simple and every-day rites as were called for. Vesta was never a purely ritual object or an imaginary figure. Fire is too obviously useful for that, and Vesta, in any Roman house of old days, before the more complicated modern domestic architecture came in (houses, under the Empire, if they belonged to well-to-do people, were much more modern and convenient than anything Europe was to see again until well into the nineteenth century), was nothing else than the ordinary fire used for cooking and heating. It burned on a hearth towards the back of the main room (originally the only room), the *atrium*, and on the opposite side, that towards the road or street, appeared the visible presence of another deity, almost exclusively Roman, Janus.

The name of Janus is connected with *ianua*, which means the outer door of a house. As a common noun, it signifies a gate or barbican, such as gave entrance to and exit from a walled place like Rome or any other considerable town in the ancient world. The name for the whole structure, in common parlance, was *porta*, but *ianus* was used in two ways, besides being the name of the god. It could mean a large double gate standing free, a not uncommon monument in classical times, comparable, as an ornament of the city, to such erections as the Marble Arch in London. There was, for instance, a *ianus geminus*, or two-arched gateway, in the Cattle Market (*Forum Boarium*) at Rome, and a still more famous one in the Forum proper, the administrative and commercial centre of the city under the Republic and later. But it could also mean one of the archways in an ordinary gate in the city wall. So, when the clan of the Fabii undertook their heroic, if legendary, single-handed campaign against the people of Veii, which ended in their destruction by superior numbers of the enemy, they marched forth, says Livy "by an unlucky route, the right-hand *ianus* of the Gate of Carmentis". That gate faced almost due south, therefore anyone going through it out of Rome was going as near as the structure would let him to the unlucky quarter, the west, if he took the right-hand opening. We shall have something to say later concerning right and left hand in Roman divination. But Janus was also present in every house, for naturally it must have a door of some kind, however simple. Now to go through a door, whether inwards or outwards, is to begin something, and beginnings are heavily charged with magical significance, in fact with *mana*, the world over. Hence it is not to be wondered at that the opening which let the Roman into or out of his home was laden with *numen*, which took to itself a name, that of the god Doorway. Nor is it very strange that in any full-length litany which addressed itself to all powers, small and great, Janus had first place, taking precedence even of Juppiter, while Vesta came last of all. It was simply what everyone saw when he came home, first the entrance to the house, then any objects which might be in the *atrium*, then the hearth-fire burning steadily (people who have no quick means of lighting a fire do not let it go out if they can help it) at the back of the room. So important, indeed, was the entrance-door that even its parts tended to assume a *numen* of their own. Once man gets beyond building a mere hut, of reeds or other material, and constructs a solid dwelling of timber or stone, his outer door will consist of two upright posts, a threshold, a lintel, and the door proper, swinging on hinges or, as was often the case in antiquity, revolving on a pivot. Of these the threshold is often the most substantial part, being in many cases a heavy block of stone, high enough to keep mud and water from coming into the house in bad weather. It may have been priestly elaboration which decreed that this part of the structure had two presiding deities, Limentinus and Lima, the god and goddess of the threshold (*limen*), But it is no theory, priestly or other, but fact that the actual threshold was an object of considerable importance. The bride, in Rome as in many places, was lifted over it as she entered her husband's house for the first time. We know well enough why, for Catullus, in one of his two marriage-songs, tells us ; it was for the omen's sake, lest she should stumble. But others let us know that there was more in it than that, for she also must not tread on it. Furthermore, she must win the favour of the entire doorway, and to that end she anointed the door-posts before she entered. The proper unguent was wolf's fat, for the wolf is not only a formidable but also a holy beast in Roman tradition ; it is Mars' own creature. Therefore so important a part of it as the fat would be heavily charged with *numen*. One would like to be told how hunters in early days dealt with a creature at once so troublesome in wild country and so sacred ; that they killed it out of hand, with no appropriate ritual, is simply incredible, but our authors date from times when Italy was for the most part well settled and tolerably policed, at all events in the territory originally Roman. However, wolf's fat naturally grew harder and harder to obtain, and later ages were content with hog's lard, again an important part of a beast closely connected with ritual and also with the idea of fertility, the blessing most wanted in marriage by the practically-minded peasants who started the custom going, or even common olive oil. The bride also fastened wool to the posts, another lucky substance.

But to return to the threshold, we have further evidence of its importance. Plautus has given us a scene in which a young man is leaving home, as he thinks, for ever. He is supposed to be an Athenian, but, as usual in that author, the atmosphere is completely Roman. He takes his solemn

farewell of the supernatural powers, and his words are :
"Lintel and threshold, greetings, and fare you well. To-day, for
the last time, I step outside my home and my country. . . . *Penates*
of my father and mother, Lar master of our household, to you
I confide my parents' affairs, to guard them well. I seek other
penates and another Lar, another city, another country".

It hardly needs further proof that these parts of the prosaic
house-door were charged with *numen* for a pious Roman of
that day, about the end of the third or beginning of the
second century B.C.

It has already been mentioned that the floor of the house
was the haunt of uncanny presences, and we happen to know
what was done to clear them out. For some reason, May 9th,
11th and 13th was an unlucky time of year, when ghosts
were especially on the prowl. It was not the season when
the family dead were honoured, for that was February, but
the time for dealing with the houseless spirits. To do so was
the task of the householder ; it was not a public rite performed by State experts, like those which we shall deal with
in the next chapter. The ritual was gone through at midnight,
when the officiant rose and went barefoot about the house,
thus, in the old-fashioned and simple dwelling, remaining
the whole time in contact with the earth, for the floor would
be nothing else until later and more civilised ages. Making
a magical sign to keep unholy things at arm's length, he then
took nine black beans into his mouth ; beans, perhaps
because they are apt to cause flatulence, are somewhat
suspicious food to the ancients (in the Greek world,
Pythagoreans would not eat them), and a popular idea seems
to have been that they are connected with ghosts and the
realm of darkness generally. At all events, they are not uncommonly ghosts' diet. These he would drop or spit out,
saying as he did so, "With these I ransom me and mine".
It was supposed that the ghosts (*lemures*) followed him and
picked up and ate the beans, thus rendered more attractive
by having something of the flavour of man from being in a
live man's mouth. But he was very careful not to turn his
head to see them do it, a precaution regularly taken by the
officiant in any religious or magical ceremony which brings

him in contact with dangerous powers. Finally, he dismissed his undesirable guests with as little offence to their feelings as possible. He washed his hands, clanged together some sort of bronze or copper objects—probably an ordinary cooking-pot would serve his turn, for the point of it was to make a metallic sound, which spirits do not like—and finally said "Good Folk (*manes*, the polite name for the dead), get you gone".

If we pass from the floor of the house to its roof, we still find evidence that the supernatural had its part. Roman houses had no such elaborate means of getting rid of smoke as our chimneys. In the roof of the *atrium* there was a square opening, the *impluuium*, literally "rain-in place", which served at once to collect rain-water in a tank placed underneath and to let out the fumes from the hearth-fire. We have some evidence that this was on occasion the way in and out for other than normal or mortal visitants. If a man was abroad and falsely reported dead (for instance, a soldier missing on active service), he had a fairly elaborate ceremonial to go through on his return. For, having been declared dead, he officially belonged to the other world, and not to this ; his relatives, we gather from Plutarch, who is our informant here, would have celebrated his funeral rites, thus making him over to the abode of ghosts. Therefore it was not fitting, as our author justly remarks, that he should use the front door, which we have seen to be a holy thing. He must climb up on the roof and let himself down by a rope through the *impluuium*. What else he did in order to restore himself to the communion of the living, we do not know ; the thorough-going and logical Greeks in like case made him go through the form of being a baby again, that being the recognised pathway into normal human life, but there is no direct evidence for such a performance in the Roman area, though in itself it is not unlikely. As to the use of the opening in the roof as the way out for unchancy things, we have the case the priest of Juppiter, who was so holy that nothing unlucky was tolerated in his presence. Therefore, if a man in bonds managed to get into his house, he must at once be loosed, and the fetters be flung out through the *impluuium*,

lest they pollute his doubly sacred doorway. There is a
certain amount of evidence that the roof is, not only in
ancient Rome but at various times and places, a place where
things not of this world may be expected to come and go.

Enough has perhaps been said to make it clear that no
small amount of *numen* existed in the ordinary dwelling-house
of early Rome. But most of the population lived, not in the
City itself, but somewhere in the territory surrounding it,
and got their living by tilling the land or raising cattle,
especially the former, since Italians were and are no great
meat-eaters. It was not to be expected that the fields should
be destitute of *numen*, since we have seen that it existed in
such familiar objects as the boundary-marks dividing them.
It was the care of every farmer to draw around his land a
magic circle, shutting out evil and shutting in good. Several
writers tell us something of the circumambulation of the fields
(*Ambarualia*), none more charmingly than Tibullus, who,
like his greater contemporary Vergil, was country-bred and
had an affection for the old ways. What follows is largely
a prosaic paraphrase of his pretty verses in the first poem
of his second book, but with a detail or two added from
elsewhere.

The first requisite was "good words". By this neither
Tibullus nor anyone else who wrote in Latin meant pious
remarks nor prayer-formulae only, though doubtless both
would be in place. It was rather the avoidance of ill-omened
words, for in Latin as in many tongues *nomen omen*, a name,
or indeed any significant word, "means something", often
much more than it says. Thus, in calling up men for the
armed forces, it was customary to call first someone whose
name had welcome associations ; a man whose personal
name was Kaeso, "slasher", or whose family surname was
Victor, for example, would certainly find himself well up
in the list. So in this country rite, everyone would avoid,
during the ceremony, any such remark as "this field ought to
do well if we don't have another drought this year". It is
no great wonder that those concerned usually kept as quiet
as they could (the Greek verb which signifies "to say good
words", *euphemein*, commonly means "to be silent", and a

like secondary meaning attaches to the equivalent Latin phrase *fauere linguis*, "to be lucky with tongues"), except while repeating the words of the sacred litanies, which would be dictated to them, slowly and audibly, by the local expert. Next, no work must be done, not only all human inhabitants of the farm but the draught-cattle enjoying a holiday and oxen as well as men and women being crowned with garlands. These were no mere ornaments, but rather magical objects, composed of plants supposed to be lucky or well-pleasing to the gods concerned, which would thus protect the head and consequently the whole person against evil influences while at the same time instilling good ones. Later casuists exercised some ingenuity, reminiscent of that shown by Jewish rabbis in deciding what constitutes "work" and therefore a violation of the Sabbath, to make clear what, if anything, a farmer might do on a holy day. But the people concerned are not said to be idle ; rather they are busy, *operati*, at their task, which on this day is not ploughing or weeding but getting a supply of good influences, in fact of the right kind of *numen*, for their land. Thirdly, everyone must be pure, *castus*. This included sexual purity, no one being allowed to take part who had indulged his natural appetites the night before. Hence, with the growth of a moral meaning in what was originally a purely ritual word, the modern sense of "chaste" ; but to begin with there was no ethical feeling attached to it. The participant in such a rite would need all the *numen* that was to be had, and sexual relations are full of *numen*, therefore to engage in them would use up the available supply of that precious power. Equally a part of the ritual purity is the wearing of clean white clothes and a formal washing in running water, from a spring or stream. An altar would be set up, if there was no permanent one, but if there was, it would be prepared for use by having a green turf laid on top of it. The victim (Tibullus specifies a male lamb, and no doubt this was a very common choice) was then led three times around the land, followed by the farmer and all his people, in their white clothes and wearing wreaths of olive. This was one of the most appropriate materials for such a purpose. Trees which bear useful fruit are lucky (the word *felix*, which is applied to such a tree, means primarily fruitful and secondarily fortunate), and the olive is the most valuable of all in the Mediterranean region, where it is the primary source of the carbohydrates necessary to any balanced diet. Butter is its Northern substitute, and the synthetic preparations which eke out an insufficient butter-supply are the substitute for a substitute. The procession over, the victim was sacrificed, the act being accompanied by a prayer, as was always the case. A sacrifice (cf. p. 166) increases the *numen* of the god to whom it is given, and it is clearly of little use to do that unless the power concerned is told, in unambiguous terms, exactly what use his worshippers expect him to make of his heightened vigour. The gods of a legalistic people are naturally legalistic themselves, apt to keep to the letter of a contract. In this case the chief powers concerned are Bacchus (Tibullus means, or at least his ancestors would have meant, the Italian wine-god, Liber pater) and Ceres, and they are asked to give increase and keep all evil away. When the victim was killed, the next thing was to examine its entrails, especially the liver, for omens. If these were favourable, that is to say if the internal appearance of the beast was normal, it meant that the gods had accepted the offering and might be relied on to do their part, if nothing untoward happened in the meanwhile. When their portions of the victim were prepared and burned on the altar-fire, all concerned could sit down with a good conscience to the feast which was regularly part of such a rite. Tibullus concludes his poem with a brief address to his patron Messalla and a long eulogy of the rural gods, which, for he is a poet of love, shades off into an account of the love-god's activities in the countryside. All this may very well represent the traditional hymns which we know were sung on such an occasion, for he is not writing a scientific or technical account of how to conduct the ceremony, but handling his theme with an imaginative writer's freedom.

It was not only on the occasion of this formal drawing of the magic circle that Roman farmers performed religious ceremonies in connexion with their land. The Lar familiaris has already been mentioned (p. 175). His brethren were out in the fields. Roman land was regularly distributed to its owners or tenants in a sort of chequer-board pattern of squares subdivided into squares. The whole was apparently a particular application of the principle of the *templum* which must be discussed more fully later (p. 233), but for the present this much will suffice. The surveyor of the parcel of land to be assigned to Roman colonists or other future holders of the region in question took up his position at some convenient central spot. He then sighted by means of a simple instrument called a *groma* (an Italian corruption of Greek *gnomon*, a pointer) along two main lines, one approximately north and south, the other roughly east and west, so as to form a great Greek cross. These lines were called, one the *cardo*, the other the *decumanus*, though which was which was a disputed point. Now it was a simple matter to complete a quadrilateral in which the cross was inscribed, and the resulting four parts could be subdivided again and again by the same method until the minimum unit desired was reached. Thus each tenant was presented, normally and ideally at least, with a square holding, forming a larger square with three adjoining allotments. Between them would be left little strips of un- tilled land, on the lines of the local *cardo* and *decumanus*, which might serve as paths, and the central point where these met, the place where a corner of each of the four properties almost touched, was called a *compitum*, or cross- roads. Here it was customary to set up a little chapel of the Lares of the cross-roads, *Lares Compitales*, open in all four directions, so that the Lar of each farm might have free ingress and egress to the common shrine. Before each open- ing, fifteen Roman feet away, stood an altar, whereon sacrifice might be made by each of the proprietors concerned to his own Lar, at a kind of harvest-home festival, the Compitalia, which down to very late times was held on no rigidly fixed day but simply when winter came and the round of farm- work was over for the time being ; early January was the usual season. Each farmer brought his plough and hung it up before the Lares, and there was feasting and jollity for him and his family. On the evening before, a curious ceremony was gone through, which puzzled the ancients themselves, as its meaning had clearly been forgotten. A woollen doll was hung up for every free member of the household, and a woollen ball for every slave. Antiquaries explained that these were substitutes for the human beings concerned and it was hoped that the Lares, or a goddess called Mania ("the good lady", a euphemism for an underworld power connected with the dead, *manes*) would take these and leave the living alone. This, however, like some modern theories of similar nature, arises from a common confusion. The Lares are powers of the earth, who among other things help it to be fertile ; but ghosts and the vague and grim gods who rule over them are also of the earth, for there the dead are buried. Hence the frequency with which ghosts are expected to help the tiller of the soil and on the other hand the kindly powers who do help him are dreaded because of the uncanny place in which they live. The truth probably is that the woollen dummies were put where the Lares could give them some of their own *numen*, just as various objects, including ornaments worn in childhood (a Roman boy carried a locket, *bulla*, with a little charm inside it, to protect him until he came to man's estate), used to be hung up before the Lar familiaris, that he might extend his protection through them to the persons they belonged to, and such things as hair were very commonly offered to all manner of deities for a like reason. The *numen* which had thus, as it were, soaked into the doll or ball representing each individual would stand him in good stead when he resumed work on the soil which the Lares protected and strengthened. Why mere lumps of wool stood for the slaves and more or less recognisable human effigies for the free persons, we do not know. Possibly the reason lies in the terminology of Roman law. A doll, however roughly made, must have some sort of head ; head is *caput* in Latin, and the word also means legal personality. But a slave is not a person in law, he has no *caput* in that sense, therefore perhaps it was felt that a headless thing, although made of a lucky material, was a better representative. of him. Incidentally, if the above explanation of the puppets is the true one, it is an instance of what we find very commonly in early religion and magic, namely that the *mana* which is handled and directed is no immaterial thing, like the "spiritual grace" of much later and more developed cults, but material, which can be absorbed like water in a woollen ball, or put into a boundary-stone by setting it in a hole which has consecrated things, the remains of a sacrifice, at the bottom.

As to the original meaning of the name Lares, we are, as often, reduced to guessing. A plausible guess starts from the oldest form of the name, which was Las, plural Lases (*s*, in old Latin, changed to *r* between vowels), and this suggests the first syllable of the adjective *lasciuus*, "playful". They may have been the merry or jolly godlings who like to see all go well on the land and everybody full-fed and happy. Certainly this fits the pictures of them which we see in Pompeian houses, for instance, since these show them dancing and holding drinking-horns, but we do not know how old the idea is which these pictures embody ; the earliest Roman cults had no imagery at all, either painted or in the round.

A good deal of Italy was and is but ill-suited for cultivation, so beyond the farming districts stretched untilled land, much of it wooded. This, like all such territories, was haunted, and some attention must be paid to the powers dwelling in it. These were especially the Fauni and Faunae, whose names probably mean the Favourable Ones, an appellation much like those by which fairies are known in Great Britain and Ireland ("Good neighbours", "Good people" and so forth). Their number and personality were of the vaguest, and often we get the singular, Faunus. He had his festival in country districts, on December 5th, when the people of the *pagus*, or rural district, kept holiday with dances and suchlike occupations. Hardly more definite was Silvanus, He of the Forest (*silua*), another inhabitant of the wilder parts of the country. He lived so far from the town that he never came into any official State calendar, nor had a temple or priest in Rome ; but the people whose cattle pastured in his region evidently thought it well to keep on good terms with him, and his dedications, chapels and statues found their way into the city in time, after long dotting the countryside. It is not unlikely that he contributed two saints to the Christian calendar, for it was not uncommon to call him *sanctus*, "holy", as all deities were, and to make his nature doubly clear by adding the adjective *siluester*, "of the forest" to his name. Hence SS. Silvanus and Silvester may be the offspring of a misread dedication belonging to pre-Christian cult.

Thus the farmer, by simple and time-honoured rites, strove to secure for his house and land the necessary *numen* and to keep away the wrong kind of *numen*, such as ghosts and fairies might be supposed to possess. His religion expressed itself in ceremonies performed by his family alone, by himself and his immediate neighbours (the Compitalia) and by the village or rural community (Paganalia). It is interesting to see how he met the crises of individual life, birth, marriage and death.

Birth, if we will believe the official records, was surrounded by a crowd of godlings who, presumably, helped the great goddess of women, Juno, in her attendance on the mother. Lucina, when that is not a title of Juno herself, made the baby see the light (*lucem*) for the first time. Whether the little goddess who performed this one simple act, or the great one who included that among her other activities, was the earlier we have no means of determining. Levana was present when the father or his representative picked up the baby from the ground, thus acknowledging it as his and undertaking to rear it. Candelifera was there to watch over the light which always burned in the birth-room ; and so on, almost without limit. But there was one little group which was rather more real and less to be suspected of being the creation of some theoriser. A woman in childbed is doing a thing which can still appear wonderful, if any capacity for wonder is retained, to the best-informed modern, however much he knows of the physiology of reproduction, and to an early Italian it must have been clear that *numen* was present. Now, the world over, the hostile powers hate fertility, and injure it and fertile persons and things if they can. But they also hate, at least the Italian ones did, evidence of the normal activities of mankind, such as ordinary housework, which indeed even the benevolent deities seem to dislike, for the everyday tasks of spinning and so forth were not done on feast-days. So the mother was protected by those homely means. When her baby was born and had been laid on the ground (to receive *numen* from Mother Earth, or perhaps to get his soul from the same source), picked up again and attended to (there was, according again to officialdom, a little goddess Cunina who looked after the child in the *cunae*, that is the cradle), three people were set to work guarding the house all night against the uncanny things from outside (some said that Silvanus was likely to come and make trouble). One of them chopped at the threshold—we have seen that it was heavily charged with *numen*—with an axe, one pounded it with a pestle, as if he were pounding corn on it, the third swept it with a besom. From these actions there sprang three minor deities, Intercidona, Pilumnus and Deverra, i.e., Cut-in-Two, Pounder and Sweeper. How much the country people believed in their existence we do not know, nor does it greatly matter ; in such cases a name is not of primary importance, for we have no evidence that anyone prayed to them, and it is in prayers and charms that it is essential to have the right name. But they certainly continued to use this piece of magic late enough for the authors we have to learn of it and record it.

The child, once past babyhood and able to understand what was going on, was himself, or herself, something of a sacred person. Boys, as already stated, wore a little locket containing a lucky object, probably a phallus, which scares away evil things, and also, when in full dress, did not use the plain white outer garment of their elders but a *toga praetexta*, a cloak with a purple fringe or hem. Magistrates also wore it, and the reason was the same ; the boy and the magistrate had certain sacral duties. The magistrate had to perform or take part in sundry religious rites in his official capacity ; the boy was an acolyte (in Latin *camillus ;* his sister was a *camilla*) to his father in the performance of the family rites. We know little of the details, but we have seen (p. 177) that a son of the house made the daily offering after dinner to the domestic gods, and we can guess from the public cult of Vesta (cf. p. 201) that the little girls helped their mother to tend the hearth and honour its goddess.

Marriage, in Roman ritual, has all its three parts well developed. If a woman is to marry into another family, still more into another clan, as was the usual rule in Rome, at least in early days, she must be severed from her own group, and therefore from its gods. But the gods may feel injured at losing a worshipper ; therefore it is well to show a little seemly reluctance at going away. Hence the show of violence to a Roman bride, who was torn from the arms of her mother, a business in which it used to be fashionable to see a relic of supposed primitive times in which wives were got by kidnapping ; better acquaintance with the history of the rite has shown us that there never was a time when that was the universal and respectable custom. Being so separated, and so no longer her father's daughter nor under the protection of the *numen* of his house and its gods, she is in a dangerous position, for she is not yet a wife and so has no husband to extend the protection of his *numina* to her. Therefore she must be very carefully guarded from head to foot, and Roman families took all possible precautions, in the most logical fashion, for all these customs are quite logical and rational, once the underlying assumptions are made. She wore, even in later times, an old make of under-garment known as a "straight smock" (*tunica recta*) ; in old days she would wear a *toga* over it, of the same fashion as her brothers' outer garments, but later this style went so out of use that to call a woman a "toga-wearer" in classical times meant that she was a prostitute ; respectable women wore a sort of long gown known as a *stola*. But her most conspicuous garment was her veil, made of yellow-dyed material, or sometimes red. Either colour was lucky, and thus her head and face were shielded ; the garment was called a *flammeum*. Her hair, which had previously been parted with a spear—ill-omened things cannot abide iron—was arranged in six locks, thus giving her a lucky number either side of her head, and wound with woollen ribbons or fillets. Like all persons engaged in business of religious importance, she had a wreath on her head, worn under the veil and composed of flowers and herbs gathered by herself. Thus she was well enough guarded against danger from above. Her waist was girdled with a woollen sash, tied in a particular style of knot, called, at least as far back as our information goes, the knot of Hercules. Behind her, and touching her, came not a bridesmaid but rather a bride's matron, a woman living in a first marriage, and so having about her none of the doubtful *numen* which would attach to widowhood (in early days there were no divorces). Front and sides were guarded by three boys, all of whom must have both parents living. One went before her, carrying a torch of whitethorn, a lucky material ; one held either arm. She herself carried a distaff and spindle, for the same reason, probably, as prompted the precautions taken at a birth (above, p. 189). Finally, to keep away all sounds of ill-omen and very likely to drown any charms an ill-wisher might recite, all the wedding-guests and everyone else who was there to look on joined in a shower of jokes, the broader the better, for indecent jokes are good magic, directed against bride and bridegroom, and also in shouts of *talassio*, a word so old that no one knew what it meant, except that it was the right thing to shout at a wedding. Nuts were thrown about, and the whitethorn torch (it seems to have been one of five torches, but we know nothing about the others) was thrown down, scrambled for and carried off. One of the reasons for this was that if husband and wife disliked each other, she could bring about his early death by putting it under the marriage-bed on the first night, and he hers by burning it at a grave.

On lifting the bride over the threshold (see p. 180), the third part of the marriage ceremony began. She had been severed from her father's house and brought safely through her period of temporary godlessness ; it remained to make her a wife. On her arrival, while she was still before the door of her future husband, she was asked, apparently by the bridegroom, who she was, and must answer with the puzzling formula : "Where thou art Gaius, I am Gaia". No one has ever satisfactorily explained these words, for a Roman wife did not take a new name. If she was, for instance, the daughter of a Fabius, her only legal name was Fabia, though she might have some personal name in her own home, for instance Tertia, or its diminutive Tertiola, if she was the third child.

and Fabia she remained all her life, married or not, though, if her husband was called Claudius, i.e., was a member of the Claudian family, she would be commonly known as "Claudius' Fabia" (*Fabia Claudii*) to distinguish her from other women of her original clan. The most likely suggestion is that Gaius is an old clan-name here, not a personal name, as it was in classical times, and that she meant "Whatever clan (or family) you belong to, I too belong to it henceforth", for that, in fact though not in name, a wife did. Be that as it may, measures were taken to assimilate her to her new household. After the ceremony at the door, she touched fire and water, the common materials of purification, thus burning and washing off her own strangeness, such remnants of the *numen* of her father's house as might cling to her, and any bits of bad magic she might have picked up on the way, and coming into contact with two essentials of life in any house. For that these things are fundamental and essential was a fact expressed elsewhere than in the marriage ceremony ; when a man was declared outlaw, the Roman formula was that he was excluded from water and fire, which henceforth none might share with him or let him have. In the *atrium* of the new house stood the bed of the Genius (*lectus genialis*), just opposite the entrance-door. It may have been originally the marriage-bed, for the oldest Roman house was one-roomed, but it remained in ritual use much later than this. That no human beings occupied it was a small matter, for its essential occupant was the Genius of the man or, as may have been the case, of his family. The word *genius* means "begetter", and personifies that particular kind of *numen* which enables the line to continue, generation after generation. This much we can still make out ; all else about the Genius is conjecture, for he is thickly obscured by confusion with a quite different Greek figure, the personal *daimon*.[1] It is possible that the sacred bed had another occupant. A Genius belongs to men ; there is some evidence that a woman had connected with her a sort of female counterpart to him, the Juno. However, the testimonies to the existence of this figure are none of them ancient enough for us to be at all sure that

[1] See *Ancient Greek Religion*, p. 144.

she belongs to the earliest stratum of Roman religion. But the ceremonies we have described were not all that the bride had to go through. She had with her three coins ; one of these she handed to the bridegroom, one she laid before the deities of the house, the third she took the next morning to the nearest cross-road and offered it to the Lares Compitales there. She was now, for the marriage was consummated on the night of her arrival at her new home, a house-mother, *mater familias*, and remained so whether she ever had children or not.

While death was no more welcome in early Italy than elsewhere, it does not appear that the native Roman belief, or that of Italians generally, added to the natural shrinking from it any extreme fear of the next world or of ghosts. Archaeological evidence from the oldest sites suggest that the living took no great pains to put elaborate barriers between themselves and the dead, and stories of hauntings, though they exist, are not common in classical Latin, and such as there are concern chiefly the kind of ghost most likely to be formidable, that of a person dead by violence and denied the proper rites of burial. There were decencies to be observed, and as usual these took the form of avoiding the wrong kind of *numen*, for it can hardly be doubted that the dead, or the powers of the world of the dead, were thought to exercise some at least. When a death occurred, the household was for the time being in a state of tabu or ill-luck, *funesta*, and consequently observed a period of mourning. The first and most obvious step to get rid of this undesirable state was to transfer the departed from the world of the living to that which was now his proper abode, the realm of the "good people" (*manes*). Popular thought concerning this was apparently of the vaguest ; it is a disputed point whether there was a native Roman god of the dead, corresponding to the Greek Hades-Pluton. Nor was there ever much distinction of individual dead people ; nothing remotely like Greek hero-cult is native to Rome. The corpse, laid on a bier of some kind, was washed, anointed, and, if that of a person of any official position, dressed in the costume befitting his rank ; we may conjecture that a common man was put into

ordinary decent attire, such as he might wear when going
about his business or pleasure in life. The body was now
taken to the burial-place, which might be somewhere on the
land the living person had tilled, or in a suitable spot set
apart for burials and cremations ; very often tombs were at
the side of roads, and all manner of constructions for the
reception of corpses or ashes were made from time to time,
varying, according to the date, the standing of the deceased,
and the amount of expense that was thought proper, from
the simplest pit in the soil or rock to the most elaborate
monument. The essential thing was that the body should be
put under earth, and if for any reason the entire corpse was
not so disposed of, at least a bone or some small portion, say
a finger, cut off from the rest had a clod of earth formally
laid upon it ; a man was buried, according to the findings
of priestly experts, when no bone of him was above ground,
and till then the period of mourning must last. Cremation
was common, but by no means universal ; for example, the
dictator Sulla was the first of his clan, the Cornelii, to be
burned. But fire was a necessary thing, for all funeral pro-
cessions carried torches, not, as some ancients and moderns
after them suggested, because originally funerals were always
at night, a proposition which has no real proof, but because
fire or light or both are regular forms of protection against
ill-luck and bad influences. The children and other kin of
the dead followed the bier, and if cremation was used, the
nearest relative lit the pyre, with his face turned away. The
grave was in a sense in consecrated ground ; it was not a
locus sacer, or dedicated spot, like the precinct of a temple,
but *religiosus*, more or less strictly tabu, and not to be lightly
approached. Certain rites, including the sacrifice of a pig,
were proper in preparing it. The corpse being bestowed in
whatever manner was preferred, the house from which the
funeral procession started was purified by sundry rites,
including a sacrifice to the Lares, and the period of strict
mourning was concluded by the *nouendiale sacrificium*, the
offering of the ninth day, i.e., by our count, eight days after
the burial, for Latin generally reckons inclusively and says,

e.g., that the tenth day of a month is four, not three, days before the thirteenth.

Such, in outline, was an ordinary funeral by native Roman rites, so far as we can reconstruct them ; a great many details remain obscure and need not be gone into here. Great families adopted, from quite early times, a much more elaborate funeral ceremony, which seems to be of Etruscan origin. In this, while the main and essential features were unaltered, the funeral procession was increased by a number of persons, including musicians, professional mourners, and, most remarkable and impressive of all, the visible presence of the ancestors of the dead. It was the custom of such families to decorate the walls of the *atrium* with wax masks of former members of the family. On the occasion of a death, these would be taken down and worn by actors who personated the earlier dead, wearing the robes of the highest office each had held and riding in vehicles appropriate to their rank. Thus a Roman noble would go to the world of the dead escorted by a long series of magistrates of the past, in full dress and sitting on their official seats mounted upon wagons. At a suitable place—in Rome, the Forum—a halt would be made while one of the family pronounced a speech in praise of the newly dead, and while the general rule was that no burial might take place within the city walls, certain families were exempt from that law, and in token of such privilege, for a moment held a torch under the bier, as if to cremate their kinsman on the spot. But all these and other elaborations, besides being much too expensive for the ordinary family, were quite inessential to the real business of getting the departed member of the family out of this life and into the next world. He was not neglected there, even after the nine days were over, but had his portion in the annual Feast of Souls (*Parentalia*, festival of parents, and so of ancestors generally), held in February, the usual month for rites of a dismal kind and for purifications. The State recognized, but did not conduct the soul-feast, for which nine days were assigned, the thirteenth to the twenty-first inclusive of the month, perhaps in imitation of the family's nine days of full mourning. The last of these is marked in the State calendars as the Feralia, but even it, according to our oldest authority on such things (see p. 200), was not barred to public business, while in the interval came two festivals of some importance, the Lupercalia and the Quirinalia, the only days of the whole series which were public holidays on which the courts did not meet and no legislative assemblies might be held. They were, however, days of ill omen for most things, for example no marriages were held then, the temples were closed and magistrates did not wear their purple-edged cloaks. These were decent and ordinary precautions to take while ghosts were about, watching their surviving relatives decorate the burial-places and otherwise attend to their wants ; but at the same time they indicate that ghosts, if properly treated, were not beings of whom any normal Roman went in panic fear, but simply senior members of Roman families, to be treated with the deep respect which every well-brought-up junior showed to his elders.

From this brief and imperfect sketch of the private cult of ancient Rome we pass to those forms of worship which were on a larger scale.

CHAPTER II

THE GODS OF THE ROMAN STATE

T H E rites of which we have hitherto spoken are generally called household ceremonies, *sacra domestica*. Not a few were celebrated by larger units ; thus a clan might have ceremonials of its own to perform and kept them up sometimes under circumstances of great difficulty. Thus, it is said that when the Gauls occupied Rome all but the Capitol, in 390 B.C., one of the garrison was Gaius Fabius Dorsuo, a member of an old and noble house. The time came for certain rites to be performed by a member of his clan (*gens ;* the word included all free-born men who had the same surname, in this case Fabius), on the Quirinal Hill, and he undertook to perform them. Taking the necessary utensils and materials and clothed in the proper garb for such an occasion, he calmly went down from the Capitol, passed through the enemy's lines, paying no attention to their shouts and totally unafraid, reached his destination, did what was necessary, and came back again, "in good hopes", says Livy, who tells the story with his usual vividness, "that he had the favour of the gods, seeing that not even the fear of death could stop him serving them". Livy leaves us to decide for ourselves whether the Gauls were simply too dumbfounded by his boldness to do anything or awed by fear of the supernatural, "to which their race", he adds, "is somewhat prone".

There were other cults likewise, on behalf of portions, not the whole, of the State, and some of these we shall have occasion to mention in this chapter. There were likewise ceremonies kept up, by permission of public authority, by artificial associations, generally known as *collegia*, but these hardly belong to early days, since they are characteristically the resource of foreigners who have no share in the State cult, adherents of some non-Roman but tolerated religion, or slaves and other little people, who, having no kinsfolk or none of any social and economic standing, clubbed together to insure decent burial for themselves when they died and in the meantime a little social life. The normal Roman of early days was born into a whole complex of communities smaller than the State, his family, his *gens* or clan, his *curia* or subdivision of the people, his *tribus*, which was a division at once of the people and the land they lived on, often having the name of a clan, perhaps other groups as well, and so needed no artificial associations. Women were less prominent outside their own households, but were by no means excluded from the State's cult as a whole, still less from the *sacra* of groups within it to which they might belong by birth or marriage. There were some particular rites in which no woman might take part, others from which all men were excluded, but both sexes had their share in the great majority of cults.

Before trying to describe the Roman state cult in its earliest recoverable form, it is necessary to say a word about the calendar, for many festivals of gods are fixed to particular days of the year, although not all are ; official language spoke of *feriae statiuae*, or fixed feasts, and *feriae conceptiuae*, movable feasts, whose exact date was determined year by year, usually within a more or less rigidly fixed period. The oldest calendar was very imperfect, consisting of but ten months, March to December, of which only the first four, Martius, Aprilis, Maius and Iunius, had names (all the above are adjectives, and *mensis*, a month, is to be supplied with them), the rest being numbered, Quintilis, Sextilis, September, October, Nouember, December ; we still use the last four names, generally forgetting that they mean respectively the seventh, eighth, ninth and tenth month. The comparatively dead season between the end of one year's agricultural work and the beginning of the following spring was not reckoned ; a phenomenon not uncommon in early attempts at counting days. Then someone, probably one of the Etruscan kings who governed Rome before the days of the Republic, introduced a better calendar, which for the first time was an approach to a true year, for it was, or tried to be, continuous. He added two months, Ianuarius, the month of the festival of Janus, which he clearly intended to begin the series, although it never did until much later, and Februarius, the month of purification (*februa* are materials used in ceremonies of purification and avoidance). In this, the calendar which served the Republic till its last days, four months (March, May, July, still called Quintilis, and October) had 31 days each, the rest 29 except February, which had 28. The total was thus 355 days, or roughly 10¼ days too few to match the solar year ; the balance was approximately redressed by inserting a short month, Intercalaris or Mercedonius, between February 23rd and 24th. This additional group of days numbered 22 or 23, and was supposed to be inserted at such intervals as would bring the total number back again to the beginning of a solar year ; in practice, the clumsy arrangement was made worse by miscalculations, accidental and deliberate (clearly, it would often be politically convenient for one party or another to retain magistrates on whose support they could depend for an extra three weeks or more), and by Julius Caesar's time the official year was far astray of the real seasons. He stopped all pretence of lunar months, instituted a solar year of 365 days, and made its length nearly right by inserting one day where once the extra month had stood, thus repeating the date February 24th once every four years. But till his time, the months were supposedly lunar, and each had three main days in it, the Kalends, or time of proclaiming (what was proclaimed, on the day of new moon, was the length of time till the next named day), the Ides, which was the time of full moon, the fifteenth day of the four long months and the thirteenth of the others, and the Nones, i.e., the Nines, eight days, as we reckon, nine by Latin count, before the Ides, and so on the seventh day of a long month, the fifth of a normal one. All other days were expressed by saying that they were such-and-such a number before one of these dates, and of this reckoning a remnant survives in our own tongue, for the other name for leap-year is bissextile year, that is the year in which the sixth (*sextus*) day, counting inclusively, before the Kalends of March, i.e., February 24th, comes twice (*bis*).

This rather complicated arrangement was not generally known in times when reading was not common (though letters were never kept the secret or privilege of any particular class) and the rudiments of astronomical science were a very rare possession indeed. But in 304 B.C. the calendar was published, and at some time, we do not know exactly when, it became customary to set up in convenient places copies of it, annotated with the names of the fixed festivals and other matters of interest. One Republican specimen of these survives, the battered but precious Calendar of Antium (*Fasti Antiates*), from fairly early in the first century B.C., also several of Imperial date, conformed to Caesar's revision, but still giving an account of the festivals, sometimes with valuable annotations, the fruit of contemporary learning. Of these festivals, a number are inscribed in larger letters than the other entries ; it is as certain as anything of the kind well can be that these are the oldest known, and from them we can form at least an outline idea of the early and comparatively pure Roman cult, before foreign ideas began to

have much effect. Whether it is in our power to get back
to a time of wholly Roman cult containing nothing but native
elements is another matter ; it is far from certain that such
a state of things existed, once that mixed settlement known
as Rome had been founded.

Starting, then, with these oldest festivals, it is to be noted
that a few of them are an extension to the State of the
domestic worship we have already learned to know. Let us
begin with the hearth. Whatever happened to other people's
fires, there was one which must always have been carefully
tended in a little early community, and that was the domestic
fire of the chief or king. So long as that burned, there was
a supply of fire for the whole people, and there is some
reason for saying that it was in a sense an embodiment of
the communal life, for life, light and fire are ideas closely
conjoined in simple thought. So it is not to be wondered at
that there was a public Vesta in Rome, and that her fire was
tended by virgins, the successors of the king's daughters,
whose official abode was close by the Regia, the building
which replaced the old palace of the kings. There were six
of these women in historical times, originally, it is said, four.
They were chosen, while still little girls, from families of
patrician origin, that is to say descended from original or
early settlers of Rome, and they served for thirty years
(originally it had been but five), during which time they
must not marry. If one of them was found unchaste, she
was not executed, for she was too holy to kill, but put into
an underground chamber in the Field of Ill-luck (*Campus
sceleratus*), and there left to die of hunger and lack of air, or
be miraculously rescued, if Vesta chose thus to vindicate her
innocence. It was an ordeal, not an execution. Her lover,
if known, was beaten to death. Their service, which was
one surrounded with high honours, was naturally concerned
chiefly with Vesta herself, though they took part in sundry
other rites as well. The ceremonial was complicated, and one
account, probably owing not a little to gossip, says that a
Vestal spent her first ten years in learning it, the next decade
in practicing it and the third in teaching it to novices. That
part of which the general public knew something was the

tending of the holy fire, the extinction of which was a serious
portent ; the Romans, says Dionysios of Halikarnassos, fear
the worst if it happens, for they take it as a sign that their
State shall be destroyed. We do not know exactly whence
this learned Greek had his information, though it must have
been from a good Roman source, but he probably has got
to the root of the matter. The fire of Vesta was the hearth
of the City and Empire, and a cold hearth is an uninhabited
house in the feeling of most peoples. Sundry means of
expiation were used, but the regular remedies included the
beating of the Vestal responsible and the rekindling of the
fire in the most primitive fashion, by friction of wood, which
must be taken from a fruitful tree, and the lighted tinder
carried to the hearth in a bronze sieve. Other rites included
bringing water for Vesta's household uses ; it must not
come from the regular water-supply of the City, when one
was instituted, but from a sacred spring, that of Egeria,
outside the Porta Capena, one of the southern entrances to
Rome. Furthermore, it must not be set down on the way
from the spring, lest its virtue should be lost by contact,
even indirect, with the earth, and consequently the Vestals
carried it in a vessel which had a narrow bottom and would
overset if put on the ground. Another piece of sacred housework was the preparation of the salt needed in ritual. This
must all be done, it would seem, by the Vestals themselves.
They started with the dirty product of a salt-pan, which
they then pounded in a mortar, baked in a jar, and (presumably after some process of cleaning, by dissolving and filtering
it) reduced finally to a hard lump, which when wanted was
cut up with an iron saw ; one of several proofs that the cult
of Vesta, as we know it, is not one of the oldest in Rome,
for we shall see later that bronze is the ancient sacral metal.
To make *mola salsa*, that is to say salted grain or flour, one
of the commonest offerings, they prepared their own corn ;
the three senior Vestals would gather, between May 7th and
14th, but only on the odd-numbered days, such ears of spelt
as were by that time to be found ripe, which they then
brought back with them, threshed and ground or pounded,
and on three occasions in the year mixed with the prepared

salt, a supply of which they kept in the shrine. These occasions were the feast of Vesta herself, June 9th, the Lupercalia of February 15th, and the Banquet of Juppiter (*Epulum Iouis*) on September 13th, an instance of their activity in other rites than those of their own goddess. Vesta, always represented by her own hearth-fire and never by an image, was housed in a small round building in the Forum, which although in our use of the word it was a temple, for it was devoted to sacral uses, was not one in the Roman sense, for it did not stand upon ground formally set apart for the use of the gods after proper consultation of the omens. It contained, besides the holy hearth, the storeroom, in which were kept a number of objects too holy ever to be seen save by the goddess's own priestesses, and therefore of unknown nature, though conjectures as to what they were bore testimony to the ingenious curiosity of not a few Roman antiquaries. The theory most in favour was that they included the Palladium, the sacred image of Athena which had been the "luck" of Troy, and was said to have been stolen from her temple there by the Greeks before they took the city. This, however, was no part of Roman tradition, but belonged to a pseudo-historical Greek theory, which, if a non-Greek people showed any signs of being civilised, was prone to declare them descendants of the worthiest opponents of Greek heroes, and so discovered that Rome had been founded either by Aeneas or by some descendant of his.

If Vesta had her place in State cult, so had the Penates. We have seen that her shrine had a store-room, *penus*, and that seems to have been their abode, as the *penates* of a private house kept watch over the more commonplace stores in the larder. Here again fancy was hard at work, and identifications of these obscure gods, who yet were felt to be important, showed much ingenuity, but little knowledge of or regard for the facts of religious history. We need have little hesitation in saying that to begin with they were the guardians of the royal store-cupboard, which no doubt was a somewhat larger and more imposing thing than that of an ordinary family, though we need not suppose it was very magnificent, for the original Roman kings were the chiefs

of a small community which still had a long way to climb
on the ladder leading to civilisation. So we may think of the
round shrine, the ruins of whose latest ancient reconstruction
are still to be seen in the Forum, as a sort of annex to the
king's house, the place where his daughters looked after the
important hearth and the stores which he, or the queen, saw
fit to keep there. There was still a trace of the old association
of father and daughter left in historical times, although the
Vestals were under the supervision of the chief pontiff when
we hear of them. On certain occasions they used to go to
the King of the Sacred Rites, the last survival of the sacral
functions of extinct royalty, and solemnly ask: "Wakest
thou, King? Be wakeful!" We do not know what these
occasions were, but may perhaps glimpse through the little
we know to an older time when the daughters of a real king
used to summon their father for some piece of ritual which
he and they had to perform together.

If the Holy Hearth was publicly honoured in Rome, the
Holy Door was not forgotten. The *ianus* in the Forum has
already been mentioned (p. 179), and there is no satisfactory
proof that it was ever anything but a ceremonial gateway,
independent of any system of fortification. It would appear
that it was used for important war-magic. As already mentioned (*ibid.*), there was a right and a wrong way for an
army to march out, and it seems probable that early Roman
armies paraded formally through this gate, with precautions
against doing so in any but a lucky direction, when they set
forth on campaign. To make this an easier and quicker
business, or merely to indicate that it was necessary, the
ianus was open in wartime, and this, as Rome's political
commitments expanded, meant that it was very seldom closed,
since she was generally at war somewhere. Hence it is not
strange that it came to be thought of as the gate of war,
within which, on the rare occasions when peace reigned, War
was imprisoned, to be let out when, at the outbreak of fresh
hostilities, the gate was once more thrown open. In the case
of other arches which bore the god's name, no such ceremonies
seem to have taken place, and we do not know precisely what
they were for, if it was not simply ornament.

Besides these deities of the house, the Lares had their place in the State cult. Since their shrines, when not in houses, were (p. 186) at cross-roads, it was no great extension to suppose them protectors of roads (*Lares uiales*), and so of those who travelled in any way, including seafarers (*Lares permarini*). Soldiers must march, therefore we know, though our information is not early, that on occasion the Soldiers' Lares (*Lares militares*) were addressed. In general, it seems to have been felt that these public Lares guarded the Roman land and its citizens much as the private ones looked after the farms and those who tilled them. Corresponding also to the ceremonial of the farm were certain rites, quite as much magical as religious, that is to say depending upon the mere performance of the ceremonial as much as on winning the favour of any god, for their efficacy.

We saw (p. 183) the Roman farmer drawing a magic circle about his lands at the Ambarualia. The indications that this was ever attempted for the territory of Rome, even in the oldest times, when it was but a few miles across, are faint and unsatisfactory, but a corresponding ceremony, the Amburbium, or circuit of the City, was used now and again ; Lucan tells us that it was tried by the Senatorial government in 49 B.C., when Caesar was on the march against them. But much older and more interesting was the very ancient cere-mony of the Lupercalia (February 15th). By all accounts, Rome began as a little settlement on the Palatine Mount, a naturally strong position west of the Forum, which in early days was handy to the river and defended during a great part of the year by marshy ground about some at least of its circuit. The boundaries of this old village, for it cannot have been much more, followed roughly the contour of the foot of the hill, except towards the river, where they swung out to in-clude the Cattle Market and the great altar of Hercules which protected traders there. This was what the Romans, perhaps then, certainly later, knew as the *pomerium* of their town, the sacred boundary, approximately following the line of the fortifications, hence its name, "behind-wall" or "wall-behind". In classical days it was still marked by a line of stones, for the old rite never ceased to be celebrated till the final triumph of Christianity. On the appointed day, two young men of good family made ready to play their parts. They met in a cave on the Palatine, the Lupercal, or Place of the Wolf. There a dog and some goats, perhaps two, were sacrificed, and the young men were daubed with blood, presumably that of the goats, which was then wiped off with wool, or perhaps goat's hair, dipped in milk. Then, naked except for a loin-cloth and carrying strips of goat's hide, they ran around the *pomerium* of the Palatine settlement, striking at everyone they met. Two interesting features of the ceremony are, that they were popularly called he-goats themselves, and that anyone, especially a woman, whom they struck was supposed to be delivered from barrenness.

The general sense of the rite is clear enough, although some details are obscure. The object of it is to trace a magic circle, thus shutting out evils, especially infertility, and shutting in good. This is done by the young men transforming themselves, for the time being, into human he-goats, the very embodiments of sexual vigour and at the same time of pugnacity. It is not by accident that the ancients supposed the performance to take place in honour of a god who might be identified with the Greek Pan, for he too is a he-goat, partly humanised. Besides infertility, another evil is to be excluded, the most dreaded of common European wild beasts ; the word Lupercus almost certainly means "averter of wolves", and a man who ran this holy course was called a Lupercus. But, and this is perhaps the most interesting point of all, no one gives us any clear and credible account of what god it was whom they thus honoured, or were supposed to honour, and it is very likely that the entire performance was pure magic, at least originally. The dog-sacrifice would serve to get the good will, or at least avert the hostility, of any uncanny powers who might lurk in the ground or the cave. The whole ceremony puzzled the Romans of historical times, and gave rise to some ingenious but unfounded theories, more than one of which has misled incautious modern enquirers.

Passing now to rites which certainly were in honour of gods, we begin with that one whose *numen* is perhaps most obvious of all, the great god of sky and weather, Juppiter.

The calendar seems to have been made and adopted too early for the most famous of his cults to be included. As Optimus Maximus, the best and greatest of all Juppiters, he had an imposing temple on the Capital, fronting south after the fashion of its Etruscan designers and having three chapels, the centre one for the god himself, while on either side were two female partners, Juno and Minerva. But the grouping is not native Italian, and in purely Roman cult Juppiter has quite other associations ; even a connexion with Juno is at least highly doubtful, and the etymology of her name is still too uncertain for anyone to say confidently whether or not she originally has anything to do with him. To worshippers with their minds full of Greek legends and popular identifications of Greek deities with their own, it was of course obvious enough ; Juppiter was Zeus, the Greek sky-god, Juno was Hera, his wife, and Minerva was Athena, his daughter. As a matter of fact the names Juppiter and Zeus come from the same original linguistic stock, Juno does much resemble Hera in her functions, and Minerva has something in common with Athena, for both are patronesses of craftsmen ; but, as has already been said, no Italian legend makes any deity the blood-relation of any other, and Rome, unprompted from outside, showed no inclination to associate these three holders of *numen*, of whom Minerva was not native, though she is Italian.

However, Juppiter was firmly fixed in the calendar, even though this one great cult was perforce omitted. All the Ides belong to him, for a very intelligible reason ; they are the days of full moon, or at least are supposed to be, and at full moon that very important piece of sky-*numen*, light, is displayed practically throughout the twenty-four hours if there are no thick clouds about. On the Ides of every month, a white wether was led along the Sacred Way, the old street which led into the Forum and was a regular processional route, up to the Capitol, and there sacrificed by Juppiter's own priest, the Flamen Dialis. Concerning this functionary something must now be said, for he represents a very ancient stratum in the complicated religious history of Rome. He had about him some of the outward marks of kingship, such as the right to be attended by a lictor, or bearer of the rods (and, outside Rome, axes) which marked the presence of a magistrate with coercive powers. He wore the dress of a magistrate, with its purple-edged toga ; his official seat, like that of a senior magistrate, was a special kind of chair known as curule (*sella curulis*). He had the right to be present at meetings of the Senate, which was originally the king's council. There are indications that his office went back to the royalty of the Bronze Age, for iron might not touch his person ; his hair and nails were cut with bronze implements. Quite possibly he was the result of some ancient political compromise, in which the king of an older bronze-using population was stripped of most of his secular powers by an iron-using people, but left with his sacral functions and treated with high respect as a holy person, belonging to the cult of a great god. Be that as it may, his entire life was devoted to the service of his deity, and not only his, but that of his household, for he must be married, and that by the most ancient rite of all, known as *confarreatio*, the central ceremony of which was the eating by bride and bridegroom of a cake made, not with wheat, but with the older and inferior grain known in English as spelt, Latin *far*. Such marriages, because they could not be dissolved otherwise than by the death of one of the parties, were rare in historical times. If his wife, the Flaminica, died, he must lay down his office, for the worship of Juppiter was not to be carried out by one person, but by a family. If there were no children, a substitute was furnished in boys and girls who had both parents living and acted as *camilli* and *camillae* (see p. 190). Apart from this, he was surrounded with a most extraordinary complex of prohibitions. Every day was a holiday for him, therefore he must not only do no work, but see none, and an attendant went ahead of him to warn anyone working to leave off till he was past. He must not come into contact with anything suggesting war, for which reason he might not see an election, for the voters assembled in their military divisions at the polls. Nothing resembling bonds must come near him ; even his ring must be cut through, or it would be too much like a fetter. We have already seen that a man in bonds was delivered if he got to the flamen's house (p. 182). This was carried so far that he might not pass under a trellis on which a vine was trained, for its tendrils suggested fastenings. He must always wear his *apex*, a kind of mitre, in the open air, that is in sight of his god, who must not see his priest otherwise than fully dressed. Even indoors, it was a comparatively late indulgence which allowed him to uncover his head, and to change his underwear he must go into some room which had no opening in its roof. Death must never come near him ; hence a funeral or any place where dead bodies were burned were forbidden to him. He must never mount a horse—another testimony to the antiquity of his office, for horses, other than native wild ones, are indeed long familiar in Europe, yet not so old-established that we cannot find traces of a time when they were new and therefore uncanny. A long list of unlucky or doubtful things must never be touched or even named by him, including a she-goat, uncooked meat, ivy, beans, meal which had yeast mixed with it, and dogs. It is therefore not surprising that slaves might not touch him ; his barber must be a free man. All possibility of evil magic was kept away, therefore he must not take an oath, for the ancient oaths regularly included conditional curses, in the form, "if I keep this oath, may good fortune befall me, but if not, ill-luck". Nor must such parts of his person as his hair-cuttings be left where an ill-wisher might find them, but carefully buried under a fruitful tree. He also must make a kind of pretence of sleeping on the ground, for the legs of his bed, from which he might never be absent for more than two nights, were daubed with mud. His wife also had numerous restrictions to observe, and herself conducted various ancient and holy rites.

But to return from the priest to the god, Juppiter, as befits a sky-god, had agricultural interests. These included the solemn business of inaugurating the vintage each year. At the Vinalia, or Feast of Wine, on August 19th, his *flamen* sacrificed a ewe-lamb, a curious victim, seeing that the usual rule is that the offering is of the same sex as the deity. After he had killed it, and before the sacrificial portions (*exta*) had been, after the Roman fashion, cooked and laid on the altar, the *flamen* solemnly cut the first bunch of grapes ; the vintage might then be carried on. Of other festivals of Juppiter we know little more than their dates, though concerning one, which came on December 23rd, we may conjecture that it was an occasion for helping the sky-god to recover his powers of furnishing light, after the darkness of the winter solstice.

Juppiter, in early cult, was regularly grouped with two other gods, Mars and Quirinus. The former of these was certainly a war-god, but it is equally certain that war was not his only function. He was a high god, with a range of activities not common in the native Roman cult, whose usual principle seems to have been that one god should exercise one kind of *numen*, not many. What kind Mars began with no one can say at this date, especially as the problem is complicated by the ancients' habit of identifying him with the Greek Ares, who was nothing more than a war-god, a divine swashbuckler. But it is well attested that his cult was popular all over Italy, including Etruria, where he was adopted, like several other native Italian deities, and his name slightly altered into Maris. Various Italian dialects had also their own forms, and Latin itself varied somewhat, calling him on occasion Mavors, for instance, or by the reduplicated name Marmar. He also has, not uncommonly, the title Gradivus, the meaning of which was already lost in classical antiquity. But that, whatever form his name took, he was not merely a god of battles is shown, among other evidence, by one of our oldest authorities, Cato the Censor (234-149 B.C.), in his curious little treatise on agriculture. He gives directions for a "vow for the health of the cattle", consisting partly in an offering of food and wine, to be made in the daytime, either by a freeman or a slave, and directed to Mars Silvanus. The recipient is distinctly a man's god, for no woman may be present nor see how the rite is performed, but there is no hint that he is warlike. He also prescribes a form of lustration for the fields, rather different from the Ambarvalia described by Tibullus (p. 183). The victims are a young boar-pig, a male lamb and a bull-calf ; Janus and Juppiter are associated with Mars in the ritual, a libation of wine being made to them at the beginning, but the prayer is addressed to Mars alone. It is quite long and explicit, and instead of praying, as one would expect if Mars was a god of war, that he would keep enemies of flesh and blood away from the fields, or give victory to Roman arms so that no invasion need be feared, the farmer asks him to ward off "diseases visible and invisible", bad weather, and other things which have little or nothing to do with war and its ravages, and to grant health to all who work on the farm. Nevertheless, his warlike functions are abundantly attested by his festivals and the nature of other deities associated with him, as will presently appear. We must therefore suppose that he was simply one of the great powers in which the Italian peoples trusted, their mighty protector and helper in both war and peace. The stormy history of early Rome is reason enough for Mars's warlike activities to have become strongly emphasised ; we shall see that on occasion not only he and other gods but so unlikely a power as Juno was thought to be capable of leading the State to battle, or defending it by force of arms.

The Roman year was ushered in by Mars' own month, which we still call, in the modern European languages, by various corruptions of the Latin name Martius. There was a festival in his honour, the details of which we do not know, on March 1st, although the Kalends are regularly Juno's day, and indeed there was a feast of married women, the Matronalia, at the same date. On the 14th—an unusual time for an official festival, since the rule is that only odd-numbered days of the month are employed for such purposes—came the Equirria, or horse-festival, the second of that name, for one had been held already at the close of the previous year, on February 27th. Both seem to have consisted in horse-races, held on the Field of Mars (Campus Martius), lying north of the older part of the City, unless the river was in flood, when they took place on the higher ground of the Caelian Hill, not far from the Forum. Horses were not used for agriculture, so it is clear that the object was to get the cavalry mounts ready for the coming campaigning season ; in early communities, fighting seldom or never took place in winter. Running, dancing and all forms of vigorous movement are well-known and common devices for increasing one's store of *mana*, and no doubt it was felt that the horses would be thus provided with needful *numen*, by the blessing of the god. Although the Ides of the month were not devoted to Mars, he was duly honoured on the first odd-numbered day thereafter, the 17th, when he had what is described as an *agonium*, a ritual word for a festival, again unknown in its details. The next lucky date, the 19th, known as the Quin-quatrus, i.e., the fifth day (counting inclusively) after the Ides, was again sacred to him ; in the times when most of our authors wrote, two curious mistakes had altered the nature of this festival. It so happened that the temple of Minerva on the Aventine was dedicated on that day, and also the true meaning of the old-fashioned word had been forgotten, and it was imagined that it signified a festival lasting five days. Accordingly, for five days in the middle of Mars' month, the Romans from the second century B.C. onwards celebrated the intrusive goddess, her protégés, the craftsman of all kinds, including those who practiced the liberal arts, and not least schoolmasters, keeping holiday, while the last-named expected a fee from their pupils. Finally, on March 23rd, the festival of the Tubilustrium was held, that is to say the purification of the trumpets.

And here it may be well to state briefly what a Roman meant by the words *lustrum*, *lustrare*, and their compounds. To "lustrate" anything is to purify it, getting rid of evil or hostile influences and, if possible, getting good influences in. One of the commonest methods, although by no means the only one, was to draw the magic circle about the person or things needing purification, as we have seen done at the Ambarvalia (p. 183) and Lupercalia. Examples of such rites are very common, and it was usual (the running at the Lupercalia was an exception) to move in a solemn and leisurely procession when performing the ceremony. Hence it is that the words often have the secondary meaning of orderly and impressive movement ; for Vergil, the clouds "lustrate" the mountain glens, that is, pass slowly over them, casting their shadows as they go. No doubt when a boy he had often seen them doing it on the higher ground towards

the Alps, the *alto Mantovano* of to-day, which lies to the
north of his native city of Mantua. But the ritual meaning
was that of purification by whatever means, and hence a
period of five years was called a *lustrum*, for then, by old
custom, the censors, who used to be regularly appointed at
that interval, would assemble the people, perform an appropriate ceremony, and so "put the *lustrum* away" (*lustrum
condere*), probably by burying the materials they had used,
with all the ill-luck or ill-doing of the period just closed
sticking to them.

But to return to Mars, during March another important
piece of war-magic took place, nothing less than a war-dance
by his own priests. These were called simply the Dancers
or Leapers, *Salii*, and their whole performance showed their
antiquity. There were twenty-four of them altogether, the
Salii Palatini and the Salii Collini, associated respectively
with the primitive settlement on the Palatine and what appears
to have been a later one on the Quirinal Hill (*Collis Quirinalis*).
They all wore bronze armour and cloaks called *trabeae*, embroidered in bright colours, red and purple. They carried
shields shaped somewhat like a figure 8 on their left arms,
and a spear or stick in the right hand. On their heads they
wore the same mitre-like covering as the flamens (p. 209), the
apex. Thus attired, they passed through the city to several
sacred places in it, dancing and leaping vigorously, beating
their shields, and singing a very ancient hymn in honour,
not only of Mars, but of a variety of gods, the surviving
fragments of which (for its archaic text was often quoted by
grammarians) still puzzle modern linguists. This obviously
was primarily a war-dance, and the impression is not lessened
by the fact that certain girls, the *Saliae uirgines* or dancing
maidens, were somehow associated with them, for it is not
very uncommon to find the woman of the tribe assisting
their men in war-magic. But not the least interesting point
is the form of their shields, which is known to be very ancient,
appears with no great variety in sundry parts of the Mediterranean, and was associated by the Romans with a legend that
the original model of them fell from heaven and the rest were
made in close imitation of it, lest the sacred thing itself be

stolen by some enterprising enemy. How important these representatives of an obsolete type of armour were is clear from the fact that the ancients commonly said, not that the Salii were performing or had ceased to perform their rites, but that the sacred shields (*ancilia* ; ordinary shields are *scuta* or *clipei*, according to their shape) were being moved, or were laid away.

For the next six months Mars had no regular worship (though of course a soldier in difficulties might pray to him as much as he saw fit, if it was done with decent observance of proper form) except for a second Tubilustrium which took place, we do not know why, on May 23rd. With October his ritual began again, for by then the summer and autumn work of the farm is over and the old campaigning-season likewise, so it was well to do two things, pass out of the condition into which the rites of March had brought the god's people, in other words dismiss the *numen* no longer needed, and procure new *numen* for the business lying ahead, the late autumn ploughing. The former purpose was achieved on October 19th, when the Armilustrium took place ; it must have seemed obvious that weapons which had been used against the enemy might be tainted with foreign magic or other undesirable forms of *numen*, for such things are as contagious as any disease, and therefore they should be purified before being laid away till next campaigning season. It may very well be, though we have no information, that if some disturbance did break out during the colder and darker time of year, some sort of observance was gone through by those who had to deal with it, but at least the "lustrated" equipment could do no harm in the meantime.

But a much more interesting ceremony, one which shows Mars in his double capacity as war-god and god of a farming community, took place on the Ides of the month, not displacing but together with the usual sacrifice to Juppiter on that day. This was the October Horse (*Ecus October*), and was conducted as follows. A horse-race was held, the contestants, as was usual in Rome, driving chariots, a vehicle which was never used, as far back as our records go, by Italians for actual war, though no doubt it once had been,

but was retained for sport, as it was in Greece also. When
it was over, the off horse of the winning team was sacrificed
by the Flamen Martialis, Mars' own priest, who had restrictions and ceremonial comparable to those of the better-
known Flamen Dialis, but less complicated and rigid. Its
head and tail were cut off ; the latter was taken by a runner
to the Regia, for no doubt in older times the king was the
only person fit to be trusted with such important magic,
and there hung up over the hearth, on which its blood was
allowed to drip. The head was fought for by the men of the
Sacred Way and the Suburra, the winning party taking it
away to its own quarter. To understand this properly, we
must clear our minds of any preconceived notions about
Mars. Very good scholars have been so blinded by the fact
that a warlike beast is sacrificed to a god who certainly has
warlike functions that they could see no further. But not only
have we the distinct testimony, handed down it is true only
in the epitome of an epitome, of Verrius Flaccus, the best
antiquary of the age of Augustus, that the rite was performed
to secure a good harvest, but we know that the head of the
horse was garlanded with loaves of bread, and also that the
blood was collected by the Vestals and kept in Vesta's own store-
room, whence it was given out at the Parilia (see p. 222) as one
of the materials for purifying the cattle-stalls. But all these
facts must not make us conclude hastily, as some, including
the present writer, have done, that the horse was one example
the more of a vegetation-power in horse shape ; we have no
evidence for this particular belief on Roman soil. It is a
vigorous beast ; it is sacrificed to a great god ; all sacrifices
produce *numen*, and this one not least. That war, tillage and
stock-breeding should all be associated with the rite in one
way or another does but prove that Mars was a great god,
one of the few who no longer confine themselves to manifest-
ing one kind of *numen*. Mars is also one of the very few
deities who found themselves cramped, not enlarged, by
identification with a Greek god. Once the notion became
general that he was simply Ares under another name, his
wider functions were so lost that it is only in quite recent
times that any attention has been paid them.

Quirinus also suffered. He had his festival, the Quirinalia of February 17th, and his priest, the Flamen Quirinalis, who with his colleagues the priests of Juppiter and Mars made up the triad of greater flamens. But of the festival we know nothing, and of the priest, by an odd chance, only that he was active on occasion at functions with which so far as our evidence goes Quirinus was not connected. He had his place in the worship of Robigus, Larentia and Consus (pp. 221, 229, and 223), but we do not know how he served his own god. Nor is the deity in much better case. Ancient tradition had it that he was of Sabine origin, an odd fact, for the Sabine dialect lacked the sound expressed by *qu*. Setting this aside, it is pretty clear that the name is an adjective, and means "of the *quirium*", and that suggests Quirites, one of the words for citizens of Rome. A modern and very plausible etymology derives *quirium* from a supposed older form *couirium*, which would mean "assembly of men", and could quite easily become *quirium* in the mouths of Latin-speaking people. It may be, therefore, that he is the god who presides over the assembled citizens of his town, whether that was originally Rome or some place in the Sabine hills. Again Greek explanations have been the death of a Roman tradition ; he was associated with Mars, Mars was Ares, Ares had associated with him, or bore as a title, Enyalios, therefore Quirinus was Enyalios, a minor war-god. Furthermore, he was Romulus, the founder, in a thoroughly Greek story, of Rome, who, again in Greek and quite un-Roman fashion, had become a god after his death and was himself the son of Mars. But for the stolid Roman conservatism which went on performing traditional rites long after everyone had forgotten what they meant, we should be entirely in the dark concerning Quirinus.

Of Juno, on the other hand, we know a good deal, though her name has given rise to much debate among etymologists, some of whom affirm and some deny that it has any connexion with that of Juppiter. Two things at least are certain, that she is not associated with him in any early Roman worship and that she is closely connected with the life of women, like the Greek Hera, with whom she was identified. It has already been mentioned that she is capable of becoming a war-goddess (p. 211). This was at Lanuvium, perhaps also at Falerii and Tibur, but not at early Rome itself, so far as we know. In the first of these places she bore the titles Sispes and Sospita, both meaning Preserver, with the honourable additions Mater Regina, i.e., Mother (in the sense already explained, p. 22) and Queen. Her statue, whose age and origin we do not know, showed her, says Cicero,

> wearing a goat-skin, carrying a spear and buckler, and in shoes with upturned toes.

The skin had the horned head still on it, drawn over the head of the goddess, who thus appeared in a sort of primitive armour, ready to fight for her city if need arose. But these cults were somewhat abnormal, and generally she had quite other functions. In Roman worship she was never the chief deity, therefore had no need to fight, for that was the business of Mars, probably also of Quirinus, certainly of Juppiter, who was worshipped as Stator, i.e., Stayer of Rout, and one of whose festivals, the Poplifugia, may possibly mean the putting to flight of hostile armies, for "army" is what *populus*, the word from which English "people" is derived, really means. Her concern for women began, it would seem, with their birth and lasted all their lives. As Juno Lucina, she watched over the entry of the baby to the light (cf. p. 189) from the darkness of the womb. As Sororia, she cared for girls attaining maturity (*sororiare* is used of the swelling breasts of an adolescent girl). As goddess of marriage, she was Juno Iuga, Juno of the Yoke, if that was not a mere translation of the title Zygia, which has the same meaning and was borne by her Greek sister. Certainly the sanctity of marriage was in her charge, for an ancient law, attributed to the times of the kings, forbade a woman living in an irregular union with a married man to touch her altar, on pain of an expiatory sacrifice. Every year there was celebrated in her honour a rude and curious rite known as the Nonae Caprotinae, that is to say the Nones of the wild fig-tree. In the times of which we have any accurate knowledge, it was conducted by slave-girls ; it is very likely that in older days the free women of Rome performed it

themselves, but the classical Roman matron was of more than
Victorian correctness and dignity of manner. Its date was the
Nones (seventh) of Quintilis, the later July. Incidentally, it
is one of the indications that the festivals in the existing
calendar are older than the calendar itself, for this important
feast does not fall within the goddess's own month of June
(*Iunius*, derived, not directly from the Latin name of Juno,
but from its Etruscan mispronunciation Uni or rather a
compromise-form connected therewith ; *Iuno* could give only
Iunonius). Putting together the various accounts we have, and
subtracting the attempts at explanation of the ancients, who
manifestly had not the least idea what it was all about, we
learn that women both bond and free joined in a sacrifice
to Juno ; that they met and feasted under a wild fig-tree
and were crowned with its leaves ; that the slave-girls were
dressed in the full ceremonial costume of free women ; and
that they had a sham-fight with each other, apparently armed
with switches of fig-wood. To a modern's broader knowledge
of the early history of religion all is fairly clear. These slave-
girls acted as the substitutes of their mistresses, whose
clothing they wore, for that part of the rite which, as already
said, was below the ladies' dignity in historical times. They
used, in their contest, in other words in a rite of mutual
beating, rods from that tree which is employed to fertilise
the cultivated fig ; for the latter is female, and only the wild
fig, which is male, has the pollen which the cultivated fruits
must have to reach maturity. They thus knocked fertility
into each other, much as the Luperci (p. 206) struck it into
any whom they met with their similar magical implements ;
for in Latin a wild fig is a goat-fig (*caprificus*), and like names
produce like effects in all magical rites. Juno thus is once
more associated with at least the efficacious name of the
creature whose hide we saw her wearing.

Juno had a further development, which she shares with
several deities connected with the life and functions of women.
The sexual rhythm of their bodies tends to fall into periods
about equal in length to a lunar month, and this tendency
was strongly recognized by the Romans, for instance in their
computation of the full time of a normal pregnancy, ten lunar

months. Hence the goddess took on a secondary association with the moon. By ancient usage, the junior member of the College of Pontiffs (see p. 228) used to watch for the new moon, and would thereupon announce the length of the month just beginning by pronouncing, in presence of the assembled people and certain others of the State clergy, the formula *calo Iuno Couella*, "Juno Covella, I call", five or seven times according as the Nones were to be the fifth or the seventh, and the Ides consequently the thirteenth or the fifteenth. What the epithet Covella means we do not know, however.

Other developments of her cult are more obscure in their origins. For example, we do not know why she was worshipped on the Arx, the ancient citadel of Rome, on the Capitoline Mountain, at the end away from the Capitol proper, where the great temple (p. 207) stood, under the title Moneta, "the adviser or warner".

Something has already been said of the cult of Tellus Mater, the earth-goddess, at the Fordicidia (p. 166). She was conjoined to Ceres, the corn-goddess, in an ancient rite never quite confined to a fixed date, though it was always in January, on two days a week apart, the *feriae sementiuae*, or festival of the sowing, whose import is explained clearly and correctly by Ovid, as occurring "when the seed is cast and the field becomes fertile", i.e., at the end of the sowing of the winter wheat which is the main crop. Ceres, it would appear, was worshipped on the former of the two days and given an offering of spelt, Tellus on the second, her sacrifice being a sow in farrow. Ceres had once a male partner, Cerus, of whom nothing more is known than his name ; foreign influence, especially Greek, gave her new associations and also functions which it is doubtful if she originally possessed. Roman gods of the oldest stratum were worshipped within the *pomerium* of the City, and this did not include the Aventine Hill, although that lay within the city limits, or what we should regard as such ; the inhabited region so outgrew its old sacral boundaries that a magistrate going from one part of Rome to another might find himself obliged to perform the rites of divination proper to one quitting his own territory and moving across the border. The Aventine, being close at hand and a convenient site, became a favourite spot for the temples of deities whose existence was recognized by the Roman government, though they were not on the same footing as the original objects of worship. One of these was Ceres in a new guise, associated with Liber and Libera, the former an Italian god of wine and the latter his female partner or double ; Italian deities not infrequently go in pairs of male and female, though they were not thought of as married, so that whichever sex it pleases them to have, appropriate formulae may be addressed to them. But the group would seem to go back by some route to the great cult of Demeter at Eleusis, where she was associated with her daughter Kore and a god Iakchos. A similarity of name caused Iakchos to be confused with Bakchos, in other words Dionysos, who included an interest in viticulture among his many activities, and so Liber, also identified with Dionysos, represented Iakchos at Rome. It is, then, a Greek cult in Italian dress, and the temple became a centre, not only for the corn-dealers who apparently had much to do with its introduction, but for the religious and other activities of the *plebs*, that part of the population which, not being able to show descent from original inhabitants of Rome or early accretions to their number, had to begin with no share either in the State cult or in its secular offices, though during the Republic they attained to both in full measure. Parallel to this political change came a change in religion, to the extent of giving real importance to several divinities who had not originally been worshipped in Rome at all, and whose festivals therefore were never added to those recorded in large letters on the calendars. But of these accessions more will be said in the next chapter. For the present, it is enough to notice that the Aventine temple was founded on Ceres' own feast-day, the Cerialia of April 19th, when again she was associated with Tellus, for that date is the next odd-numbered day but one after the Fordicidia. Another effect, it may be, of foreign, perhaps specifically Greek influence was that Ceres was regarded at times as formidable, for a mad person was thought to be possessed either by the Larvae, or ghosts, apparently much the same as the Lemures (p. 181), or else by her, and was called accordingly *laruatus* or *cerritus*. Demeter has her formidable side, for the dead are sometimes called her people and one of her titles is Erinys, or Avenging Power. This may have influenced Ceres, who naturally was identified with her, as both were corn-deities.

Other agricultural rites also were maintained, not merely permitted or regulated, by the State, and not the least remarkable was the Robigalia. It took place on April 25th, and Ovid claims to have seen the ritual ; whether this is true or he merely read a good account of it matters little.

"As I was on my way back from Nomentum," he says, "on this day, I was stopped on the road by a congregation all in white. It was a *flamen* on his way to the sacred grove of ancient Rust (*robigo*), to burn the sacrificial portions of a dog and of a sheep. I at once drew near to learn the ceremony, and Quirinus' own priest spoke thus". (He then gives the substance of the prayer, a long appeal to Rust not to damage the crops.) "Such were his words. At his right hand were a napkin loosely woven, also a chalice of wine and a box of incense. Incense he put and wine he poured into the altar-fire, also the flesh of the sheep and the hideous entrails—I saw him do it—of the dog".

Other authorities inform us that the name of the power addressed was Robigus, *robigo* being the ordinary word for the "rust" which on occasion damages wheat, and that the grove was five miles from Rome, which would bring it about to the boundary of the oldest Roman territory. Clearly the intention is to check the incursions of the disease within the limits of all Roman fields, just at that time of year when it is most likely to occur, and all manner of farming activities were introduced by the sacrifice of a dog or puppy, presumably to the powers beneath the earth, which were often supposed to be pleased with that offering ; but why the *flamen* of Quirinus in particular was employed in it is a matter for conjecture, and no explanation yet put forward has satisfied everyone.

Flora was the goddess, not so much of flowers in general, as of the flowering of the wheat and other crops. Her festival apparently depended on her coming, that is to say on the

time when the flowering occurred, for it never was fixed in
the calendar until it had quite lost its original character. The
Floralia of approximately the end of April were buried under
the Floral Games (*Ludi Florales*) of April 28th-May 3rd,
which in turn grew out of the one-day celebration of the
erection of a temple to her on the first of these dates. It was
ordered by a Sibylline oracle (cf. p. 243), which meant that
it was a Greek cult, and the loose nature of the festival, the
central feature of which was farces of a not over-decent kind
acted by courtesans (in ancient "legitimate drama", female
parts were taken by men), suggests that it was an offshoot
of one of the semi-Oriental cults which lurked here and
there under the worship of Aphrodite, one of whose titles
was Antheia, She of the Flowers. That temple was at the
Circus Maximus, in the valley between the Palatine and
Aventine, unromantically occupied in recent years by a gas-
works ; the old Flora had her inconspicuous shrine on the
Quirinal, and it was a custom to bring stalks of corn to it on
the day called Florifertum, whether that was the same as the
Floralia or not. Doubtless they were flowering, not ripe stalks.
We know even less of Pomona, goddess of tree-fruits, but
she must once have had a certain importance, for she is one
of the fifteen deities who had special priests (*flamines*) of their
own, though hers is the most junior of all.

We are rather better acquainted with the Pales, a god and
a goddess, so old a pair that the surviving authors had quite
forgotten that they were a pair at all and use the name in the
singular, making it masculine or feminine as the humour
takes them; a single entry in the Fasti Antiates (p. 200) lets
us know that on the Nones of Quintilis (July 7th) there was
some kind of festival to "the two Pales". A better known
occasion, however, was April 21st, the Parilia (etymologically,
this should be Palilia, since it means "feast of the Pales",
but such differentiation, as it is called, is very common in
many tongues). The Pales were deities of stock-breeding and
all that goes with it ; and that a festival of the kind to be
described should have taken place at a comparatively late
time in the year, when the Italian spring is well advanced,
suggests that it had its origin with some element in the

Roman population whose old home was much further north. Certainly it resembles a formal preparation of the beasts for leaving their winter quarters and venturing out to graze and live in the open.

The procedure was as follows. Every owner of stock was provided by the Vestals with the necessary materials for purification, the blood of the October horse, the ashes of the unborn calf of the Fordicidia, and bean-husks. The first two obviously can have been given but in minute quantity to each person, of the last there would be abundance. With these he fumigated his byres at dawn, having first sprinkled the beasts with water and swept the stalls clean. Various other forms of fumigation were in use at all events in the time of Ovid, but the most conspicuous, which was applied to the people concerned, perhaps to the beasts also, was to jump through the flames of a bonfire of light materials, straw and the like. There was the usual garlanding of everything and everyone concerned, and rustic sports. The sacrifice seems to have included no animal victims ; a prayer for divine protection (whereof Ovid gives us what purports to be a paraphrase, at best an extremely free one) was repeated, with the face to the east, four times. This was the individual method of keeping the day ; there was also State ritual, but we know no details of it. Nor is it clear how the idea started that the day was the anniversary of the City's foundation, a notion popular throughout a great part of antiquity and revived by the late Fascist government of Italy.

Another pair of rustic deities were Consus and Ops, that is to say Storer and Plenty. Omitting much Greek lore which conceals their real natures, for these ancient figures puzzled the later people of antiquity, we know the following facts about them. Consus had an underground altar in the Circus Maximus (cf. p. 74), which was uncovered only on his festivals. Its character may perhaps be connected, as has been suggested, with the common practice of storing corn in underground receptacles, but if so, it certainly never was such a store-bin itself nor near one, for that low-lying ground would be under water, or at least waterlogged, when the Tiber was in flood in the earlier and less well-drained ages of Rome.

A fragment of old lore concerning the god has come down to us, preserved because by some blunder it was not only wrongly understood but imagined to be the inscription on the altar itself, which is quite impossible. It runs, when properly interpreted, "Consus is mighty in the sowing, Mars in war, the Lares at the boundary between farms", thus combining in one dictum two purely rustic powers with the great god whose scope included the protection of the land and those who worked on it. That Consus's activities should extend to sowing is perfectly understandable, for if there were no bins to store corn in, where should we get the seed to sow ? It is the business of the power whose *numen* helps men to store away corn or any other useful thing also to help them get it out when they want it, and gods, both Roman and other, very commonly have functions which seem opposed, being complementary opposites. It has been the fashion of late in some places to speak of "bi-polar" activities in such a connexion. The festivals of the god and his companion were in August and December. In the former month, the Consualia came on the 21st, the Opiconsivia on the 25th. By that time, a Roman harvest is in ; the lower-lying parts of the country have generally cut their wheat by about July 31st at latest, though hilly districts may be a little later. It was therefore no inappropriate time for the deities who watched over the store-bins and their abundant contents to be celebrated. A little less obvious is the December date (Consualia December 15th, Opalia December 19th, with the Saturnalia intervening), for it corresponds to no very obvious part of the cycle of farm-work. One suggestion is that it marks the very last gathering of all, the collection of the latest olives, for these are not got in all at once, but in successive stages at not inconsiderable intervals of time. Certainly they too have to be stored, and a plentiful supply of them is welcome, and must always have been so.

The Saturnalia have been mentioned in passing ; it was the festival of a mysterious deity, Saturnus or Saeturnus (usually Saturn in English), of whom exceedingly little is really known, although many confident assertions have been made. Of one thing at least we may be fairly sure, that he is not originally Roman, for we have it on good authority that sacrifice was made to him with uncovered head. That is the ordinary Greek rite, presumably to let that important part of the sacrificer's person be open to the benign influence of the god he addressed, but a Roman cautiously muffled his head on such occasions, lest his efforts be nullified by hearing or seeing a bad omen ; for omens are of no effect and portend nothing if no one, or even if no official person, observes them. What the god's name means, we do not know. Attempts to find it a Latin etymology have so far proved fruitless, and at present it is generally supposed that it has something to do with the Etruscan family name Satre or Satria. In that case, he probably has no real name at all, but is simply "the god whom the *Satre* worship". But even this is far from certain, for our knowledge of how words borrowed from Etruscan, which in any case were not numerous, were treated, is far from complete. His chief festival, the Saturnalia, originally on December 17th, but later extended to three, four, five or even seven days, to begin with resembled the Greek harvest-feast of the Kronia[1], for during it there were no social distinctions, slaves had a holiday and feasted like their masters, and all restrictions were relaxed, one being the prohibition on gambling with dice, which was supposed to be in force at other times of the year. It was, however, a more thoroughgoing season of jollity than the Kronia, at least in historical times, "the best of all days," says Martial. Civilians and soldiers alike celebrated it, it was usual to choose by lot a Lord of Misrule (*Saturnalicius princeps*, "leading man of the Saturnalia"), and gifts were exchanged. Although the date is different, it seems probable that its customs, blending with those of the New Year festival and with the northern Yule, had their share in producing the traditional merry-makings of Christmas (cf. p. 296). However, there are indications that Saturn had a grim side to his character, for not only is he identified with Kronos, and through him with unlovely Semitic gods worshipped on occasion with human sacrifices, but his cult-partner is Lua Mater, whose name, if, as seems probable, it is Latin, is to

[1] See the author's *Ancient Greek Religion*, p. 67.

be connected with *lues*, "plague, pestilence, blight", while of her cult we know this much, that arms taken from the enemy were on occasion dedicated to her by burning them (clearly a piece of sympathetic magic, to spoil the arms the enemy still had), a rite which she shares with Mars and with his cult-partner Nerio, an obscure goddess made more obscure by her becoming identified with Minerva.

Agriculture, with which it has commonly been thought that Saturn was somehow connected, had a few other deities, mostly quite minor. Liber Pater, the wine-god, has been mentioned ; there are not a few obscurities connected with him. His name is identical with the word signifying "free", in the sense of free-born, not a slave, and on his feast-day, the Liberalia, March 17th, it was customary for young men to put on the man's toga (cf. p. 190) for the first time, on which occasion they were escorted to the Forum by their friends and relatives.   Liber is also a title of Juppiter, which may or may not be due to a translation into Latin of Zeus Eleutherios ; and naturally Liber became identified with Dionysos (cf. p. 220). The precise connexion between his various activities, and between him and Juppiter, cannot be said to have been clearly explained as yet. Another deity of wine was Medetrina, a goddess whose existence seems due to the festival called Medetrinalia, on October 11th, when it was the custom formally to taste the product of the recent vintage, not yet properly fermented into wine, with the formula "I drink new and old wine, I heal (*medeor*) my illness, new and old". In passing, a minor deity of the fields should be mentioned, because her name has been much misinterpreted in ancient and modern times. This is Mater Matuta, who had a festival, the Matralia, on June 11th, and a temple in the Cattle-Market. A perfectly satisfactory explanation of her name has come down to us, and is due to Varro ; she looked after the ripening (*maturescentia*) grains. This fits the time of her festival, not very long before harvest, also the fact that her feast was in the hands of free married women, for clearly her share in the provision of *numen* for the fields was important enough to demand the attention of these traditional practitioners of farm-magic and doers of the lighter farm work. It equally explains why no slave-woman might take part ; slaves are foreigners, and what should they know of the way to approach the native goddess ? Equally, it makes it clear why some Greek theologians thought she was the same person as their own Eileithyia, the goddess of birth ; if she can ripen the fruit of the ground, why not that of the womb, seeing that the equation between Mother Earth and human mothers runs through all ancient religion and magic ? But the same root which gives Latin its word for "ripen" produces several words which signify "early", especially early in the day. So the notion came about and is not yet quite departed that she was a dawn-goddess. It is refuted by the fact that she had a cult. Dawn—Eos in Greek, Aurora in Latin—is a pretty figure of mythology and folk-tales, whom no one is known to have worshipped in the whole ancient world.

Water had of course its deities, the best-known of whom is Neptunus (usually curtailed to Neptune in English), a not very important god of fresh water, who never became a god of the sea (the Romans were and remained incurable landlubbers, though necessity compelled them to voyage for trade and to maintain a navy) until he came into contact with the Greek Poseidon, which explains why he was sacrificed to at sea with Greek and not Roman ritual. His feast, the Neptunalia, was on July 23rd, a very natural time to appeal to a power who could give water, in the heat of an Italian summer when streams were low and fires likely to break out among the houses. His cult-partners were Salacia, apparently the goddess who makes water spring up (*salire*) from the ground, and Venilia, about whom nothing more is known. More important, in Rome at least, was the god of the Tiber, though he does not seem to have borne in ritual the name of his river ; it has been guessed that Volturnus, a god of probably Etruscan connexions, who had a *flamen* of his own, was the Tiber-god, but this is simply a guess, and its author, Mommsen, backed it up by some very bad etymology. Whatever the deity was officially called, he had some interesting ritual which gave rise to a whole class of Roman priests, the *pontifices* or bridge-builders, whose name is commonly Anglicised into "pontiffs". Their original business must have been to appease the river when it was necessary to throw a bridge over it, thus putting it and its god in the magically inferior position of being under the feet of those who walked across. A little of their magic we know, for it survives in a very old rite, much discussed and misunderstood in antiquity and by moderns, that of the Argei. This word (its etymology is uncertain) signified certain dummies of reeds, in an old-fashioned costume, and also the chapels, twenty-seven in number, in each of which one such figure was kept till needed. On May 14th, an even-numbered day and therefore a strange and unusual one for any public ceremony, for the Romans believed firmly in the luck of odd numbers, these puppets were taken to the old wooden bridge, the Pons Sublicius, which spanned the river, and there, in the presence of the pontiffs and the Vestals, were solemnly thrown in. The only reasonable explanation, as demonstrated by the late Sir J. G. Frazer, is that they were surrogates for human beings, and the river was expected to accept them instead of drowning real men who used the bridge. Why the number was twenty-seven and not some other we cannot tell ; it may be related to some ancient subdivision of either the City or the ground on which it stands.

Other deities of water included Fons, a sort of collective god of all fountains or springs (*fontes*), and a few more, mostly obscure and sometimes doubtful, while numerous minor godlings presided each over some one stream or spring. For all sources of water, especially of drinkable water, are holy in most countries, and not least around the Mediterranean, where a good water-supply, such as Imperial Rome acquired and the modern city has regained, is not always easy to come by, especially in summer.

Fire had, besides Vesta, its gods and goddesses, two of whom, Cacus and Caca, were perhaps those presiding over the fire of the chief's hut in the old Palatine settlement ; at all events we know that Caca had a ceremonial like that of Vesta, and the position of the latter's shrine in the Forum, not a part of the oldest Rome, is one of several indications that she was not the oldest sacred hearth. A very different god was Volcanus (Vulcan in English), whose name is certainly not Latin, for its nearest connexions seem to be with Crete and Etruria, and whose original functions were connected with the volcanic phenomena which we name after him. He too had a festival in hot weather, when his destructive fires were most to be feared, on August 23rd, when he was given a sacrifice likely to please a fire-god, live fish being thrown into flames. Thus getting the sort of victim whose habitat would generally protect it effectively against him, he might be the readier to spare land-dwellers, their crops, houses and cattle. Inevitably, in time he was equated with Hephaistos, the Greek smith-god, who had himself begun as a deity of volcanic regions, and so passes out of native Roman religion into the cult and mythology of the all-pervading Greeks. His partner Maia was still more effectively hidden, for, her name happening to sound like that of Maia the daughter of Atlas, mother of Hermes in Greek legend, her original nature was almost completely forgotten.

The gods of the underworld received their dues at Roman hands, but with cautious reserve, for no one wanted to come into too close contact with such powers while in this life. The State did not directly concern itself with the placation of ghosts, whether members of Roman families or kinless and homeless phantoms, but it set aside days on which they might be dealt with according to custom by individual households. The Lemuria of May have been mentioned (p. 181), also the soul-feast of February (p. 196), the *dies parentales,* or days for *parentalia,* such rites as are due to a departed father or mother, and so to dead kin generally. But there were a few deities who seem to belong to the same sphere. It is said by sundry ancients that *parentalia* were given to two women of old days, Tarpeia and Acca Larentia, or Larentina, for the name varies a little. It needs no great research into the facts to see that they are minor goddesses, whose activities were somehow connected with the underworld, but whether or not they were actually rulers over the

dead we do not know enough to say. Evidently their ceremonial was like enough to that conducted at a grave to point
to their being other than the familiar and friendly givers of
numen to the crops. Dim and unsatisfactory memories exist
also of a deity called Vediovis, that is to say "not Juppiter",
who was important enough to have two temples dedicated
to him in Republican times. It possibly is he whom Dionysios
of Halikarnassos means when he says that if a client wronged
his patron or a patron his client

"he was liable under the law of treason which Romulus sanctioned,
and if found guilty might be killed by anyone who chose to do so,
as being a victim to Zeus of the underworld".

But it is perhaps more likely that Dionysios is merely giving
Greek definiteness to the grim Roman formula concerning
such an offender, *sacer esto*, let him be removed from ordinary
life and relations ; the word *sacer*, which is very like the
Polynesian term "tapu", has a double meaning. A *res sacra*
is a piece of property of some kind made over to a god, and
therefore, as we should call it, holy or sacred ; but a *homo
sacer*, a man thus severed from the uses of everyday life, is
rather a person accursed, left for the gods concerned, or some
particular god, to deal with as may seem fit to divine wisdom.

But generally, the lower world was thought of as the home
of the Manes, or Di manes, the "good folk" or "good gods".
The usual form of inscription on a tombstone stated that it
was dedicated to the *di manes*, and this was particularised
by adding the name of the deceased, either in the dative
("to the Good Gods and especially to So-and-So") or in the
genitive ("to the Good Gods of such a-one"). A name which
not infrequently meets the student is, however, that of Orcus.
It is a disputed point whether this is Latin at all ; there is
a Greek underworld figure, Horkos, "the Oath", presumably
that power who punishes perjurers, in this life or the next,
and the Greek *h*, never a strong aspirate, tended to disappear
and may well have been lost altogether in the passing of the
name from one language to another ; Latin derivations, however, are not entirely given up, and it may be proved that
Orcus is really a native god, possibly a sort of a Roman

Hades or Pluton. Pluton himself was, in the period of strong Greek influence, adopted by Roman theologians and mythologists, if not actually in cult, his name being either Latinised by dropping the final *n*, or translated as Dis Pater, "the wealthy one who has authority".

In so short an account as this many Roman deities known to be old must be omitted, especially as nothing is known of the functions of some of them. But mention may be made of one curious little goddess whose name seems to spring from a ritual formula. On the Ides of March, that is the first day of full moon in the year, it was customary to pray that one might live in and through the year (*annare perennareque*) in comfort. From the stems of these two verbs a name, Anna Perenna, seems to have grown up, and to her the festival of that day was dedicated. It was a popular ceremonial, involving a picnic in the open or under temporary shelters, on the banks of the Tiber, during which everyone drank as much as he could, for he hoped to live as many more years as he could drink cups of wine ; Ovid remarks drily that some assured themselves of a very long life indeed by this means. Anna, who was a real enough goddess to have a sacred grove in Rome, fell a prey to mythologists, owing to the fact that her name sounded rather like the Semitic Hannah, and Dido, queen of Carthage, was provided with a sister of that name in a story immortalised by Vergil.

The worship by the State of these deities was highly organised. At the head of the Roman clergy stood the Board of Pontiffs (*collegium pontificum*), which included, besides the Pontiffs themselves, who originally numbered three, but were successively increased to six, nine, fifteen and sixteen, the Flamines, of whom, besides the greater ones serving Juppiter, Mars and Quirinus, there were twelve more, some so obscure to us that we do not know to what deities they were assigned, the Vestal Virgins, and the King of the sacred rites (*Rex sacrorum*), the inheritor of the priestly functions of the real kings. Save for the chief pontiff (*pontifex maximus*), who was the head of the State clergy, he outranked all his colleagues. He was the only priest who must be that and nothing else ; presumably it was felt to be neither logical nor perhaps politic for one who was a king, even if only in name, to be also a republican magistrate. The greater flamens seldom held any secular office, owing to the onerous nature of their duties ; but there never was a priestly class or caste, nor was the clergy ever in a position to enforce any decisions it might make, even in purely religious matters. Its function was to advise, the advice being tendered to the executive officers of the State, who, if they accepted it, would see that it was carried out. It also guided the actual performance of any rites which might be decided upon, or which were regularly performed as a matter of course. In time a very large sacral literature was accumulated, but it dealt with ritual, not with doctrine, for the sufficient reason that Roman religion, like that of most ancient peoples, had no doctrine and nothing which could be called a creed. It was universally assumed that there were deities, and that they possessed *numen*, which might be used for the practical benefit of mankind. It was the business of the experts to discover and teach how best to induce the gods to do as men wished, also to ascertain whether they were willing to do so, or approved the actions begun or contemplated by their worshippers. To achieve this, it was proper to know the right names and epithets by which to address the powers in question, for a prayer cannot be addressed to no one. It was also essential to know the proper ritual, and often highly advisable to keep it secret, lest enemies should learn of it and use it against Rome instead of for her. If any god or goddess was known to favour a foreign power, it was lawful and prudent to induce him or her to desert, and for that purpose there existed a rite of "calling out" (*euocatio*) by which such deities might be drawn from their former abodes and brought to Roman territory, under promise of a better cult there than they had had before. It was in this way that Minerva was got from Falerii after its capture by the Romans in 241 B.C., and given a shrine on the Caelian Hill in Rome. In like manner, Juno Regina owed her temple on the Aventine to her quitting Veii when Camillus captured it ; the temple was dedicated in 392 B.C. It is clear that in all this there was an element of sheer magic ; there was also a strong element of bargaining, for the Romans were a legal-minded people who understood excellently the obligations of both parties to a contract. So on occasion they made contracts with gods, drawn up by skilled clerical draughtsmen and providing for all manner of contingencies. A very famous one has come down to us. When it became evident that the Second Punic War was to be a long and hard-fought struggle, with Hannibal in Italy and threatening Rome itself, Juppiter was appealed to and promised a sacrifice of the whole increase of the flocks and herds for a year if by that year, half a decade ahead, he put the Roman people in a satisfactory position. The deed, when drawn up, was approved by the Assembly. But in return for so great a gift, the god was to waive certain rights which he might normally insist on ; the Romans were to be considered to have done their part even if irregularities were found in the method of sacrificing, if the offering were made on the wrong date or by an unqualified person, and also to be quit of responsibility for any beasts who might die or be stolen before the time came to offer them.

A further business of the clergy was to discover the will of the gods, to the extent at least of knowing whether they answered "yes" or "no" to a proposal made to them, as for instance, to give their blessing to some public act about to be commenced. Here lay the functions of the Augurs, literally the Increasers (by magical or other supernatural means), whose office had already shifted its emphasis by the time we first learn anything about them from any process of "increasing" anything to the more passive observance of the signs by which the divine will was made known. The usual process was as follows. The diviner began by tracing out a limited region within which he would look for signs, a *templum*, as it was technically called. This he did by indicating visible landmarks, as (the example is from Varro), "yonder tree, whatever kind it is, which I know I have named, shall be the left-hand boundary of my *templum*" and so forth. The space thus marked out was divided, as by the *cardo* and *decumanus* of a land-surveyor (cf. p. 186), into right and left, front and back ; signs within it had their understood significance, according as they appeared in one or another of these quarters. Since the diviner regularly faced south, left-hand omens were generally lucky, being from the east, the quarter of sunrise and so associated with light and all that it stands for. The usual signs were derived from the flight and cries of birds, hence the name for the taking of omens is *auspicium*, literally bird-watching, and anyone who had the official right and duty of looking for such signs in preparation for a piece of public business was said to have *auspicia*. A subordinate, for instance a junior officer on service, was governed by the *auspicia* of his senior, on whom devolved the responsibility for the subordinate's action and the official credit for any success. As in other priestly business, the augurs themselves were simply the expert advisers, whose part was to see that the watching for omens was properly done, or to do it themselves if so instructed by the legal authority. In later times the whole business degenerated into a mere farce. An action having been determined upon for secular reasons, good omens would be officially announced, even if none or only bad ones had actually been observed ; the responsibility rested on the person announcing them, and the gods, if they had not meant to approve the action, had their legal remedy in punishing that person. On the other hand, if it was desired to impede any public business, it was open to a magistrate who disapproved of it to announce bad omens and so bring it to a stop, or even to proclaim that he was going to "observe from the sky", as the technical phrase had it, and so suspend action until he had made his report. Some late Republican legislation was intended to stop this wresting of what had been a serious religious observance into a tool of political trickery.

Besides these great priestly *collegia*, or boards, and the later officials with whom the next chapter will deal, there were numerous minor bodies. One of the best known to us was the Arval Brothers (*Fratres aruales*), a very old priesthood, revived by Augustus, whose records were carved on stone in the precinct of their goddess, the Dea Dia, and have been largely preserved. Their chief business was a series of complicated ceremonies carried out every year, having for their object to secure *numen* for the crops. Of the Salii and Luperci we have already spoken (pp. 213 and 205). But on all alike fell the task of seeing that everything connected with the State religion, whether a sacrifice, the dedication of a temple or altar, the taking of *auspicia* or anything else was done according to the traditional methods, known by long experience to be agreeable to the supernatural powers, and that any failure in ritual was put right by an expiatory sacrifice or other proper means. To observe all these rites most scrupulously was the characteristic expression of love and duty (*pietas*) towards the gods. Such observance ("care and ceremonies", Cicero calls it) was binding on all right-thinking Romans. To bind is *religare*, and the feeling of uneasiness if anything in this sphere was not properly performed was therefore *religio*. All the sacred precautions could be summed up by styling them the *religiones* of the Roman people, perhaps the nearest equivalent in Latin to speaking of their religion. The result of performing them in the absolutely correct manner which ritual prescribed was the maintaining of peaceful relations with the deities, comparable to the peaceful relations between one State and another when both sides scrupulously observe the terms of a treaty concluded between them. Hence a Roman spoke of the "peace with the gods", *pax deorum*, and strove, prompted by his *pietas*, to secure it.

It was thus not a very exalted religion. Its objects were material, a sufficient food-supply, protection against physical dangers such as fire, success in war, increase by natural means of the population and their cattle. Nevertheless it was decent, marked by no immoral rites and encumbered by no frivolous or savage myths concerning gods and men. It seems to have been felt that the gods did not make wanton use of their *numen*, but dealt honestly and intelligibly with men who were honest with them ; that they were possessed of that *grauitas*, the disposition to take things seriously, which a Roman admired in his fellows. The very vagueness of the conceptions left a mystic or saint, if early Rome bred any, free to read what exalted ideas he would into the traditional cults, unencumbered by either dogma (of which Greek religion was equally free) or mythology. Left to itself, the old religion of Rome might in time have risen into something lofty and pure ; but we shall see that it was not left to itself, and what good qualities it might have developed were so buried under foreign accretions that it is only in the last two or three generations that we have formed any clear conception of what it was.

CHAPTER III

STRANGE GODS

It was not to be expected that a small state like early Rome, lying in the middle of Italy and on the great natural trade route, the Tiber valley, should long be left undisturbed, in religion or anything else, by the powerful influences about her. Immediately to the south were the territories of the Latin League, of which, from the earliest known times, Rome seems to have been a member, rising to be its head in place of the older state of Alba Longa, of which it is reputed that Rome itself was originally a colony. To the north lay the Etruscan confederation, a loose union of cities whose ruling class and some part at least of their population came originally from Asia. They had a high civilisation, a splendid architecture, a language differing entirely from any other in Europe and still unintelligible to us, a developed industry, an art greatly influenced by Greek models yet with original features, and a religion which, while it borrowed freely from Greek and Italian cults, had characteristics of its own, notably its extremely elaborate divination and the ceremonies with which its expert practitioners sought not only to foretell the future but also to delay the coming of an unwelcome event. Equally characteristic was the rich, complex and fantastic picture which they had formed of the other world and the experiences of the soul after death. These are portrayed on the walls of the elaborate tombs of their nobles and have a flavour at

times of the heavens and hells of far Eastern religions, mixed
with such familiar conceptions as the banquets and sports
of the blessed in something like a coarsened Greek Elysion ;
all very different from the shadowy Manes of Roman cult.
These people established a dynasty in Rome, the fall of which
led to the foundation of the Republic, and their contributions
to the religion of the City they ruled for a time, while not
affecting its fundamentals, were not inconsiderable. With
more or less probability, at times with something like certainty,
we may trace the following elements of Roman cult to the
Etruscans ; the dress and insignia of the magistrates, all of
whom had priestly functions, the style and orientation of the
older temples (*aedes sacrae*), the *templum* itself, although that
has been credited, not without plausibility, to the Bronze
Age inhabitants of pre-Etruscan Italy, the use of cult-statues
in worship, the elaborate funerals of nobles, and something
at least of the methods of divination. These last, however,
were not fully Etruscanized. The Etruscan experts, as already
said, claimed to foretell the future ; a Roman augur hardly
did more than learn whether or not the gods approved what
was actually begun or purposed, whether or not an offering
was acceptable to them. For further details, and especially
for an interpretation of any happening supposed to be preter-
natural and therefore ominous, official Rome resorted to what
were rudely called the "gut-gazers" (*haruspices*) of Etruria,
who never formed part of the Roman clergy but were summoned from time to time to give their opinion. Not all
Romans believed in them, for at least the elder Cato remarked
that he wondered they could see each other without laughing,
but the skeptics were in the minority. Their characteristic
method, as their nickname implies, was to sacrifice a beast
and examine its entrails, especially the liver ; there survives
a bronze model of the liver of a sheep inscribed with names
of gods in Etruscan characters, and we know something, from
Latin references to works by Etruscans on the subject, of the
methods used. They were curiously like those employed by
the Dyaks at the present time, as may be seen at length in
the great work of Hose and McDougall, *The Pagan Tribes
of Borneo*. We have seen that Saturn may be an Etruscan

god, and several other deities have with more or less likelihood been traced to the same people. On the whole, however, Etruscan influence upon Rome was superficial, touching several externals of the native religion but leaving its fundamental character, so far as we can judge, unaltered.

Naturally, other Italian communities of a culture very like that of Rome itself and of about the same development could effect no profound change in its religious life. They did, nevertheless, give the Romans several new deities, whose shrines, while not admitted to the charmed circle of the *pomerium*, stood within the boundaries of the City, on such places as the Aventine. Their adoption was due to various causes. Diana, a goddess of forests who helped women by giving them children, was the chief deity of the Latin League. Her shrine was in a sacred grove, *nemus*, not far from Aricia ; its site was near the modern village of Nemi. Rome, apparently while still under the Etruscan kings, had ambitions to become the head of the League, and in connexion, it would appear, with these set up a new and comparatively imposing cult of the goddess on the Aventine, where some few features of the temple and its attendant ceremonies still bore witness in historical times of her native character, before she was hidden under the personality of the Greek Artemis, whom she really did resemble to a certain extent. Minerva has already been mentioned as one of the triad worshipped in the Capitoline Temple (p. 207); there is no evidence that she had any cult in Rome earlier than that, but afterwards she possessed several and took an important place, although just outside the closed circle of the oldest deities, as patroness of all manner of handicrafts and, later, of fine arts. An interesting importation was Fortuna, otherwise Fors Fortuna. There are some fairly definite indications that she was originally an agricultural deity, and a little evidence that she had some connexion with Mater Matuta (cf. p. 226). In time, however, perhaps because so much in agriculture depends on causes outside the farmer's control, she became, like the Greek Tyche, a goddess of luck or chance, and as such was worshipped in many parts of Rome, and also elsewhere, under a variety of titles, such as Fortune of the Men, of the Women, of Maidens, and so forth. That she was not of the oldest Roman group of deities is clear from her having no festival, also from the story that she was introduced by King Servius Tullius, the last monarch but one of the traditional list, which is to all intents and purposes the same as saying that her cult, while old, is not of the most ancient. She may have come in from Antium (Anzio), where she was multiplied into two Fortunes, or from Praeneste (Palestrina), where she had a very famous oracle ; Antium also possessed such a shrine, but we know little about it. If so, however, she must have lost some of her powers on the way, for in Rome she was not oracular.

A few gods originally Greek seem to have reached Rome by way of Italian cities. Two of the most noteworthy are the divine twins, Kastor and Polydeukes, sons of Zeus and Leda, or, as they are called in Latin, Castor and Pollux, colloquially "the Castors". A picturesque tale, modelled on existing Greek legends, stated that at the battle of Lake Regillus, 499 B.C., they had appeared at the head of the Roman army and afterwards brought news to the City of its victory over the Latins. The facts about them are that they, particularly Castor, who overshadows his brother, were patrons of the Roman cavalry, the *equites*, and of the class from which it was drawn, originally young men of good families. The nearest place from which the twins could have been brought to Rome is Tusculum (Frascati), where they were worshipped from quite early times. A very interesting fact, attesting their early arrival in Rome, is that their temple stands (for the extensive ruins are still visible) inside the *pomerium*, in the Forum itself, near the shrine of Vesta.

Within a still older *pomerium*, however, is another Greek importation, Hercules, whose name is one of several Italian corruptions of Herakles. The ancient line followed by the Luperci (p. 205) swings away from the base of the Palatine at one place, for, as Tacitus puts it,

The furrow which traced the boundaries of the town began at the Cattle Market . . . to take in the great altar of Hercules.

The Cattle Market (*Forum boarium*) is on the side towards

the river, a natural place for traders coming up or down
stream to meet the early inhabitants of Rome and exchange
their wares for such things as living cattle or their meat,
tallow and hides. But for foreigners to meet peacefully in
this way is, under early conditions of society, not a light
thing ; to insure the safety of all concerned, it is well that
the spot should be under the protection of a god whom
buyers and sellers alike will recognise. Herakles' adventures
had won him the reputation of a great traveller, and it seems
to have been thought that he would have a fellow-feeling
even for less warlike and powerful wanderers than himself,
the merchants who went up and down the country in early
times. Also, he had a great reputation for averting evil of all
kinds, as in his earthly life he had rid the world of many
formidable beings who plagued it. At all events, in Italy he
had become a protector of merchants, to whom they would
dedicate a tithe of their profits in gratitude for his help. On
occasion he was thought to disclose buried treasures also.
So, since in many parts of the Greek world he was worshipped, not simply as a hero, or venerable and powerful
ghost, but as a full-fledged god, Italian merchants seem to
have adopted him as a patron, hence the erection of his altar
on this trading-place. The cult is said to have been originally
in the hands of two Roman clans, the Potitii and Pinarii, of
whom the former had died out by the end of the Republic ;
it was alleged that this extinction followed upon their impious
selling of the secrets of the cult to State-owned slaves, at the
instigation of Appius Claudius (one of a family of pestilent
innovators), while he was censor in 312 B.C. At all events,
the ritual was in the hands of the State officials from that
time on ; it was Greek in character, the sacrifice was a heifer
which had never been yoked, and the libation was made from
an old wooden goblet said to have once belonged to Hercules
himself. No other god might be mentioned during the rites,
and the precinct was so holy that no dogs and no flies ever
ventured to enter it. But Hercules was so little felt to be a
foreigner that an Italian equivalent was found for him, in the
person of an old and obscure god, Semo Sancus Dius Fidius.

A minor deity with a great future who was not of the

oldest stratum of Roman cult was Venus. Her name is curious ; by analogy with other nouns of like formation, it ought to be neuter, signifying something like "delightful appearance", which meant, not the beauty of women, but that of a piece of well-tilled ground, especially, it would seem, a vegetable-garden. At least, the dealers in vegetables and pot-herbs celebrated her festival on August 19th, the dedication-day of her temple. She cannot have been a very old importation, for Varro says he could find no mention of her in any ancient document ; but, for some reason now obscure, the idea grew up that she was the same as the Greek Aphrodite. Aphrodite in turn was the Greek name for the goddess anciently wor-shipped at Mt. Eryx in Sicily, and therefore this deity, around whose shrine a great deal of fighting went on in the first Punic War, was called in Latin Venus Erucina. Early in the second Punic War, when the presence of Hannibal with his invading army in Italy made men's minds very uneasy, a number of precautions were taken to secure the favour of all manner of gods, and one of these was a con-sultation of the Sibylline books (see p. 243), which advised that a temple be erected to this goddess. That was accord-ingly done, in 215 B.C., while another followed during the next century, in 181. It so happened that this latter shrine was founded on April 23rd, which was the day of the so-called Vinalia Priora, or earlier festival of wine, the day on which the grape-juice of the last year's vintage, having now fermented enough to be drinkable, was formally drawn and a libation of it poured out to Juppiter before any human lips tasted it, thus bringing the new, and therefore dangerous, liquid into contact with the wholesome *numen* of the god. It was not officially called wine (*uinum*) on that occasion, but *calpar*, a word which, to judge by its cognates in other languages than Latin, is derived from the name, not of the contents of the vessel used but of the vessel itself. It is a nice example of sacral caution. Wine is what men commonly drink, at least in a wine-making country ; until it has been made safe for drinking by the beneficent influence of Juppiter, it is safest to call it simply "that stuff in the pitcher". How-ever, the coincidence of date gave rise to a common mistake ;

most people, although scholars and priests knew better, fancied that Venus was the goddess of the festival, and it became the day on which prostitutes made sacrifice to her. This is an example of undesirable foreign elements making their way into sober and decent Roman ritual ; some of the Oriental goddesses who were identified with Aphrodite, and therefore with Venus, had temple-harlots in their service, and the goddess of Eryx was one of them. A more respectable development, but still quite un-Roman, was the connexion between her and the great Julian family. They explained their name by saying that they were descended from a certain Iulus, son of Aeneas. But Aeneas (Aineias in Greek) was in mythology a son of Aphrodite ; in other words, the junior branch of the Trojan royal family, which seems to have survived the destruction of the city, was somehow associated with the local mother-goddess worshipped on Mt. Ida, near Troy. Therefore Aphrodite, or Venus, was the ancestress of that house which gave Rome its earlier Emperors, and from the time of Augustus on her cult was important. That Venus of Eryx in particular was honoured in this connexion was due to another development of Aeneas's legend, which credited him with founding her temple.

Other gods were Greek pure and simple, one at least not even changing his name when he came to Rome. This was Apollo, who was so widely worshipped in the Greek-speaking world that any nation in contact with Greek civilisation, even indirectly, was sure to hear of him. The Etruscan dynasty, like all Etruscans, had Greek contacts, by no means always friendly, and their people adopted the cult of so great a god quite early ; one of the most impressive monuments ancient Italy has left us is the famous statue of Apollo from Veii, a marvellous and awe-inspiring piece of Etruscan art, which shows the god at his most terrible. It is not surprising, therefore, that the Etruscan kings of Rome are represented as consulting the oracle at Delphoi on occasion, nor that they are credited with having acquired the Sibylline books for Rome. At quite an early date verses were current in Greece, supposed to be the inspired utterances of women known as Sibyls (*Sibyllai*), a word of unknown origin. That their inspiration came from Apollo was the generally received doctrine, for he tended to attach all diviners and prophets to himself by one means or another. One of these women was said to have lived, or even be still living, for she was credited with a life of 1,000 years, at Cumae, on the coast, not far west of Naples. Doubtless her legend and her prophecies had been brought by the Greek settlers in that part of Italy. A collection of verses supposed to be hers was in the possession of the Roman government from an early date, whether it was actually got by the Etruscan kings or not. It was kept in the Capitol, under the care of a priesthood whose duties extended to all new cults. They were the Two Commissioners for Ritual (*duouiri sacris faciundis*), whose numbers were increased till finally there were fifteen of them. Only they might consult the mysterious verses, and even they only by order of the secular authorities. Hence we know little of the contents of their collection, or of the later one which succeeded it, for Augustus got a new one together when he rebuilt the holy place, burned down during the civil wars between Marius and Sulla, in 83 B.C. He selected, from the many books offered from various quarters of the world, especially the supposed homes of the different Sibyls, those which he considered genuine, burned the rest, and stored the chosen prophecies, not in the Capitol, but in the base of the great statue of Apollo in his new temple on the Palatine, one of the most magnificent in Rome. For Augustus had a deep devotion, real or simulated, to Apollo and set up in his honour what was practically a rival cult to that of Juppiter, so that from this time onwards Roman official religion had two centres, one on each of the venerable heights overlooking the Forum. The older temple, however, lost little of its prestige, and was still the place to which, on the successful conclusion of a campaign, the triumphal procession made its way, though now it was always headed by a member of the Imperial house, as perpetual commander-in-chief ; a subject could get no more than the right to dress on formal occasions in the elaborate (originally royal) costume of one who had celebrated a triumph.

However, Apollo did not have to wait for the Empire

before being received and adequately housed in Rome. The immediate cause of his admission was perhaps some pestilence, for the oldest prayer to him of which we have any account was that uttered by the Vestals, and in this he was addressed as Physician and Healer (*Apollo medice, Apollo Paean*). Certainly he was called Physician in connexion with his oldest temple, vowed in 433 B.C. during a sickness and dedicated two years later. It stood outside the *pomerium*, near the river bank, and succeeded an older and smaller shrine. One of the new ceremonies of the second Punic War was the institution of games in his honour, which soon became annual. These in themselves were nothing new ; Juppiter had long enjoyed a similar celebration, the Roman Games, made annual in 366 B.C., and the Plebeian Games were instituted about the same time as the Apolline, for they became annual in 216. But Apollo, being a Greek, liked Greek amusements, and his games were marked above others by the adoption of Greek dramatic performances, alongside of the Italian sports, the most characteristic of which were combats of gladiators. Actors, who were "Dionysos' craftsmen" in Greece, became "Apollo's guests" (*parasiti Apollinis*) in Rome, though they were also under the patronage of Minerva, like any other skilled workers. Their art, in its more serious forms, was never really popular, for even comedy, which had some quite good exponents during the second and third centuries B.C., languished afterwards and gave place to farce and ballet. One reason for this no doubt was that drama had no roots in the native religion, Etruria only having some few performances of a semi-dramatic character. The Greek states to the south did indeed have a certain amount of drama of their own, but never very highly developed ; the inspiration of Roman dramatists in their more "legitimate" plays came from Greece proper.

Something has been said of the Greek cast which the worship of Ceres assumed (p. 220). Another Greek figure was that of Mercurius, or Mercury, as he is generally called in English. Like Hercules, he was a god of traders, and whatever his Italian origins may have been (it is not undisputed that he was ever a purely native god, and certainly he was not originally Roman), he came in that capacity, an important one belonging also to the Greek Hermes. He was an early importation, whatever the exact cause of his coming, for he was given a temple in 495 B.C., if our records are to be trusted for so ancient an event.

We know definitely when a later Greek figure arrived in Rome, the patron of physicians, Asklepios, whose name took the dialectical form Aesculapius in Roman mouths. His cult, as a great inhabitant of the underworld, who continued his healing activities mostly by means of visions granted to those who slept in his temples, was not widespread even in Greece till towards the end of the fifth century B.C., when it became extremely popular. About a century later, in 293 B.C., a pestilence was ranging in Rome, as commonly happened there, owing to the ill-planned and crowded streets and the general ignorance of hygiene. A Sibylline oracle advised them to seek the aid of Aesculapius, and a mission sent to Epidauros, one of his principal shrines, came back with a sacred serpent, a common enough epiphany of the deity. According to tradi-tion, it slipped overboard as the ship with the ambassadors was coming up the Tiber, and landed on the island which stands in mid-stream opposite the mediaeval ghetto. Here a shrine was erected in honour of the god, and like many of his places of worship it became a sort of hospital or sanatorium ; Aesculapius was given Salus as his cult-partner, corresponding to Hygieia (Health) in his Greek cult, and to this day his influence may be said to continue, for the church and hospital of S. Bartolomeo now occupy the place. The island itself, in commemoration of the god's voyage, was given in antiquity the shape of a ship.

In 249 B.C., during the long-drawn first Punic War, when war-nerves were a common phenomenon, certain portents moved the Senate to authorise a consultation of the Sibylline books, and this time the advice was to hold games in honour of Pluto and Persephone (or, in Latin, with a translation of one name and a mispronunciation of the other, Dis and Proserpina) for three successive nights, and to repeat them once every *saeculum,* a period variously computed by the Etruscans, from whom it was derived, but generally fixed

at either 100 or 110 years. This was duly done, at a place
on the Campus Martius, in the northern part of Rome, called
Terentum, which, according to a natural conjecture of ancient
scholars, owed its name to the cult having originated in the
Greek city of Tarentum (Greek Taras, now Taranto). The
next celebration took place a little more than a century later,
in 146 ; after a longer delay, Augustus celebrated the games
in a new form, keeping up the nocturnal rites but adding
brilliant shows on the corresponding days, in honour of
Juppiter, Juno, Apollo and Diana. This was in 17 B.C., and
justified by a highly artificial calculation of the dates when
earlier periods had ended ; it was only to be expected that
some of his successors did not wait for so long a time to
elapse before celebrating so magnificent a ceremony and thus
setting their own greatness on something like a level with
his, but we need not go into the later occasions and the rival
chronologies on which they were founded. It should be noted
that in Imperial times the name of the festival was changed,
and it was no longer called, as it had been, *ludi Tarentini*
or games of Tarentum, but *ludi saeculares*, that is games
marking a *saeculum*.

So much for actual Greek gods. A wider influence,
however, than could be exercised merely by the reception
of a few new cults was felt by about the third century B.C.
A critical date is 217 B.C. It was apparently not unheard of
in the native worship to have sacred feasts at which the
deities were supposed to be present ; they were represented
by bundles of herbs, known as "heads of gods". But in that
year such a banquet was held (the Latin name for it is
lectisternium, i.e. the preparing of couches such as diners
reclined on by Greek custom), in honour of gods grouped
in Greek fashion and represented by statues. On the first
couch were Juppiter and Juno, husband and wife in the
Greek identification of them as Zeus and Hera. On the next
lay Neptune and Minerva, who to a Greek were Poseidon
and Athena, the ancient deities of the Athenian akropolis.
Then came Mars and Venus—Ares and Aphrodite were
Greek cult-partners of long standing—Apollo and Diana (in
Greek mythology, Apollo and Artemis are twins), then the

two fire-deities, Volcanus and Vesta, finally two closely associated with the corn-trade, Ceres and Mercury. Only the last two groups make any reasonable sense if we start from the presuppositions of Roman cult ; the rest are pure Greek. From that time on we have abundant evidence of the growing Greek influence, both in cult and in every-day thought. Greek myths are assumed as known in dramatic authors, and attached to Roman deities equated with Greek ones. Old groupings begin to break up ; thus Saturn, who was identified with Kronos, presumably because of the resemblance between their festivals, was paired no longer with Lua but with Ops, whom some freak of theology interpreted as Kronos' consort, Rhea. Consus, her real cult-partner, was not easily identified with any Greek god (some guessed wildly that, since his altar lay in the Circus, and horse-races were held there, he must be Poseidon, Lord of Steeds), and so, like several other such deities, retired into the background. The vague old figures became clear-cut personalities of the Greek type, and Greek statues, or imitations of them, housed in temples built after the Greek pattern, were more and more to be seen all over Rome and Italy.

It was unfortunate that these once bright Olympian figures came to be widely known at a time when they were losing their lustre for their originators. The failure of the traditional deities of Greece to preserve the city-states which had long worshipped them was causing much religious unrest,[1] with tendencies towards individualism in worship, a search for new and more satisfactory cults, and an abundant crop of theories, some of a decidedly skeptical nature. One of the shallowest of these, that of Euhemeros (fourth and third centuries B.C.) was taken up in Rome not long after its author's own day by Ennius (239-169), the greatest of those writers who made Greek literary methods familiar to Rome. His Latin translation or adaptation of Euhemeros' romance, in which under the form of a traveller's tale he set forth his theory that the traditional gods were kings and other noteworthy persons, deified after their death by admirers or flatterers, made far more impression in Rome than

---

[1] See *Ancient Greek Religion*, p. 100.

it ever had in Greece, because the Romans seldom had either a philosophical or a historical training such as would have helped them to detect the weaknesses of such a doctrine. About a century later, the view held, for instance, by Polybios the historian, as it had been by sundry others before him, gained some ground ; it was, that religion in general was nothing but a deep political scheme devised by early rulers and moralists to awe their subjects into good behaviour when human devices for detecting and punishing their irregularities were not likely to succeed. Hence, together with the very cults which in their hey-day might have added vividness and variety to the sober but rather dull native worship, came tendencies to disregard all religion, except for the maintaining of the State ceremonies which were part of the machinery of government. The last two centuries of the Republic saw a decline, becoming more and more rapid, of religion in Rome, and with it the loss of a good deal of what the Romans called *religio*, the scrupulosity which had once marked their conduct and led, among other things, to such excellent results as a careful keeping of sworn obligations. No doubt much unenlightened feeling and not a little sheer superstition was got rid of in this period, but it is to be doubted if the average educated man of the age of Cicero was either on such a high level morally or so likely to develop for himself a religion or a philosophy which could guide his conduct as his ancestor of some two hundred years earlier had been. It was a weakness of the Roman mind that in most departments of knowledge not immediately connected with the needs of everyday life and the necessary carrying out of routine public duties they were far too prone to adopt Greek conclusions ready-made and too little able to criticise them radically, or to form any fresh opinions for themselves. Hence it is that there never was a Roman school of philosophy in any proper sense of the word (teachers of philosophy and groups of persons interested in it did exist), nor any Roman science, unless it be jurisprudence.

One idea taken over from Greece was that gratitude for benefits constituted a good reason for paying divine honours. Since the gods were traditionally the givers of good things, if good things came from any source, that indicated the presence of something like deity. This, properly understood and followed out, might have led to a form of religion by no means degraded ; what it actually caused was not only such a theory as that of Euhemeros but strange freaks of cult. Plutarch has a story of "the man who sacrificed an ox to his benefactor", and can give the name of the sacrificer ; one Pyrrhias of Ithake thus honoured an old man who had made him rich in return for a great service. The remarkable thing about this folk-tale, for such it undoubtedly is, is that Plutarch, a pious and learned man, shows no signs of blaming Pyrrhias for his eccentric way of showing gratitude. Much more important was the quite common deification of men of high rank, especially kings of the Hellenistic kingdoms which sprang up in the ruins of Alexander the Great's empire. This was most commonly done after their deaths, but not infrequently in their lives, and to speak of a reigning prince, directly or by implication, as a god was a commonplace of courtly language. Hellenistic philosophy, too, held that to be truly royal a man must have in him something which exceeded ordinary humanity.[1] Another development belonging to this period is the occasional cult of an abstraction ; thus it is said that Timoleon, the Corinthian patriot to whom Syracuse also owed a temporary freedom from illegal absolutism, is said to have had a private chapel to Automatia, or "that which happens of itself", in commemoration of the good fortune which had attended his most daring undertakings.

All these tendencies are reflected, at one time or another, in Roman cult. Abstract qualities, which were rarely worshipped in Greece, though to personify them is one of the commonest figures of speech in their poetry, enjoyed much veneration in Rome. One reason for this is probably that the average Roman had little power of abstraction, as is shown by the comparative rarity of abstract nouns in the language. It has been ingeniously suggested that the origin of such words is not the philosophical process of seeing and naming a quality which many things have in common, but rather the belief in a supernatural power which gives certain qualities,

[1] Cf. *Ancient Greek Religion*, p. 102.

and there is little doubt that this is true in some cases. Fear, for example, under its Greek name, Phobos, has not the form of an abstract noun at all, and the evidence is fairly cogent that the word meant originally a supernatural being who made men take fright and run away in battle. Good Faith (Fides) is quite an ancient divinity in Rome, her cult being ascribed to Numa ; that is to say, no record existed of a time when she was not worshipped. She was associated with Juppiter, naturally enough, since the sky-god, who sees all that men do, is everywhere a favourite witness to oaths and treaties, and the three senior *flamines*, that is the very core of the oldest clergy, in the service of the three principal gods of the most ancient State cult, used yearly to go to her shrine on the Capitol and offer sacrifice. Juventas was another dweller on the Capitol and associated with Juppiter ; she watched over the *iuuenes*, the men of military age, from the time they put on the men's toga till they were too old to be liable to army service. A few more old deities were of like kind, and it seems a very natural way of expressing the presence, actual or hoped for, of some special kind of *numen* to attach such a name to it. But in the later period which we are discussing, cults of abstractions pure and simple sprang up thickly. When Concord (Concordia) was first given a temple by the great M. Furius Camillus, in 367 B.C., no doubt she was still the author of that *numen* which made all Romans hold together in times of stress. But when L. Opimius restored it in 121 B.C., to commemorate the end of the disturbances due to the Gracchi and their abortive reforms, we may suspect the intrusion of a more abstract idea, such as might in later time have expressed itself in an allegorical painting or statue, while we need have no doubt that the future emperor Tiberius, when he re-dedicated it to Concordia Augusta, in A.D. 10, was simply personifying the good relations between the members of the Imperial house. Cults of Concordia now grew up all over the Empire, often with titles added to show what particular sort of agreement or "team spirit" was meant. Yet more certainly abstract was Clementia Augusta, who reflected the mercy which the Emperors, some of them with justification, claimed as a corner-stone of their policy. A cult directed to a colourless figure of this kind was a respectable way of issuing official propaganda or of displaying decorous loyalty, and hardly more.

If we wish to understand how little deification might mean, from the point of view of any reasonable theology, we cannot do better than to examine the correspondence of Cicero after the death of his beloved daughter Tullia. He was a man of strong family affections, and she apparently was an amiable woman, who probably returned his natural feeling for her. We are well acquainted with his views on philosophical matters; he was an Academic, which meant much the same as an agnostic. Certainly he had no deep convictions concerning the destiny of human beings after their death, still less a persuasion that his daughter had become something superhuman and powerful on leaving her body. Yet he cherished the intention to erect nothing less than a temple to her. Several letters to his closest friend, Atticus, treat of the matter; he busied himself with choosing a suitable site for the building, and reiterated that it was not to be a tomb or funeral monument of any kind, but a shrine (*fanum*) which could not be mistaken for anything else and should be respected as such by later owners of the ground on which it was to stand.

"It is a shrine I want", he declares, "and I won't give up the idea. I am anxious to avoid any likeness to a tomb, not so much because of the legal penalty [on excessive expenditure upon funerals] as because I must have as near as possible a deification" (or apotheosis; he uses the Greek word).

If therefore a tender-hearted man's somewhat extravagant but natural and genuine grief could find such an expression as this, we need not wonder that when a really great statesman like Augustus did immense good to the general welfare by putting an end to the continual civil brawls, which often rose to devastating wars between rival parties, and establishing a stable and not oppressive government, many were perfectly ready to worship him, and he even had to check a tendency which was repugnant to some of his Italian subjects, not because they thought it blasphemous—that was a Jewish and later a Christian reaction to the prevalent Emperor-worship—but because it was not Roman, and conservatism was a force to be reckoned with. Two motives seem to have inspired those who kept up the cult of him and many of his successors. To some, it was a recognized means of showing gratitude and loyalty ; many established gods were nothing but men to whom such an honour had been paid in the past, and Augustus was quite as good as any of them. To others, what they were worshipping was the divine element really existing in Augustus, which in due course would depart to its proper place in heaven. That is what the poets of the time say, adding that they hope the departure will be long delayed ; and what is a piece of dutiful metaphor to them, was probably plain fact to the minds of many plain people. In Italy, the official compromise was to worship his genius. Whatever the genius may originally have been, by that time it was the spiritual double of a man, which came into and passed out of this world with him, ruled his life and was pleased if he enjoyed himself ; to "indulge the genius" is to eat, drink and be merry, while to "cheat the genius" is to live miserly. But throughout, the genius remained divine, a proper object of worship for a man and all his household, and therefore in the case of the genius of one who received the title of "father of his country", a very proper being for his "children" to adore. Once Augustus, or any popular Emperor, was dead, Graeco-Roman sentiment was well satisfied if he was formally declared to be divine and so given a cult and priests as the latest addition to the hierarchy of gods, for nothing in ancient belief obliged anyone to suppose that the deities formed a close corporation to which no one else might ever be admitted. However, it should be clearly recognised that this practice of deification and all that it implied were an importation from the Greek world. It is instructive to listen to Cicero once more, speaking, no longer as a bereaved father, but as a Roman senator, and discussing the proposal to give divine honours to Julius Caesar.

Conscript fathers, do you think that I would have moved what you unwillingly voted for, to blend funeral ceremonies with prayers, to bring into the commonwealth a pollution past atonement, to enact that we should pray to a dead man ? I say nothing of what man it was. Let it be Lucius Brutus, who himself rid the State of kingly tyranny and whose posterity, after nearly five centuries, display the like valour by the like deeds ; even so I could not be brought to let any dead man intrude into the awful presence of the immortal gods, or allow the State to worship one whose tomb is there to receive the rites of the departed.

We thus find, by the end of the Republic, a strange unreality in Roman religion. The ancient festivals and many new ones subsisted, indeed were often popular, for one of the chief means of marking them was to hold public shows, including the ever-welcome displays of gladiatorial combats and fights with wild beasts. Most of the old priesthoods remained in existence, though not all ; the office of flamen Dialis, with its burdensome tabus, was vacant for seventy-five years after the death of its last Republican holder, in 87 B.C. Matters of ritual remained under the control of the pontiffs, who often were asked their advice and by whose authority not a few ceremonies were added, altered or forbidden. The position of augur remained respectable and sought after ; the list of members of that venerable college includes the names of Sulla the dictator, Pompey the Great, Hortensius and Cicero the orators, Mark Antony, Julius Caesar and other leading men. It is interesting to remember that of these, Caesar was an Epicurean and therefore believed neither that the gods were interested in what happened in this world nor that they sent signs of any kind, while Cicero kept an open mind on divination, inclining towards disbelief. But many temples had fallen into ruin or were left unrestored after accident or the ravages of war had destroyed them. Such opinions as are expressed in surviving documents bear testimony to the sheer ignorance of even the best-informed as to the true characteristics of the national cult. Religious machinery was freely used for sordid ends in the endless political squabbles. False swearing was a commonplace. The whole atmosphere of the educated classes was one of indifference to religion, combined with a polite observance of such of its forms as were at once traditional in public life

and not particularly burdensome. Yet the following generations saw a great and growing interest in such things, and
from two to four centuries later the best minds in the Empire
were deeply concerned, not simply with questions of conduct,
but with mystic experiences, minute points of theology, and
controversies between one highly transcendental faith and
another. It shall be the task of the following chapter to try
and trace some at least of the causes of this remarkable change.

CHAPTER IV

AUGUSTUS AND THE REVIVAL OF RELIGION

THE adopted son of Julius Caesar, Octavian, or, as he
subsequently was called, Augustus, was one of the greatest
and most astute statesmen ever born. Coming to manhood
in the midst of civil commotion, at the end of some three-
quarters of a century of increasing disturbance, he left behind
him at the close of his long life an ordered State which,
despite the follies and vices of not a few of his successors
and many of their underlings, withstood all strains for over
three hundred years, during which occurred the longest
periods of peace that Europe had ever known or has seen
since. In theory, what he had done was to restore the Republic
in its best and most enlightened form. To quote his own
words, from the memorandum of his achievements which
he caused to be inscribed in several parts of his Empire :

In my sixth and seventh consulates, having put an end to civil
wars and being by universal consent in supreme control, I handed
over the commonwealth from my own power to the good pleasure
of the Senate and People of Rome. . . . Thereafter, although
I enjoyed greater prestige than my fellow-magistrates, I had no
ampler powers than theirs.

All, therefore, was supposedly as it had been before, and

Rome governed herself through the traditional and consti-
tutional machinery inherited from the past, while paying
attention, as many political thinkers had been urging her to
do for a century or more, to the advice and example of her
leading citizen, the *princeps* or chief man, to whom, incidentally, it had been found expedient to delegate for the time
being certain extraordinary powers. Whether anyone seriously
believed this formula we may well doubt ; but that it was
the ostensible basis of the early Empire is quite certain. The
detail that the "chief citizen" had under his hand the entire
military and naval forces of the State was judiciously kept
in the background, and it was an evil day for Rome when
it became no longer a secret that any Emperor owed his
security to them. Augustus was content with real power ;
later rulers wanted and ultimately got both the substance
and form of absolutism.

From early in his career, the new monarch surrounded
himself with a halo of religious veneration. His title, given
him by the Senate, carefully avoided everything other than
that, and though Greeks frankly referred to him and his
successors as kings (*basilês*) no Roman ever called them anything of the kind. The word *augustus* means him or that in
which something, namely *numen*, is increased ; its first two
syllables are identical with *augur* (see p. 233). Long before
the first and greatest holder of the title was born, Ennius
had spoken of an *augustum augurium*, a sign of divine
approval, heavily charged with *numen*, which had authorised
the foundation of Rome. It was therefore in keeping with his
position that one of his principal tasks was to restore, not
only the ancient morality of his people and their old and
deep-seated respect for law and order, but their religion. To
this end he revived half-forgotten priesthoods, saw to it that
candidates for such posts as those of the Vestal Virgins and
the various flaminates were forthcoming, built or re-built
temples in many places, but especially in Rome, inaugurated
new worships, as that of the Palatine Apollo (cf. p. 243), and
himself eagerly accepted the post of chief pontiff as soon as
it became vacant by the death of his former colleague and
rival, Lepidus, who had fallen into complete political

insignificance but was scrupulously spared to perform such of the duties attached to his holy office as he chose to fulfil. Religion became respectable and, what was at least as important, loyal. The greatest poem of the generation before, that of Lucretius, had taught Epicureanism and thundered against the degrading superstition which made men think that the gods could be angry with them, or indeed cared in the least what they did or how they fared. The greatest poets of Augustan date vary between the outspoken remark of Ovid that it is expedient to have gods and therefore we should think that they exist, and the profound piety of Vergil. How sincere Augustus himself was is a question which is never likely to be answered ; it is, however, possible to see what materials he had to work upon and to what extent he made his Romans what they once had been, the most scrupulously pious of mankind.

It must in the first place be noted that no strongly antireligious feeling existed anywhere. The uneducated went on with their traditional practices, or such of them as survived, especially the old-established rites of the country-side, and, we may suppose, entertained vague and uncritical beliefs corresponding to them. Among the educated, there were many who had no religious beliefs, but few if any who objected to religion existing or would do anything actively to oppose it. Most Romans, if they took an interest in philosophy at all, were either Stoics or Epicureans ; probably the numbers of both had grown considerably in the last half-century or so, for while in Cicero we catch something of the tones of a missionary making an unfamiliar doctrine known, in Augustan writers it seems to be assumed that most people have at least a general knowledge of the tenets of the principal philosphers. Of these schools, the Epicureans taught that gods existed, and had the outward appearance familiar from art and literature, but that their abode was outside not only this universe (we should say "solar system") but the innumerable others which they postulated as existing. They had not created anything, they were not troubled with the moral or other government of any of the worlds ; being perfectly happy, they had no onerous duties of any kind, but

lived in a blissful state of contemplation, apparently of their
own perfections and bliss. Yet they may have had a certain
passive and involuntary influence. It has been acutely pointed
out by Dr. Bailey[1] that Epicurean religion (he is speaking
of the more thoughtful Epicureans) was a contemplative
adoration of these beings, and that, according to one of the
recorded utterances of Epicurus (341-270 B.C.) himself, the
emanations from their divine bodies were productive of much
good. For Epicureanism allowed of no realities which were
not corporeal, distinguishing merely between grosser and
finer material substances. The ideas men have of the gods
are due to the impinging on the substance of the human
mind of a kind of very tenuous shells of fine matter which,
being continually thrown off the bodies of the gods, as off
every other object, make their way through the intervening
space and reach our senses in a more or less undamaged
condition. These fragments, therefore, of beings perfect in
every way, might greatly improve a receptive human adorer
by putting into him something of a nature far superior to
humanity. Hence a consistent Epicurean might well do as
the founder of the school had done and take part in the
conventional and established worship of his country, while
retaining his own opinions of the nature of the beings to
which it was addressed and the efficaciousness or otherwise
of the rites used.

The Stoics, on the other hand, came by a very different
route to a not dissimilar result, as indeed was the case in
many matters of ordinary conduct. Their philosophy was
deterministic, teaching that everything was minutely fore-
ordained by an all-wise and benevolent Providence. Furthermore, they laid great stress on the validity of universal
customs and beliefs ; this was one of their reasons for holding
divination to be a real science, for there is no people on
earth which has not some way of trying to foretell the future.
Where a popular practice or story appeared to be childish
or immoral, they were very ready to discover in it some
profound allegory, and especially to allegorise the popular
gods, largely by extremely bad puns of the sort which then

[1] *Phases, &c.* (see Bibliography), p. 225 and notes.

passed for etymologies. Since the universe and all its parts are divine (Stoicism has been described as a materialistic pantheism), many of the gods fitted at once into their places in the Stoic scheme. The chief deities, says Varro, voicing Stoic doctrine as he usually does, are Heaven and Earth. Now Juppiter is the heavens or the air ; therefore Juno, being his wife, is Earth ; she is called Queen because she rules over all earthly things. The sun and moon are plainly divine ; but the sun is Apollo (this is an older theory than Stoicism, for it goes back to the fifth century B.C., and Stoicism is of the third), and Artemis, who is the same as Diana, is the moon. In this way every god could somehow be brought into the wide net of their doctrine and regarded as nothing but a popular presentation of their philosophy. Therefore the originators of the conventional cults had been good Stoics, whether they knew it or not, and consequently there could be no possible objection to participating in the rites their ancient wisdom had established for the guidance of posterity.

The two principal schools, then, to one or the other of which most educated Romans of the day attached themselves, were not likely to offer any opposition to a restored and augmented cult of the State deities. There was another, of some importance towards the close of the Republic, which would be still less inclined to object. This was neo-Pythagoreanism, a curious mixture of philosophy, mysticism and magic which found its adepts in Rome. They possibly included Nigidius Figulus, the most learned man, except Varro, of the last generation of the Republic, but better known to later times as an astrologer and diviner. However, they were more prominent in connexion with a certain Quintus Sextius, head of a short-lived and unoriginal school of Roman thought, who blended some Pythagorean elements with his Stoicism and was succeeded by his son and a few other disciples. Sextius himself was a contemporary of Julius Caesar, and the best-known Roman to be influenced by him and his followers was the younger Seneca, tutor of the emperor Nero and one of his victims. Such men would certainly not oppose a movement intended to restore the ancient pieties of the country, especially as it went with a serious attempt to bring back the moral principles which the earlier Republic, not undeservedly, was credited with observing.

Among the unphilosophical part of the public, which was always greatly in the majority, there were some at least who cared for the arts, and to them no doubt the appearance of many handsome temples and good statues was welcome. The Augustan cult was a splendid one, and may be assumed to have gained some popularity for that reason. A further influence in its favour was the genuine feeling which many had that divine events were taking place. The poets, as so often, reflect this, and interpret it in their own way. No poem of Vergil's is more famous than the fourth Eclogue. In this extraordinary and beautiful composition, included in his collection of pastorals but explicitly striking a higher note than the rest, he hails the coming of a new and better time, which presently, although not at once, shall bring back the primal innocence and happiness of mankind, Hesiod's Golden Age, the "reign of Kronos" of Greek popular tradition. A child is to be born, the son of a great but human father, who shall rule the world, see the Iron Age disappear after the last wars have been fought (and even they shall have the character of noble exploits, marking a return to the Heroic Age of Hesiod's series), and attain to the society of gods. What child and what parents he means, and what his materials were—he himself names a Sibylline prophecy, but we know no details—are highly controversial points. Of the general meaning there is no doubt ; all things are to be made new, by divine help. The date of this poem is 40 B.C., not very long before the establishment of Octavian's power by the defeat of his great rival Antony in 31. There are in fact some indications, though confused and doubtful after the lapse of time and because of the imperfect state of our documentation, that the end of an age, a *saeculum* of some kind, was indeed expected about then by some people. One form of this belief is reflected in a story told by that ancient commentator on Vergil who is traditionally called Daniel's Servius, in memory of Pierre Daniel, the scholar who first published him. A certain Etruscan diviner, when the comet which startled the general public by appearing at the time of Julius Caesar's funeral games was attracting attention, declared that it marked the end of the ninth and the beginning of the tenth *saeculum* of his traditional system. He added that the gods were not willing to have this secret revealed, and would show their displeasure by his immediate death ; and there and then, before he could finish what he was saying to the assembled people, he dropped dead. Whether or not this particular event ever happened is a small matter ; the important fact is that sometime about the date of Octavian's rise to power and the conferring on him of his great title such feelings as gave rise to the fiction, if it is one, were not uncommon. But the doctrine of ages of the world, each of which has its own characteristics, good or bad, is in its origin a piece of Oriental mysticism. The existence, therefore, of such a belief and the quest for signs of the end of one period and the beginning of another and better one were essentially religious phenomena. The holders of such beliefs expected supernatural powers of some kind, gods new or old, stars (for astrology was daily gaining influence) or some impersonal but superhuman fate, to bring about the change. It was never supposed to come about through natural and historical causes, such as the enactment of new and better laws or the improvements in government which the merely human wisdom of able statesmen might suggest.

There are, moreover, indications that conjectures were rife as to what power was going to intervene and improve the state of the world. Vergil declares openly that Apollo is now reigning, implying that he is at least the initiator of the new Golden Age. Horace, in an ode written probably not very long after Vergil's poem, certainly before Actium (31 B.C.), after painting a direful picture of the portents which proclaim the wrath of heaven against Rome for the sins of the civil wars, culminating in the murder of Caesar, asks what deity will rescue the nation, and hesitates between Apollo, Venus, Mars and Mercury, implying that the last-named has taken human shape, that of Octavian, and will bring about, not a new age, but a return to more prosperous times and better relations with Heaven. All four of these are connected in one way or another with the Imperial house, especially the first two ; and since Horace was himself a man not particularly interested in religious affairs, certainly no pietist, it is a reasonable supposition that he is reflecting in poetical language thoughts which were in the heads of some at least of his fellow Romans.

Augustus, then, whatever other motives he may have had and whatever may have been his personal beliefs, was using an existing current of feeling which looked and hoped for an era of prosperity due to divine favour expressing itself in and through him and his family. That this should take the form of increased attention to the outward expressions of worship, priesthoods, temples and magnificent festivals, was inevitable, seeing that the revival had governmental authority behind it. The hopes of his contemporaries were to be a considerable extent fulfilled, for he did succeed in establishing a workable system of government for the Empire, removing many of the most glaring abuses, and at least making personal respectability among the members of Roman fashionable society a thing not to be set at naught, as it often had been in the immediately preceding generations. One thing is fairly certain concerning him, that he believed strongly in his personal luck or destiny, a not uncommon characteristic of men who have risen quickly to high power ; it will be re-membered that it was found in an extreme form in Hitler. In Rome, such a belief had been quite characteristic of several prominent adventurers. Sulla had taken the *cognomen,* or surname, of Felix, that is to say "lucky" or "fortunate." Julius Caesar's one outstanding belief seems to have been trust in his fortune ; a famous story concerning him is that he cheered the master of a small vessel in rough weather by assuring him that he had "Caesar and his luck for shipmates" and so would come to no harm. In the case of Augustus, the belief took an astrological form, character-istic of the times. According to Suetonius, he consulted an astrologer and, being persuaded to give particulars of the time of his birth, was astonished to see the expert spring up from his seat and prostrate himself before him.

"Thereafter," adds the biographer, "Augustus had such con-fidence in his destiny that he published the scheme of his nativity and stamped an issue of silver coinage with the sign Capricorn, under which he was born".

Actually, he was not born but conceived when Capricorn was on the eastern horizon and therefore his horoscope-sign ; he was born under Libra. But Capricorn is a royal sign, therefore better suited to his ambitions, careful though he was never to style himself king.

Here it may be well to explain briefly the strange pseudo-science of astrology (commonly known in antiquity as *mathesis*, "the learning", i.e., the science *par exellence*, and its practitioners as *mathematici* from their subject or *Chaldaei* from the country of its origin). It depends upon the theory, generally received by ancient astronomers, which puts the earth in the centre of the solar system, and consequently the general acceptance of the Copernican cosmography marked the end of it in educated belief. Since the rays of the seven planets of ancient astronomy (Saturn, Jupiter, Mars, the Sun, Venus, Mercury, the Moon, in the order of their relative distances, real or supposed, from the earth), naturally fall upon the centre of the system, that is to say on the earth's surface, and since they are divine, or instruments of destiny, or at all events capable of influencing whatever they shine upon, it follows that they must determine the lives and fortunes of those who are born under them, in other words of every human being, to say nothing of other animals. How they determine it is a matter of calculation, for the potency of any planet varies according to its position in the sky at a given moment, relative to the earth itself and to the other planets, also to the signs of the zodiac. Every planet has its house, the sign (sometimes more than one) in which it is in familiar and friendly surroundings, also its exaltation, the position at which it has its maximum power, its depression or humiliation (*tapeinoma* in Greek), which is the position of its minimum power, and furthermore, it may be the horo-scope, that is to say exactly on the eastern horizon at the time of the birth (or conception) of the child in question, or at the zenith or nadir (in Latin *summum caelum*, *imum caelum*), or in some other significant position. But the signs of the zodiac also have each its potency ; for instance, a

child born under Aquarius, that is to say when some degree
of the constellation of that name is horoscope, will have a
life in some way connected with water ; he may for example
be a fisherman or sailor, or a skilful swimmer, or he may
die by drowning, according to the other features of his scheme
of nativity, in other words the position of the heavenly bodies
at his birth. By combining the indications of the planets with
those of the signs and, to a lesser degree, those furnished by
other constellations than the ones included in the zodiac, all
possible destinies may be worked out with considerable
minuteness. The rules, in time, grew to such an extreme
complication that an astrologer had always a loophole of
escape if his predictions were too flagrantly falsified ; some
obscure detail of observation or calculation might have been
overlooked, or the exact moment of birth not have been
rightly given, or one of the many and conflicting authorities
have misled him on some essential point. On the whole,
their forecasts gained much credence, so much so indeed
that they were often discouraged by the State ; clearly, it
would be dangerous if some ambitious subject were told
that his nativity destined him to be king, and enquiries as
to the exact length of days allotted to the reigning Emperor
were much too close akin to a plot against his life to be
looked upon with any complacency. Theoretical arguments
against astrology, enforced by examples of its failure (including the recurrent one, that twins do not always lead the
same kind of life) were common, and were eagerly taken up
by Christian apologists, for the Church always officially
opposed astrology, though with indifferent success. Arguments on the other side were not lacking ; for instance, the
argument of the twins could be countered by the celebrated
answer attributed to Nigidius Figulus, in explanation of his
surname, which means "the potter". Setting a potter's
wheel in motion, he flicked it twice in rapid succession with
a paintbrush, and then stopped it. The marks were far apart.
He then pointed out that the heavens moved much faster
than the wheel, and so the time between the birth of one
twin and another would be more than enough to give them
a different scheme of nativity, and therefore different

destinies. Astrology also appealed in a varying degree to literary men, and one, a versifier of considerable ability named Manilius, contemporary with Augustus and his successor Tiberius, has left us five books of clever hexameters on the subject. With eloquence and a show of reason on both sides, the controversy went on till long after the close of antiquity, until at last the heliocentric theory of the universe, when its truth could no longer be doubted, left it impossible to imagine the influences of the heavenly bodies converging on a moving earth which was no longer in the centre for them to converge upon.

But astrology was in its origin the fruit of Mesopotamian worship of the heavenly bodies, and therefore religious in its nature. That the stars were divine was a doctrine taught by several philosophic schools, and therefore most of those who accepted astrology perforce took up an attitude towards the phenomena of the skies which was not naturalistic, or not wholly so. As time went on, astral worship concentrated, so to speak, chiefly in the cult of the sun, which was not altogether foreign to Italy, since the Sun and Moon appear, though not prominently, among the ancient deities of the City. It was encouraged by two strong influences, that of oriental cults, of which we shall have to speak later, and a growing tendency of theologians to explain traditional divinities as either solar or lunar, generally the former, which in late antiquity was so widespread that Macrobius (flourished about A.D. 400) declares almost all gods are equated with the sun.

Almost a corollary of astrology was magic. In a simple form this was native to Rome ; Chapter I has given us examples of ancient rites which seem to have been intended not so much to induce a god to exercise his *numen* in the desired direction as to get hold of a sufficient supply of it for the operators to use for their immediate purposes. The Twelve Tables, the most ancient Roman code of laws, forbade two forms at least of sorcery, the use of a noxious charm, *malum carmen* (which, by a quaint misinterpretation of later lawyers, was taken to mean a defaming poem, and so gave rise to a law of libel) and the practice of making a neighbour's

crops leave his fields and come magically to those of the
sorcerer. But a new and more learned era of magic was now
in full bloom. It was an ancient belief, widespread and in
no wise confined to the speakers of the two classical languages,
that gods could be induced by a moderate amount of prayer
and sacrifice to remit the penalties due even to great sins.
The stars, divine or not, were seldom thought to be so easily
entreated ; they went on their unchanging courses, and their
influences were exerted on all alike. Hence the desire to get
somehow out of range of their powers. Their influence moved
from the heavens inward, hence it did not affect the gods,
whose seat was above the stars. Obviously, man could not
rise to such heights himself, at least not in this life, though
here and there doctrines of Greek or Oriental origin found
converts according to which after death the soul might pass
through successive stages of advancement until it finally
became a god. Such a destiny, however, was not for the
ordinary run of mankind, whose virtues were not so lofty
as to deserve such promotion. But magic might hope to give
the adept power over, at least, some of the lesser beings in
the long series which led up to true godhead. For, in the
magicians' creed, which was not theirs only, every god was
at the head of an elaborate series of *daimones*, or supernatural
powers which, though less than divine, were considerably
more than human, and moreover was in sympathy with a
section of the universe, working down through heavenly
bodies to earthly ones, till finally it ended in a plant or other
familiar object. Thus it was possible to get into touch with
a deity by performing the proper rites on a particular flower,
or the like, and the process was vastly facilitated by knowing
the proper, that is the mystical or magic, names of everything and everyone concerned. Therefore a powerful and
expert sorcerer could bring himself into contact with a being
so great that no star and no fate had power over him, and
so, as it were, take the whole apparatus of mortal destiny
in rear. Such ambitious sorceries, however, do not seem
to have been greatly credited in Italy, where foreign magic,
although it was not uncommon, appears to have dealt largely
in elaborate curses, by which all manner of powers were

pressed into service for such things as lovers' quarrels and the disabling of horses against which the curser wished to bet, or in the harmless performances of herbalists, whose simples were made potent by being gathered at the astrologically right moments and under the appropriate magical auspices. Fortune-telling by magical means was common enough, and included necromancy ; some accused particular wizards of killing human victims, either because their entrails gave surer signs of the divine will than those of the lower animals, or to make potent charms out of parts of their bodies, or to press their ghosts into service. But it was regularly foreign practitioners who were supposed to perform such doubtful rites as these. Thessalian women had a great reputation for witchcraft ; it is a diviner from Armenia or Kommagene who, in Juvenal, will consult the entrails of a murdered boy if those of a fowl do not tell him enough ; later, Simon Magus of Samaria is supposed to have used the soul of a child he had put to death for his wonders. It is probably largely a matter of climate that the documents relating to sorcery which we have come from Egypt, where papyrus will keep indefinitely in the dry air, but the impression gathered from the evidence that we have is that Romans and Italians generally neither practised magic much themselves nor lent the names of their native deities to it ; the Egyptian books of magic and other sources of information show us a miscellaneous throng of Greek, Egyptian, Asiatic and newly invented supernatural beings whose names, together with curious combinations of meaningless letters, are used as words of power. Magic was on the whole a disreputable thing in the capital, at least until later times than those of Augustus.

But other ways of putting the individual into touch with divinity were not unpopular. As usually happens when a state grows large and complex, the ordinary man or woman was apt to feel inferior and powerless, the plaything of forces in this world and the other which were much too strong to be resisted. The reaction to this was naturally of different kinds for different temperaments. The Stoic saint (for that sect did not lack them, as it also had martyrs to boast of) found comfort in perfect acquiescence to perfect wisdom. The fates, says the Stoics' best-known Latin exponent, Seneca, lead the willing but drag the unwilling. Peace of mind was to be had by meditation on the truths of philosophy, especially the central dogma of Stoic ethics, that there is nothing good save virtue, nothing bad save vice, all else being indifferent ; wherefore a perfectly good man, a Stoic ideal sage, is the equal of a god, for the circumstance that the god lives for ever, or at least a whole world-age, and the sage does not, makes no moral difference, and so is of no account. Their finest poet, the lovable young satirist Persius, has a lofty conception of worship, which is also good Stoic, as might be expected. He hates ostentation and extravagance, "what is gold doing in a holy place ?" and holds that the most acceptable gift is a pure heart,

"justice and piety blended in the soul, holiness in the inmost parts of the bosom, a noble heart deep dyed in righteousness. Give me these offerings for our temples, and coarse meal will be accept-able sacrifice enough."

At the same time, Stoicism preached as a duty the taking of an active part in public affairs if opportunity arose. It was unfortunate that many of its exponents were so imbued with a sentimental republicanism that, besides their creditable protests against the misdoings of bad Emperors, they were at times guilty of factious opposition to good ones, and thus brought philosophy in general, as well as their own school, into disfavour. Despite the part, judicious and otherwise, which they thus played from time to time in the affairs of the State (their most famous public man was of course the Emperor M. Aurelius Antoninus), Stoicism was a strongly individual philosophy, and its chief aim was the good of the individual's soul.

If there were philosophers who thus made their philosophy very nearly a religion, there were religious sects with a tinge of philosophy. The Roman state as a rule persecuted no one's belief ; even its attitude towards Christianity is not really an exception to this. But it had a deep-seated dislike to anything resembling a secret society, and its experience of secret religious rites had not been encouraging. In 186 B.C., the Senate had felt obliged to take swift and stern action against an outbreak of Dionysiac mysteries over a great part of Italy. According to the official account, preserved in substance by Livy, while the text of the actual decree has come down to us, the movement started from Etruria, which had proved a fruitful ground for the missionary activities of an obscure Greek priest of the cult. Under his guidance, initiations at first of a few, later of considerable numbers of both sexes began to take place, and under cover of the excitable religion of their god[1] the adepts began to indulge in immoralities and offences of all sorts ; so at least it was alleged, and it is unlikely that we shall ever know what proportion of mere scandal and gossip and what percentage of real fact underlay the accusations. The State, which had abundant machinery for suppressing foreign and unauthorised cults, put it prompt- ly into force, thus getting rid, according still to the official apologists, of the makings of a dangerous conspiracy not only against private morals but against public authority. Hence- forth any persons whose conscience bade them worship Dionysos must get permission to do so, perform their cere- monies without secrecy, and allow only a small number to be present, unless special leave was granted.

This, however, was very far from being the end of secret or semi-secret worships in Italy. In the nature of things, we do not know a great deal about them, for many of them probably were quite illegal, not having been through the necessary process of registration and authorisation to make them "tolerated cults" (*religiones licitae*) in the eyes of the law, and naturally, since they were private, extant literature has next to nothing to say about them. Archaeology is rather more informative, and a number of monuments of one kind or another throw gleams of light upon the subject. One of the most famous is the Porta Maggiore basilica. Discovered by accident during the first World War, this subterranean building has the lines of a Romanesque Christian church, a basilica in the technical sense. It apparently never was used, for no traces have been found in it of ritual of any kind

---

[1] For the worship of Dionysos, see *Ancient Greek Religion*, p. 60 foll.

except a few bones under the floor which probably represent a foundation-sacrifice. Its walls are covered, especially those of the apse at that end where the altar would stand if it were a Christian church, with mythological scenes in stucco, some of them coloured, to which there is little doubt that an allegorical meaning was attached. For example, one handsome medallion shows the rape of Ganymede, and it is probable that this alludes to the carrying off of the soul, presumably to a higher life than that on earth. It is not unusual to speak of this strange monument as Pythagorean, but in the absence of any text or inscription, it is wisest not to be dogmatic. It seems to have been stripped in antiquity of all movable furnishings, and we may not be wrong in supposing that the sect, whatever it was, which used it was quickly suppressed as a *religio illicita* or unauthorised superstition. It was thought for a while that it might be connected with the unfortunate T. Statilius Taurus, who, according to Tacitus, was accused at Agrippina's instigation, chiefly of magical practices, and committed suicide in A.D. 53. No real evidence for this was forthcoming, but this much may be taken as certain, that the basilica was constructed for some congregation including persons of wealth and taste, who could command the services of skilled workmen and very tolerable artists to make their place of worship secluded and handsome. Another famous monument is at Pompeii, the celebrated Villa Item, on the outskirts of the town, on the walls of which are a great series of frescoes, again the subject of much discussion, but certainly connected with Dionysos and as certainly showing some of the rites of some kind of initiation. Much else has come to light in one part or another of the country, and amid all difficulties of interpretation, and after making liberal allowance for mythological or religious subjects being used by decorators merely as ornaments, it is clear that the religious life of Italy under the early Empire was lively. This does not mean that the traditional public cults, or their new fellows, the worships set up by the early Emperors, were neglected in favour of these less-known expressions. On the contrary, they seem to have been maintained with considerable zeal, especially those which pertained directly to the Imperial house. To be the *flamen* of Augustus, when he died and was officially deified, was no small distinction, and there were minor posts in connexion with the cult which give harmless play to the ambition of little men (not least of lower-class Italians) to have a title of some kind and a show of official duties to perform. These, however, were matters rather of tactful Governmental policy, to attach as many individuals as possible to the régime, than of religion properly so called. More to the point is the existence of a great number of little associations which had at least a flavour of religious sanction. These were quite legal ; a decree of the Senate laid down the maximum number of meetings they might hold and other matters, important to the general public policy of not allowing private organisations to be of any formidable size or power. They often described themselves as the "worshippers" (*cultores*) of this or that deity or little group of deities ; and they often were really nothing more than burial clubs, which collected a subscription from their members and in return undertook to give any one of them who died in good standing a respectable funeral, with the usual accompaniment of a funeral feast, often on a very modest scale. But that some of them were really little congregations of people who had some common religious interest is suggested by the fact that we have an inscription in rather halting verse put up by a *cultor Verbi*. In other words, we have some reason to suppose that an occasional group of Christians, in days before their religion had won its way to State recognition, disguised themselves under this inoffensive and legal form, substituting for the name of any recognised god, Roman or foreign, that of the divine Logos of the Fourth Gospel. If they did so, members of other unrecognised religions may have done the same.

At all events, be the organisation of these private cults what it may, there was a considerable and growing demand for a personal religion, and not least for one which should assure its adherents some hope of reward and advancement in another world, if not in this. The very feeling of helplessness in face of the great forces of the State and of Destiny led, as might be expected, to two results at least among the non-philosophical who could not find comfort in so rarified an atmosphere as that of Stoic speculations. One was a mere cynical indifference ; life was of no great consequence, death ended it once and for all, therefore there was nothing about which anyone need concern himself very much. Tomb-inscriptions give evidence enough of this. There is a stock formula, occurring in both Greek and Latin, which runs : "I was not ; I came to be ; I am not ; I care not". It is so familiar that Latin-using monumental masons often repre-sented it simply by the initial letters of the words. The other was the hope, doubtless vague in detail and unsupported by any reasoned scheme of eschatology, of some kind of con-tinued individual life after death, in which the liberated soul might enjoy the fellowship of superior beings. One very pretty example of this is probably to be found in the sarco-phagus and wall-painting commemorating a small child, Octavia Paulina, who died when seven years old and was buried in a vault belonging to her family. The former shows a little girl winning a wrestling match against a Cupid of the familiar childish type, often called an *amorino*. The latter is a kind of children's Elysion. A chariot is shown carrying, not Pluto with the ravished Persephone, but another *amorino* holding a small girl, and approaching an open place where a number of other children are playing around a statue of Hekate the infernal goddess. It is difficult, in this as in very many other cases, to determine how much is the result of serious belief and how much is mere pretty fancy on the part either of the child's parents or of the artist they em-ployed ; but if the former be the case, we can parallel the pictures from literature. To die is often spoken of as a victorious achievement ; the child on the sarcophagus is winning her wrestling-match. Mystic initiates, as we shall see in the next chapter, not infrequently pass through the experiences which their gods once had ; little Octavia apparently is undergoing the same adventure as Persephone. It is quite possible that her parents belonged to some mystic sect and even that she herself had been through a ceremony of initiation, which was by no means confined to adults.

However, the best-known of these cults, which seem also

to have been the most influential and popular, were not of
native Roman, or even of Greek origin, but came from
farther east. It is therefore time to discuss the Oriental cults
which made their way into the Roman world.

CHAPTER V

ORONTES INTO TIBER

IN a celebrated tirade against foreign elements in Rome,
Juvenal uses the phrase which gives this chapter its title.

"Fellow-citizens," he says, "I cannot bear a Greek Rome ; and
yet, what percentage of our slum-population is Greek ? Syrian
Orontes flowed into the Tiber long ago and carried with it their
language and their habits".

Oriental influence, indeed, was already old when he wrote
these lines, early in the second century A.D. In 205 B.C.,
Hannibal was no longer a serious menace, but he was still
holding a remote corner of Italy, and the people, strained
by a desperate war which had lasted for twelve years, were
but too ready to believe and fear every portent that was
reported to them from any quarter. Showers of stones (doubtless volcanic lapilli) had occurred several times, and the
Sibylline books were consulted. The response elicited from
them was, according to Livy, to the effect that "when a
foreign foe had invaded Italy, he could be driven out and
vanquished if the Idaean Mother were brought from Pessinus". This was a Phrygian city, one of the most famous
seats of a cult characteristic of Asia Minor and the neighbouring countries, that of the Great Mother. All over the
Near East, though by no means confined to that part of the
world, there was an early worship of a deity, varying in name
and unessential attributes from place to place but always
having one central characteristic ; she was fertile, the mother
of all things that live on the earth, and often of the gods,

or some of them, as well. Who her husband was, or if she had one, was a question not very important, and therefore producing no single consistent answer. At Pessinus, it was a minor deity, Attis, who was supposed to be her favourite, and concerning him an extraordinary tale was told. After sundry adventures connected with the goddess and her affection for him, he had castrated himself, and according to some accounts at least had died in consequence. His action was imitated by the priests of the goddess, the Galli, as the Greeks and Romans alike called them. The deity herself was commonly known as Kybelê or Kybêbê, and sometimes identified with the much less savage Greek Rhea. The object of this horrible rite of self-mutilation was probably in its origin an attempt to give the goddess more of the kind of *mana* she needed for her everlasting task of reproduction ; the severed parts were consecrated to her, while the Galli, if they survived, continued to be her ministers, but henceforth dressed like women. The Romans duly sent an embassy to the East, which went first to Delphoi to get Apollo's own assurance that the prophecy of his votary was true, then on to Asia, where, by the good offices of a friendly king, Attalos of Pergamon, they got possession of a shapeless black stone which "the natives said was the Mother of the Gods", Livy informs us, and brought it to Rome, where its arrival, at least according to legend, was heralded by a miracle, and its custody entrusted to a young member of the great family of the Scipios, who for reasons unknown to us was adjudged to be the best man in the whole State. The holy stone was temporarily lodged in the temple of Victory on the Palatine, where later a shrine was built for it and games, known as the Megalesia, or Festival of the Great (Mother), instituted in its honour.

Everything about the native cult of the goddess, especially the mutilation of the Galli and their outlandish dress and rites, was repugnant to Roman sentiment, therefore, having obeyed the divine command by receiving her, they took measures to keep her respectable and Roman, so far as was possible. The stone was set in the mouth of a decent statue of human form ; the priests were allowed occasionally to go about collecting contributions for their deity, but Romans were strictly forbidden to become Galli themselves. It would seem that the foreign priesthood, except for certain occasions, kept itself to the precincts of the temple ; these public appearances were, besides the begging expeditions, the annual ceremonial bath of the goddess, in the little river Anio, on March 27. But from an early date in the Empire (our evidence, such as it is, points to the principate of Claudius, A.D. 41-54), the old rules were relaxed. Roman names, though principally those of freedmen, appear in inscriptions among the priesthood, and the one day of the March festival was extended to five, with a preliminary observance on March 15th, the "entrance of the reeds", as its somewhat clumsy Latin title seems to have run. The cult-legend related this to Attis, who had been exposed when newly born and found by Kybelê in a reed-bed. The main ceremony, however, preceded by seven fast-days involving abstinence from bread, was the "entrance of the tree", a new-cut pine, carried by the Dendrophori or tree-bearers. Mystically, the tree was the dead Attis, and as such it was garlanded with violets and wrapped in linen. It is clear enough that the original Attis was one of those deities of vegetation who are born and die with the plants. The next day, spent in mourning and lamentation for the dead god, was followed by the wildest period of the whole rite, the Day of Blood, when the Galli lashed and cut themselves (presumably this was that familiar savage funeral rite, the offering of blood to the pale and bloodless dead) and their number was increased by the self-mutilations of novices whom fanaticism impelled to join their order. The following night, preceded by a period of strict fasting, was apparently spent in further laments for Attis, until, presumably early in the morning, the officiant proclaimed (in Greek verses, according to our informants ; no doubt the language of the cult had been Westernised to that extent) :

"Be of good cheer, initiates, seeing that the god is saved ; for we too, after our toils, shall find salvation".

Fasting and lamentations were now at an end, and the

next day, the Hilaria or Rejoicing, was spent in expressions of joy, apparently as wild as the mourning had been. It is no surprise that the Day of Rest followed ; and after it the original rite of the bathing of the goddess was carried out with all pomp and ostentation on the date which was that of the original shorter feast, March 27th.

It would be hard to imagine a performance more thoroughly unlike Roman ritual, or one fuller of morbid excitement. The date being fairly well on in the spring, something like a May Day would not be abnormal among any population which depended on the land for its sustenance ; dancing, merry-making, and a certain amount of general licence are the marks of such celebrations of the returning season of warmth and fertility, and associated with age-old ideas of the proper way to secure *mana* for the fields and for the flocks and herds. But the frenzy of the Great Mother's festival could scarcely be paralleled by anything European, ancient or modern, and that it should have been not only tolerated but popular in Rome shows clearly that the tone and sentiments of the population were changing. Juvenal was not far wrong when he implied that it was becoming an Oriental or at least a Greek city. The native Italian stock was perhaps diminishing, certainly not increasing much. The birth-rate among the higher classes was deplorably low, while the lower classes contained numbers of unemployed, or at best casual labourers, descendants of small farmers who had found conditions on the land impossible for them and so had betaken themselves to the doles and cheap amusements of the capital. Mixed with them was a great and increasing number of freedmen, who either had been slaves themselves or were the descendants of slaves, therefore were foreigners who could not care much for Roman traditions, while their own had been broken by exile and the often extremely degrading conditions of servitude. It is significant that by no means all were even Latin-speaking ; Greek inscriptions, put up by persons of freedman status and others, are common, and it is well known that the epistles both of St. Paul and St. Ignatius (martyred early in the second century A.D.) to the young Church of Rome are in

Greek. This miscellaneous rabble of nominal Romans, mixed with resident foreigners, had lost its last semblance of political power under Tiberius, when the elections of magistrates were transferred to the Senate in A.D. 14. It still, however, could be troublesome if it rioted, so the standing governmental policy was to keep it in good humour ; but little or nothing was done officially for its moral or educational improvement. It is therefore no wonder that non-Roman influences, good or bad, were rife.

One of these owed its beginnings to Sulla's campaigns in the Near East. His soldiers there came into contact with the goddess Ma (i.e. Mother) of Cappadocia, whose followers were even noisier than the Galli in their ritual. They were armed with swords and axes, with which, when wrought up into a frenzy by wild dancing attended by loud music, they cut themselves freely. They were supposed to be possessed by their goddess, and under that influence could prophecy ; as one of them foretold that Sulla would win against Marius, his great rival, he favoured the cult and let it be introduced into Rome, where it continued after his death in 78 B.C., and the "people of the shrine" (*fanatici*), as the Romans called them, were a familiar sight and sound in the City under the early Empire. The goddess herself was identified, owing presumably to the warlike appearance of her followers, with Bellona, the Roman war-goddess, associated with Mars, and so was commonly called by that name in Latin. She was, it would seem, no very formidable rival to the Great Mother, being indeed too much like her to constitute a counter-influence.

Kybelê's rites continued to increase in popularity, and were enlarged by two different kinds of ceremonial, the one savage and revolting, the other containing at least the germs of a lofty religion. The former, which can be traced back to the second century of our era, though its ultimate origins are obscure, was the notorious *taurobolium*. The word is Greek, like many of the technicalities of all these cults, for Greek, in forms more or less corrupt and degenerate, was the lingua franca of the Near East by that time, few of the native languages ever having more than a local popularity, for few of them had any literature at all, and a language not commonly written will not spread far beyond its native place. In Greece itself, none of these religions had much vogue.[1] *Taurobolium*, then, means properly the shooting of the bull (by means of arrows or other missiles), which indicates that the practice began somewhere in a district containing wild cattle. A bull was stood over a grating which covered a pit, and there killed with a hunting-spear. The person for whose benefit the rite was performed was in the pit, and received the blood from the slaughtered beast all over his body. He then emerged and the congregation bowed in veneration before him, for he was, as inscriptions assure us, "reborn for ever", although others, more modestly, limit the "new birth" to twenty years. In some cases a ram was substituted for the bull, but the effect was the same ; the man thus reborn was or became in either case a priest of the Great Mother, at least normally. It is fairly clear that the originators of the rite meant to acquire, by the blood of the sacred animal, perhaps an avatar of some god, something of his divine power and nature. The worshippers of Kybelê do not seem to have had so clear-cut a belief, though they held the ceremony to be very efficacious, and one of their most interesting inscriptions indicates that they somehow attached moral attributes to their savage performance, which they expressed in language derived ultimately from the Zoroastrian scriptures, the Gathas.

The other development was a comparatively spiritual and exalted cult of Attis. We have already seen that his worshippers were on occasion addressed as "initiates", and that they celebrated his death and resurrection with pious zeal. It will be remembered, also, that they were invited to base their own hopes of "salvation after their toils" upon the deliverance from death of their god. It would seem, therefore, that they were in some measure identified with him, a not uncommon phenomenon in cults, not so much of the classical world proper, as of those regions lying just east of it. The best-known form of the belief, which reached Greece at a fairly early date, perhaps the seventh century B.C., was that a worthy worshipper of Dionysos could gain, under

[1] See *Ancient Greek Religion*, p. 129.

certain circumstances, such identification with the god as to be called by his characteristic epithet, Bakchos. But it is likewise the central feature of the worships we are now discussing, which generally are known collectively as the mystery-cults. It seems likely that anyone who had undergone the *taurobolium* was "reborn", not as a human being but as Attis ; and apart from this unpleasing method of attaining permanent or temporary deity, we have a fragment of the ritual of a more sober cult. One of the Christian controversialists to whom we owe not a little knowledge of the later forms of paganism, Firmicus Maternus, who preached against what had once been his own religion or one like it with all the zeal of a convert, says in his interesting tract, *On the Error of Profane* (i.e., non-Christian) *Cults*, that the pagans had certain passwords, the result of "the devil's teaching", and that one of them, which he gives both in the original Greek and in a free Latin translation, ran :

I have eaten from the timbrel ; I have drunk from the cymbal ; I am become an initiate of Attis.

He then proceeds to thunder against it with all the force of his rhetorical powers and explain how much better is the Christian Eucharist. To those who look at such things calmly, away from the atmosphere of religious controversies now long dead, it is an interesting formula, for it bears a resemblance which can hardly be accidental to one adduced by Clement of Alexandria as belonging to the Eleusinian Mysteries.

I fasted ; I drank the *kykeon ;* I took from the sacred chest ; I wrought therewith and put it in the basket, and from the basket into the chest.

The *kykeon* was a ritual drink containing water, meal and some other ingredients. Clement also knows a fuller version of the formula concerning Attis, in which the initiate mentions two more sacral actions, carrying a vessel called a *kernos*, of very ancient fashion and used in other mystic rites as well, and entrance into the *pastos* or marriage-chamber. Naturally, these formulae are not explicit ; they do not, for instance,

tell us what the Eleusinian initiate took from the chest nor
what he "wrought" with it, nor why the votary of Attis
carried the *kernos*, what the marriage-chamber was nor what
he did in it. His co-religionists would know, and the profane
were meant to be left uninformed. But from what we know
or can guess concerning rites of this kind, we are left with
some information. The devotee of Attis ate and drank from
sacred utensils, musical instruments of oriental types used
in the service of their deity. He thus partook of a sacred
feast, the food and drink being charged with the holiness of
the god. At some time during the ritual, whether the occasion
to which the password refers or not, the initiate drank milk,
and as that is the food of babies, it was interpreted by some
at least as a symbol of rebirth. There exists a late but interesting treatise by one Sallustius, probably that Sallustius
who was a friend of Julian the Apostate, Emperor 361-363
A.D. and would-be restorer of paganism, which explains it so,
and furthermore, finds in the whole series of rites, from the
cutting of the pine-tree onwards (see above, p. 274), a deep
allegory of the return of the human soul from its present
unworthy environment to the company of the gods whence
it sprang. Sallustius is far from being an original thinker,
and it may be taken as certain that his interpretations were
those of many pious followers of this or similar religions.
Thus we find that out of a cult originally grotesque, revolting
and founded upon notions belonging to a barbarous stage of
human development, there could arise, with the admixture
of a little Greek philosophy, a faith anything but degraded,
though hampered with the need for explaining away many
features of ritual which no Westerner would welcome save
under the influence of a conviction that in these barbarian
practices there lurked ancient wisdom and a system both
metaphysical and ethical which was worthy of admiration
and adoption.

The spiritual adventurer of Roman Imperial days was not
confined to the cult of Attis in his search for a personal
religion to satisfy his aspirations. The Egyptian cults had
taken a new and less markedly national form under the
Macedonian dynasty of the Ptolemies, and had spread from

Egypt into parts of the Greek world, and thence to Italy. Like Attis, the gods of the Nile had adopted Greek as their means of communication with foreigners, though deep veneration for the ancient and mysterious-looking cult of their native land was certainly one of the influences which made for their success. Osiris, whatever he may originally have been, had certainly become by the time of which I am now speaking a dying and rising god, in that respect like Attis and also like the Thraco-Phrygian Dionysos, with whom indeed he was often identified, though perhaps not for that reason. The Egyptian legend, probably not much distorted from its native form, although Greek influence is patent here and there, was well known to Plutarch, who is indeed our chief authority for it. He omits, as he plainly tells us, certain "superfluous and needless" details, and the rest is, in outline, as follows. Osiris, Isis and Typhon (Set, a very ancient Egyptian god whose cult had given place to that of Osiris, with the result that Set was represented as desperately wicked) were three of the five children born at one time of Rhea, i.e., the native goddess Netpe. Osiris and Isis, lovers from the very beginning, became husband and wife, and Osiris rose speedily to be a beneficent and mighty king. But Typhon was frantically jealous of him, and by a trick persuaded him to lie down in a coffin which exactly fitted his body (as an Egyptian mummy-case would). He and his confederates immediately put on the lid, made it fast and threw the coffin into one of the mouths of the Nile. Isis, in wild grief, searched for her husband and at length found the coffined body, which so far revived that Isis had a son by it ; she already had one child, the god Horos. Typhon and his confederates, however, were still on the watch, and this time stole the body, cut it into fourteen pieces and cast it into various places, whence Isis, slowly and with infinite pains, recovered nearly all. She then trained her son to be a formidable avenger of his father, and when grown he fought and defeated Typhon, whom, however, Isis would not put to death, to Horos' great wrath.

Osiris, among a people with so lively a belief in a corporeal and material survival of death as the Egyptians, naturally enough became a ruler of the dead, since his body had at last been rescued, but he was something more than that, even in Egyptian belief pure and simple. For historical and other reasons, there was a great tendency in that country to identify different gods and ascribe attributes to one which originally had belonged to another ; a phenomenon which appears also in Graeco-Roman religion and is known to moderns by the clumsy name of syncretism. It need not therefore surprise anyone that Osiris tends now and again to be confused with Rê, the great sun-god, to the extent at least of having some solar traits himself, and also with the god of the Nile. In these capacities he is not a god of the dead, at least not of them alone, but of the living. Certainly he was concerned with living men in the form his cult assumed abroad. Egypt also had celebrated rites which, to a Greek, suggested his own mysteries, at Eleusis or elsewhere, in which mourning for the loss of Osiris was followed, it would seem, by rejoicing at his recovery. These accompanied him, in forms which may very well have been modified and elaborated on the way, into the Greek-speaking and thence into the Roman world.

However, the gracious figure of Isis, the divine wife and mother, was still more striking and popular. The various mother-goddesses already existing were less formidable rivals to her than might have been expected, for the same tendency to syncretism enabled her to be simply identified with them. In the *Golden Ass*, to which we shall refer shortly, she appears to the hero and tells him that she is called the Mother of the Gods in Phrygia, Athena in Athens, Aphrodite in Cyprus, and so forth, but Isis is her real name and the Egyptians know her own rites. What was unedifying or grotesque in her legend was explained away by allegories, or simply omitted, and she was exalted in the belief of many thousands as à deity full of grace and of power to help in this world and the next, with whom were associated a number of doctrines often vague and fantastic, but not degrading. Especially, it would seem, resident foreigners in Italy and the poorer classes generally were fascinated by her, though her worshippers were by no means confined to the lower ranks. In her cult, something new to the west was introduced. As already mentioned, a Roman god, or for that matter a Greek one, had nothing corresponding to the daily and hourly ritual of the more elaborate Christian ceremonials. Isis had ; and the fact that her clergy had their continual round of duties in her service must have impressed those who saw them with the idea of a *numen* ever present and ready and willing to listen. She and her attendant deities, Osiris himself, Anubis, Horos and the Ptolemaic Graeco-Egyptian god Sarapis were something new and exciting, which as long as the Egyptian shrine was present in Rome was at the very doors of the faithful. Governmental opposition was in vain. The Egyptian gods' chapels were torn down four times in ten years (between 58 and 48 B.C.), but they always rose again, and at last, in 43 B.C., the provisional government which immediately succeeded Julius Caesar thought of building a temple at public expense. This was not done, and shortly afterwards the rivalry between Octavian and Antony which culminated in the Battle of Actium and the capture of Alexandria, Antony's capital (31 and 30 B.C.) made everything connected with Alexandria and Egypt unpopular. But the goddess was not to be denied ; repeated prohibitions of her worship within Rome, or at least within the sacred *pomerium*, were evaded, and at last the half-mad Caligula, in or about A.D. 38, put up a temple to her in the Campus Martius, practically in Rome though sacrally outside it. This one of his acts remained unchallenged ; the various scandals aimed at the Egyptian priesthood died down and Isis and her retinue enjoyed Imperial favour thenceforth.

We are in a position to estimate what her cult meant to a pious, or rather pietistic, mind, that of the rhetorician, mystic and perhaps dabbler in magic, Apuleius of Madaura in Africa (second century A.D.). We have from him a brilliantly written romance, the *Metamorphoses*, otherwise known as the *Golden Ass*. His plot, which is Greek and probably a folk-tale originally, tells of a young man, by name Lucius, who by mishandling a charm turns himself into an ass and can resume his human shape only by eating fresh roses. In his attempts to get this remedy, he passes through a long series of grotesque and not always edifying adventures, told with great verve and in a rich, though intensely artificial style. At last Isis appears to him, tells him to snatch a rose-garland from her priest at her spring festival, claims his devotion and promises her protection in this world and the other. He follows her directions, and in due course is initiated into her mysteries. Apuleius cannot, naturally, divulge any details of what he (for there is little doubt that at this point he is describing his own experiences) went through, but his hints are enough to be interesting. He approached, he tells us, the bounds of Death and trod on the threshold of Proserpina, returning thence through all the four elements. He saw the sun at midnight, drew near the gods of the lower and the upper worlds and worshipped them face to face. In the morning, he was exhibited to an adoring congregation in the full dress of a sun-god. Later he passed through two more initiations and became one of the minor clergy, of an order which had its seat in Rome and claimed to have been founded in the days of Sulla.

We thus see that the Egyptian deities had to offer (though, as Apuleius clearly indicates, not at cheap rates) a most impressive ritual, well calculated to stir intense feelings in those who underwent it, and leading, in the case of the more devout, to something not unlike a monastic life. For those who felt no such vocation, there were lesser degrees of intimacy with the deities, down to mere occasional attendance at the temple-services, which indeed it was said by ill-wishers were made excuses for more earthly pleasures, in the shape of assignations of lovers. Juvenal has no better epithet than "procuress" for Isis, and a very bad scandal in the days of Tiberius led to one of the periodical suppressions of the cult and the crucifixion of the priests in A.D. 19. How much of all this was mere gossip, such as naturally forms around a foreign cult kept partly secret, and how much was founded on fact, it would be idle to ask now. For those philosophically inclined, explanations of the legends and rites were abundant, and might lead them into all manner of interesting and transcendental speculations, of a kind then popular. For all alike, it was a personal and moving religion, dependent neither on

the formalities of State cult nor on the mere vagaries of
private piety, and it had also, what counted then for a great
deal, the prestige of an immemorial antiquity. Ancient
civilisation had by that time lost the fresh self-confidence
of its earlier days, and reverence for the supposed deep and
mysterious wisdom of those who had lived long ago, especially
in foreign lands, was common. These men were nearer the
gods, and therefore more likely to know the truth concerning
them, and from their teaching had sprung all that was best
in Greek theology. No life of a philosopher, save those of the
more materialistic schools, such as Epicurus, was complete
without an account of how he went abroad, generally to
Egypt, to learn wisdom from the native priests. Here and
there such stories have some foundation in fact ; for example,
there is evidence that Plato was interested in both Persian
and Egyptian ideas ; but the exaggeration in most of them
is gross, and some are doubtless pure fiction. One very quaint
outcome of this craze for ancient and foreign revelations has
proved acceptable to modern researchers. The Christians
shared it, and were interested to prove that the Hebrew
religion was the oldest in the world. In this attempt, they
studied the Greek chronologers with great diligence, and so
it comes about that much of our knowledge of indispensable
dates for ancient history is derived from material preserved
by controversialists such as St. Cyril of Alexandria, Eusebios
the ecclesiastical historian and his translator and supple-
menter, St. Jerome. The results at which these men arrived
for the earlier periods are of course grotesquely wrong, but
the data they preserve are often of high value, for the com-
putations of ancient scholars, especially the Alexandrians,
were often exact for fully historical times, not far wrong even
as far back as the eighth century B.C., and not seldom
suggestive for events more remote than that. Their great
weakness, that they knew little of archaeology and nothing
of scientific methods of excavation, has been supplied in
modern times.

The cults with which we have been dealing attracted all
classes and professions ; we have now to expound one which
was largely military. The god Mithra (Mithras in Greek)

had long been worshipped in Iran, a region whose influence was widespread and felt in the West, for after the overthrow of the Persian monarchy by Alexander the Great, there was a political revival, culminating in the establishment of powerful dynasties, first foreign and later native, in Persia and the neighbouring countries, while the cultural exports never stopped. Zarathustra, the Zoroaster of Graeco-Roman tradition, had founded a lofty religion in his native country, which, mingled with elements often quite foreign to his ideas and principles, spread in all directions, resulting in cults so different from each other as modern Parsism in India and the mysteries of Mithra in the Roman Empire. The fundamental aspect of his teaching was its dualism ; the universe, to him, is the seat of a long-drawn war between the powers of good and evil, whereof the latter, though destined to ultimate defeat, is so strong as to make the contest a real one in which the forces of good readily welcome human aid. Zoroastrians, therefore, formed a veritable church militant, and it is thus not surprising that Mithraism, the most famous and popular development of the Persian religion in the West, appealed especially to regular soldiers. They were not, indeed, Mithra's first votaries in Italy. According to a much quoted passage of Plutarch, in his life of Pompey, the pirates whom that general suppressed, though ruthless in their desecration of other people's shrines, had a religion of their own, centring about Olympos (one of the two mountains of that name in Asia Minor, not the traditional seat of the Greek gods), where

they performed certain strange sacrifices and secret rites, whereof those of Mithras survive to this day and were taught by them.

Pompey, who was inclined towards mercy when it was politic, spared many of the pirates when they surrendered to him, and settled them in Italy, where Vergil afterwards knew one of them, quite reformed and an enthusiastic and skilled market-gardener. But it would seem that they brought their gods with them, and that from this rather unpromising source the religion spread. However, there were plenty of other opportunities for Roman armies to become acquainted with Persian or partly Persian rites and doctrines during their many campaigns in the Near East, and we need not suppose that the pirates were the only missionaries.

There were at least three features in the new cult which made it attractive to a variety of minds. In the first place, like all dualistic systems, Zoroastrianism and its offshoots offered a solution of the existence of evil in a world the rightful ruler of which is a good and wise God. Plainly, if there is another power, almost as strong as and diametrically opposed to the good deity, which continually wars against his sovranty, it is no wonder that evil should often meet with some measure of success, bringing, for example, plague and famine on innocent populations. Not a few philosophers, from the time of Plato onwards, thought such a doctrine worthy of serious examination. In the particular case of Mithra, there was another dogma attractive to some philosophers at least, those of the more transcendental schools. Their idea of deity was so exalted that they had difficulty in reconciling his infinite greatness and purity with any sort of contact with the low and material affairs of mankind, and the need of some kind of intermediary was widely felt. "Mediary" (*mesites*) is precisely what Plutarch, in another passage, styles Mithra. Here, then, was a venerable revealed doctrine ready to confirm theories of the existence of beings less than fully divine but much superior to mankind which were already current. Next, and this is not unimportant for that age, Mithraism seems to have had a fairly developed moral code of its own ; at all events, Zoroastrianism had, and the emperor Julian knows of "commandments" (*entolai ;* it is the very word which, while still Christian, he would have used of the Decalogue), given by Mithra to his followers. After several centuries of moralising philosophy, many forms of which had been popularised and were known in outline to all and sundry by writings and lectures, a religion which paid no attention to ethics would have had little chance of wide acceptance. The State cults, which remained almost entirely matters of ceremonial, were for most people no more than a part of the decent formalities of life, especially public life. In the third place, Mithraism had a strict discipline and a hierarchic series of grades which seem to have made it especially attractive to soldiers. Mithra himself, in the East, had often been the patron of warlike kings, and some part of the technical language of his cult had a military flavour ; one of the grades of initiation was that of Soldier (*miles*).

From a number of fragmentary sources, written and unwritten, it has been possible to patch together something like an outline picture of Mithraism, though the gaps in our knowledge are very many, no Mithraic treatise having survived, if indeed any such were ever written, and much of our information coming either from opponents of this and all non-Christian cults, or else from sacred carvings and emblems easily understood by initiates, but never meant to be intelligible to outsiders. So far, then, as we can understand it, Mithraism had its sacred legend, as indeed all cults had, and according to this, Mithra was miraculously born from a rock, and after various episodes caught and tamed a huge bull, obviously a supernatural creature. This beast he afterwards sacrificed. This act is the central thing in Mithraism, and occupies at least as prominent a station in the decorations of their places of worship as the Crucifixion does in Christian art. We know, partly from Oriental sources, partly from the many surviving representations of the scene, that from the bull there sprang the plants and animals useful to mankind, although the emissaries of Ahriman, the evil power, tried to prevent this happy result. Mithra also entered into relations with the Sun-god, is shown feasting with him and riding in his chariot, and indeed is himself often identified with him, one of his commonest titles in dedications being *Sol inuictus*, the Unconquerable Sun. As such, his birthday is at the time of year when the sun, passing the winter solstice, begins to move towards his summer position and consequently to lengthen the days in the northern hemisphere. This was fixed at December 25th, hence the traditional date of Christmas is of Mithraic, not Christian origin. This is but one of several indications of a certain influence of the rival cults on one another ; it is possibly a borrowing in the other direction which lies behind a common scene of the adoration of the young god by shepherds.

Those who wished to devote themselves to the service of

Mithra entered upon a complicated series of initiations, seven in all, the names of which are preserved for us by St. Jerome, with some doubt as to one of them, which seems to have been miscopied, and no certainty that he has them in the right order, for he mentions them only in passing, while speaking of the destruction of a Mithraic sanctuary by a fanatical Christian official. They are, including the doubtful name, Raven, Bridegroom (?), Soldier, Lion, Persian, Sun-runner (Heliodromus) and Father. The holders of all these grades were men, women having no part or only a subordinate one in this religion. The initiations comprised sundry tests of the neophyte's courage and determination, remnants likely enough of older rites of a more savage kind, and it may have been purely a matter of choice how high in the order anyone tried to rise. How it was determined that the holder of a lower grade might be allowed to proceed to a higher one, we do not know.

Mithra himself was a righteous god, as befitted one of the allies of Ahura Mazda, the Zoroastrian deity. He was "holy" (*sanctus*) according to many mentions of him on inscriptions. He loved the truth and hated lies, for lies are of Ahriman. His followers were comrades, presumably with mutual duties. The ideal of purity which was an essential part of all Persian religion seems to have been no merely ceremonial affair for them, but to have had its moral side as well. We may safely take it that the faithful follower of this Persian god led a clean life and, at least towards his co-religionists, one of honour and honesty. His reward was to be in the life to come, and here the Zoroastrian ideas of the ultimate salvation of the good when the wicked, along with Ahriman himself, are consumed by the fire which shall end the age, were modified by astrological doctrines with which Zarathustra himself never had anything to do. Astrology taught that the human soul, on its way to earth, passed through the spheres of the seven planets, and from each of them got the appropriate passion, lust for instance in the sphere of Venus, anger in that of Mars and so on. Indeed, it has been plausibly maintained that the canonical list of the seven deadly sins is astrological and pre-Christian in its origin. Whether this is so or not, it would seem that the seven Mithraic grades correspond to the seven planetary spheres, and that the finally delivered soul, protected by the god from the assaults of the evil powers, would rise through these spheres, losing at each one of the passions which had troubled him on earth, to a realm of perfect light and purity. This last idea, that the souls of the good go literally to heaven, was not peculiar to Mithraism, but common to several faiths of that time ; we see it in Christianity, in one of the most misunderstood passages of the Apocalypse, where the spirits of the martyrs are "under the Altar", meaning the constellation of that name, which in Mediterranean latitudes is always low on the horizon. They are newly dead, and so have just arrived on the borders of the sky. But it is very much older than St. John the Theologian. A kind of forerunner of it appears as early as Aristophanes, who mentions a belief that stars are souls of the dead. But the coming of astrological belief brought a much more elaborate form of it, somewhat as sketched above, while before that, the doctrine, common to several schools of philosophical and semi-philosophical thought, that the human soul is of divine origin and may in time ascend to the place whence it came, led to the natural corollary, that the just ascend to the presence of the gods, or at least to some lower region of their dwelling-place, such as the moon, conceived as the dividing-mark between the imperfect world in which we live and that in which, owing to the absence of dense and stubborn matter such as earth and water, the immutable laws of the universe are perfectly obeyed.

Much more might be said, did the dimensions of this book permit it, of other cults which came in from the East or contained Oriental elements and found their followers in the Graeco-Roman world of the Empire. But what has been said may serve to mark their characteristic features,—a central doctrine of a god friendly to man, often a suffering god (Mithra, to judge by his expression in many works of art, sacrificed his bull only at great violence to his feelings), in many cases one who dies and rises again ; a process of initiation, often elaborate and long-drawn-out ; and a code which included moral as well as ceremonial precepts. In all alike, personal salvation and happiness after death were assured to the faithful ; in all alike, the deity worshipped had strongly astral connexions, identification of all manner of important figures, not Mithra only, with the Sun being extremely common.

It is thus evident that when Christianity became widely known and was no longer conceived by the average person to be merely a new and disreputable variety of Judaism, it found the ground well prepared for it. Even its Scriptures, the Greek versions of the Old Testament, though not much read (well-informed writers like Tacitus and Strabo show complete ignorance of them), still had spread beyond the Jewish nation, for Judaism was then an actively propagandising religion, and converts and enquirers were numerous. As soon as they were known, they won attention. Here were documents professing to go back to the very beginning of human history, to be direct revelations and to contain forecasts of events which afterwards took place. Moreover, they agreed in many places with the deeply respected prophecies of the Sibyls (cf. p. 242); for the critical powers of that age were seldom developed enough for it to be suspected, what is now very evident, that the Sibylline verses generally current were blatant forgeries, drawing for much of their material on the Jewish documents themselves. If understood according to schools of allegorical interpretation which had established themselves in the Greek-using world since about the beginning of our era, the Scriptures contained in a more authoritative form the teachings of some of the most popular philosophies, notably the current developments of Platonism. They preached, along with a complicated ceremonial code, a lofty morality and a monotheistic theology. Even the extraordinary foreigner's Greek in which they were expressed was no great handicap, for it was little if at all worse than what many of the new hearers used themselves, and many of the oddest phrases had the attraction of sounding very mysterious. Now came a set of new teachers, who proclaimed with the utmost courage and zeal, despite all the handicaps under which an unauthorised cult laboured, and despite occasional local outbursts of savage repression, that the predictions in these venerable documents had been fulfilled in a Person born so recently that he could be dated by reference to figures familiar to everyone, such as Augustus, whose life-story was encumbered by no unedifying or fantastic legends, whose doctrine was of the purest and loftiest, and whose death was declared to have been followed by a triumphant resurrection, quite after the approved pattern, while his return in the full glory of divinity was almost hourly expected. About the new doctrine there soon gathered a ritual elaborate enough to be impressive, but again marked by no repulsive features, and containing the essential element of initiation into mysteries, namely those ceremonies, especially the Eucharist, which were not for outsiders, and to which catechumens were admitted only after sufficient instruction in the articles of their new faith. Here again was a strong point, which the young Church shared only with Judaism ; regular instruction was to be had, and as time went on, those intellectually inclined could receive more and more elaborate philosophical teaching, of good enough quality to attract some of the best minds of the early Christian centuries. If we may judge by what is left of the arguments on the other side, the Christian apologists, with all their faults, were neither so credulous nor such bad logicians as their opponents. For the less intellectual, there was a feeling of comradeship in a great adventure. To adopt Christianity was always more or less dangerous until the acceptance of it as a State religion by Constantine. Those who died for their faith did so in the fervent hope that they should be richly rewarded in a future life, while in the meantime all were assured of the support of a growing community which not only recognised in theory the equality of its members with each other but outstripped all other religious bodies in the practical generosity with which it dealt with its poor. That the new religion was of Eastern origin was in that age no handicap, but rather the reverse. The asceticism which grew up within it during the first few centuries of its existence was nothing new or peculiar, but was shared with several other cults of longer standing.

Since there were many points of contact, both in ethics

and in metaphysics, with other religions, it is not remarkable that several mixed systems grew up, classified by the Christian writers as heresies and often marked by most fantastic doctrines, formed of elements from very diverse sources. Doubtless there were many more compromises of which we hear nothing. The story told of the emperor Alexander Severus, that his private chapel contained figures of Orpheus, Abraham and Christ, may not be true, but there is nothing in it essentially incredible. Such phenomena as the appearance of Orpheus in Christian art and of Christian names in pagan magic are indicative of the broad-minded readiness of many to take and use anything that attracted them in any of the miscellaneous systems then available. It will be seen that the most popular, Christian and pagan, had in common several features, namely a doctrine of something like redemption through the efforts of a supernatural being, a moral code, a ritual, and a hope of blessedness in a future state. Hence, although conversions were normally from paganism, or Judaism, to Christianity, quite genuine conversions also from Christianity to paganism in one of its more refined and philosophic forms were not unheard of ; the case of the emperor Julian was the most celebrated, not the only one. No importance, of course, attaches either to the frequent apostasies from Christianity during the persecutions or to the general movement towards it when it was assured of Imperial support ; such things are unheroic but human and natural reactions.

One class of the population, however, was reluctant to give up its old traditional practices under the influence either of Christianity or of the other foreign religions. The country people went on much as before with their ancestral ways of getting the *numen* they wanted for their fields and their beasts. A reflexion of this is seen in the shift of meaning of the word *paganus* itself. Originally it was soldiers' slang, about equivalent to "civvy", meaning one who stays at home in his village (*pagus*) and does not join the forces. Hence it came to mean one who was not a soldier of Christ, not a member of the Church militant. But more than one of the fathers implies that to them the word means "rustic", rather one who is too stupid to see the truth of Christianity than too timid or unenterprising to join it. This attitude lasted in the countryside after the opposition in the cities, centering around the sentimental and antiquarian revival of paganism in Rome itself during the last generation or two before its official extinction, had collapsed before governmental edicts. It was part of the politic and tactful wisdom of the Christian clergy that they did not merely destroy but replaced in the country districts, giving the farmers, for instance, a substitute for the vanished Ambarualia (see p. 183) in the blessing of the fields with the Litania Maior, while ancient local holinesses were kept everywhere under new names, wells for example all over the civilised world becoming the wells of saints instead of local godlings and losing none of their reputation for healing and other good powers in the process. A little remains to be said of such substitutions in the final chapter.

CHAPTER VI

SURVIVALS

IF anyone set out to write a history of the survivals of Graeco-Roman cult in the Western world, the "remaines of Gentilisme" as John Audrey called them in 1686/87, he would find himself committed to a long and learned treatise involving a wide review of European folklore from the date of that edict of Theodosius (A.D. 392), which formally prohibited all forms even of private pagan cult, down to the present day. Furthermore, he would be obliged to examine in detail many features of the history of the declining Empire itself, and unravel the complicated story of how the cult of deified Emperors and of the Genius of the living one passed in time into a theocracy in which the ruling monarch was treated as already divine, and from that into an absolutism in which the sovrans were official defenders of the Faith (or, as occasionally happened, of the prevailing heresy of the time) and still ruled by divine right. He would have to pass under observation isolated struggles between the old ways and the new, such as the occasional killing of a too zealous cleric who tried to interfere with the rites of some remote country district, the slow disappearance of the old festivals from the calendars and from popular memory, or the conversion of surviving temples into Christian holy places (Apollo did not finally yield his hold on Monte Cassino, for instance, till St. Benedict put up his monastery there in 529). He would have to consider at length the extent to which the very names survived ; there is, for instance, reason to take San Miniato at Florence as being originally nothing more than the Holy One painted with *minium*, the traditional red pigment with which Etruscan and Roman statues of gods (in this case perhaps Juppiter, or his Etruscan equivalent Tinia) were daubed. He would find abundant room for the exercise of his judgment on the question to what extent this or that prominent man of the later times was anything more than a purely nominal Christian ; Ausonius of Bordeaux, in his day a writer of great popularity, who enjoyed favour and preferment under the emperor Gratian (murdered A.D. 383), is a case in point. Certainly he was no fanatic for any kind of religion, and was puzzled and distressed when his friend Paulinus of Nola embarked upon the pious courses which led in time to his canonisation. He would need to study the lives of missionary saints and other Christian worthies, trying to discover whether, when they are said to have replaced this or that Roman cult by their own faith, they were really doing so or attacking some native Gaulish, German or other deity, roughly identified with a familiar mythological figure. The whole question of the transit from serious belief in stories of the traditional gods to half- or quarter-belief in what ancient theorists called "poets' theology" and from that again to literary ornament so harmless that no one any longer objected to it, would occupy him at some length. He would give much attention to the question to what extent the more popular saints are, as has been epigrammatically

said, "successors of the gods", and, even before that, to the
very vexed question of the amount of influence exercised
upon Christianity itself by the various mystery-religions
which, as we have seen, were its competitors and to a great
extent prepared the way for it. The ecclesiastical calendar
would force itself upon his attention, with its many dates
reminiscent of pre-Christian festivals—St. Joseph, for
instance, occupying the date of the Quinquatrus (see p. 212),
March 19th, while the Annunciation supplies the place of
the Hilaria (p. 275), St. Mark that of the Robigalia (p. 221)
on April 25th, St. Cyprian replaces Juppiter on September
13th, and so forth, raising for each date the problem whether
we have to do with replacement or mere coincidence.
Obviously, nothing of this kind can even be attempted in
the concluding pages of a short outline ; it seems, therefore,
better to take a single example, the development of a late
ancient festival into that modern one which is most universally popular, Christmas.

Two very ancient themes unite in this festival. One is
the importance of all beginnings, and consequently of the
beginning of the year. Now the solar year may begin naturally
at any one of four points, the two solstices and the two
equinoxes, and all four have been used by one community
or another at various times. The Roman calendar, as reformed by Caesar, began where ours does, with January 1st,
which of course is not a solstice now and was not in his day,
but is fairly near it, too near for any lengthening of the
daylight to be perceptible. The other is the widespread
tendency to set the powers of cold and darkness at defiance
just when they are at their most formidable, in the dark
days of mid-winter, the northern Yule. In Europe, this is
also a season when, in the old rustic economy at least, food
is abundant for the time being, especially in the north, when
there was not until fairly recently enough winter fodder for
all the cattle, and so a number of them were slaughtered late
in the autumn and their flesh salted down or consumed on
the spot. It is thus a season when it is possible to feast and
make merry, and the impossibility of doing much farm-work,
owing to the state of the weather, gives further opportunity

for a holiday. At this time of year, then, Rome had a series of popular holidays, the Saturnalia of December 17th (p. 225), the Compitalia of January (p. 186), and, newest of all, New Year's Day, the Kalends of January. Under the early Empire, this was not yet a great holiday, but had its observances, because it was a beginning. Presents (*strenae*, French *étrennes*) were interchanged ; they seem to have been of trifling value, consisting of sweet things, such as honey, and small coins, the equivalents in symbols of the good wishes which were interchanged, for clearly they express a hope (or even may be taken as a charm) that the year may be both pleasant and profitable to the recipient. Courts of law were closed, the new magistrates formally entered upon their office with the usual sacrifices to Juppiter on the Capitol, and everyone performed some small piece of his usual work, no doubt something which he could finish quickly and well, in hopes that everything he did at his occupation might likewise be done easily and thoroughly during the next twelve months. It was, then, a festival partly at least official, certainly encouraged by governmental recognition, which extended to elaborate developments of the *strenae*, originally not even the simple presents which the early Empire knew, but merely twigs, probably to be used for the decoration of the house which was a feature of this and of all manner of other feasts. As the Empire went on, they became more and more expensive, included presents of great value to the Emperor and still more valuable ones made by him in return, and finally became such a burden that the emperors Arcadius and Honorius limited their amount in A.D. 395 and Leo abolished them in 458, so far at least as the loyal offerings were concerned ; what subjects chose to give each other remained their own concern, as before. By that time, these gifts were connected, not with New Year's Day proper, but with January 3rd, the day on which it had been the custom to make formal vows for the welfare of the Emperor, hence the name Vota which it commonly bore.

So far as the general public was concerned, the festival had but small beginnings. The first of every month was a festival from very ancient times, hence no one objected to

celebrating January 1st ; but it had not even been officially
the beginning of the year till 153 B.C., and had no particular
hold on popular affections. However, as it was the greatest
official day of that season, and as it fell but a fortnight after
the widely popular Saturnalia, naturally enough usages
belonging to that festival came little by little to be transferred to it. The Compitalia likewise contributed to it, since
it lay between the two ancient feasts ; this would give it
country support also, for with the passing of the richer
classes especially to the city, turning over the actual care
of their estates to slaves or free subordinates, the Saturnalia
had became more the feast of town-dwellers and their households there, the Compitalia the winter holiday of farm-
workers. Gradually the Kalends, now a festival several days
long and leading up to the Ludi Compitales of January
3rd-5th, became perhaps the greatest holiday time of the
whole year, when everyone feasted, made merry, gave and
received gifts, and incidentally, as before, sought for favourable omens. It was thundered against by a succession of
Fathers of the Church and numerous Councils, but with
very little effect either on its merriment or its superstitions.
Popular astrology, with its doctrine that the destiny of anything, including the business of a year, could be foretold by
consulting the stars at the beginning of it, had got its hold
on the people before the Church was ready, and to put down
any popular festival is generally possible only by substituting
another for it. We shall see that gradually this was done for
part of Western and Northern Europe.

But the Roman Empire was a very extensive territory
with a most miscellaneous population, and the Roman
customs, as they spread, met and mingled with all manner
of foreign rites. In the East, the winter festival season was
crossed with sundry local customs, some very old. The most
notorious of these was a descendant of the Babylonian Sakaia
at which there was chosen, not the harmless "chief of the
Saturnalia" (p. 225), but a mock-king who, after a brief period
of unrestrained honours and pleasures, was put to death,
and there is evidence that this was actually done, at least
occasionally and among some units of the army, in Roman

garrisons in the East. Another was the custom, also, it would seem, tolerated rather among soldiers than civilians, of going about in disguise, making broad fun of all manner of people, including the most respectable and highly placed. In the Keltic and Germanic regions of the West, another disguise-ment was met with ; here the mummers went about dressed as various kinds of beasts, probably a remnant of some seasonal festival of native gods, Gaulish or other, for in Gaul at all events gods often were represented under forms other than human. Thus custom after custom, Roman and foreign, accumulated in various parts of the Empire upon what had once been no more than a rather accentuated celebration of the first day of an officially important month. The Church authorities were extremely disgusted, but their attempts to make January 1st into a fast-day or at least a sober Christian holiday met with but poor success. To this day, January 1st is a time of considerable popularity in the Mediterranean regions, and not least in Greece, where, somewhat Christian-ised as the feast of St. Basil, it continues to be a time of traditional merry-makings and amusements, accompanied by good wishes and well-omened actions to introduce the New Year.

But the East, despite invasions and other political upsets, remained the most cultured part of the disintegrating Empire. In particular, it never became illiterate nor unable to use so civilised a thing as a calendar, with its astronomical basis and its computation of a series of days, calculated in an orderly manner from a fixed point and beginning again as soon as that point is once more reached. It was very different with the barbarous peoples who flooded the West. No such notion as a regular solar calendar had as yet entered their heads. They did indeed pick up from the Gauls, who had taken very kindly to Roman culture, some notion of the planetary week, and had gone so far as to find equivalents among their own gods for Juppiter, Venus and so forth, which still survive in the English, German and Scandinavian names for the week-days. They had in their own language sundry words vaguely denoting seasons, such as summer and winter, which are things anyone can perceive for himself and not periods consisting of a given number of days each. But a regular year, and therefore a New Year's Day, was strange and even meaningless to them, and was not likely to be made popular by the ecclesiastical objections to the New Year celebrations, for what culture and learning the new-comers got was, as is well known, conveyed to them from the same source which gave them such tincture of Christianity as they could, slowly and with many difficulties, be persuaded to accept. But, although they had no regular year, they had certain festivals, fixed approximately though not exactly, from which they might reckon, and one of these was the feast whose name in its English form is Yule. This was not a day but a period, and came in winter, after Slaughter-month, in which the superfluous cattle had been killed and their meat stored for future use. So far as can be guessed from later usages, the only ones of which we have direct knowledge, it was a time of feasting and of rites intended to counteract the darkness and cold of winter and assist the coming of brighter weather. This is characteristic rather of Northern than of Southern Europe, for obvious climatic reasons. The prominence even now of lights and green decorations at Christmas seem to be survivals of this ancient native magic.

Roman and Christian influence now provided the northern people with a calendar date around which such usages might centre. The Mithraic festival of December 25th, the Birthday of the Invincible Sun (see p. 287), had been politicly taken over by Christianity, with a characteristic piece of re-interpretation. The Sun in question was in future not to be the Persian god, but the Sun of Righteousness spoken of by the prophet Malachi, which by the quaint methods of interpretation then and for long after in use was identified with Christ. There being no plain indication in the Gospels of the time of year when the Nativity took place, there was nothing to prevent its being fixed on that date, and this was accordingly done, and some ingenious if unsound chronological arguments found to support it. To a festival thus Christianised there could be no ecclesiastical objection, such as continued to attach to New Year's Day, at all events in those regions where beast-masquerades were prominent and popular. Hence to keep Christmas, or rather the Christmas season, the Twelve Days from then to Epiphany (January 5th) was a procedure which combined pious observance with the maintenance of old local custom, and thus what had not been originally the chief Christian festival by any means (that is rather Holy Week and Easter) became the most lastingly popular in the north. The later stages of its history, for instance its attraction, under Protestant influence, to itself of the observances of St. Nicholas' Day (December 6th), the transfer to it of divinations belonging either to New Year's Day or to the older Yule season, the Presbyterian objections to it, which have had the quaint result of giving New Year's Day its old importance again, at least in Scotland, and, latest phenomenon of all, the spread of the German Christmas tree to other countries, cannot be gone into here. They are interesting, but their investigation is full of traps for the incautious, since it is but too easy, if several customs closely resemble each other, to suppose them historically connected when no descent can be proved for the later ones from the older. The complete history of Christmas can never be written, because so much that is probably contributory to its customs was never recorded and so cannot be examined by a modern researcher, dependent as he must be upon documents for events of antiquity or the early Middle Ages. I have attempted no more than a brief outline of those features in this venerable festival which seem to have a real connexion with usages belonging, if not to Rome itself, at least with some of the motley populations of the Empire.

Of influence of the earliest, or native, religion of Rome on later times there is not much. A tendency, rather than a survival, which it has in common with existing beliefs is, as has been suggested with a good deal of plausibility, the somewhat minute distribution of functions among certain popular saints. Thus, although several saints are reputed in general to heal diseases, St. Agatha is popularly invoked to cure pains in the uterus, St. Apollonia to cure toothache, St. Clare can help sore eyes, St. Eutropius dropsy, St. Helena haemorrhage, while so great a saint as Peter the apostle has

developed a speciality under one of his titles ; as St. Peter
in Vinculis he can so influence thieves as to make them
restore the stolen property. All these examples are from the
Vosges and were living beliefs in the nineteenth century, if
not later. It would be rash in the extreme to find here a
survival of actual Roman cult or theology, as instanced in
the minute division of functions between deities mentioned
in our first chapter. As there explained, that was by no means
wholly popular, but in large measure an artificial priestly
development. But such a development seems to have rested
upon a real tendency in the people, and it is not too much
to say that a like frame of mind is to be found in this and
similar phenomena of later date. What has survived here,
then, is not the ancient religion itself, but some part of the
mentality which made it acceptable.

Another survival took a form characteristic of the credulity
of both late antiquity and the Dark and Middle Ages which
succeeded it. The learned magic which was common throughout the Roman Empire was not forgotten, but continued in
quite recognisable forms, heavily frowned upon by Church
and State alike—the Church finally forged a very efficacious
weapon against it by equating it with heresy and thus beginning the organised and widespread persecution of witches
and wizards—but persisting, the more so as unbelievers in
the reality of the Black Art were scarcely to be found until
well after the Revival of Letters. Learned theory on this
point was in its essence a continuation of the Greek, or
Graeco-Oriental, system of demonology which had been
widely accepted from about the fourth century B.C. onwards
and was all but universal towards the end, being given forms
different in detail but the same in their fundamental principles
by Christians and pagans alike. A natural conclusion there-
from, since it was also an accepted doctrine that the pagan
gods were evil spirits, was the popular impression that the
learned and famous men of antiquity were all "philosophers"
and so versed in occult arts. Vergil held a high place among
these sages, according to a tradition which seems to spread
from Naples, the city where he was buried, and become
known about the middle of the twelfth century ; to take but

one small instance of his expertise, that interesting twelfth-century guide-book, the *Wonders of Rome* (*Mirabilia Romae*), informs visitors that the Viminal is the spot where

Virgilius, being taken by the Romans, went forth invisibly and departed to Naples, whence comes the saying "Go to Naples".

But all manner of other writers, including Galen, Hippo-krates and many more, both Greek and Roman, had a like reputation. One bit of magic connected with Vergil had a long life. Any book which is reputed to contain great wisdom may on occasion be used as an oracle ; the consultant opens it at random, puts his finger on a word or words and looks to see what they are, interpreting them with as much ingenuity as he requires or possesses into an answer to whatever question is troubling him. Homer was so used occasionally by Greeks, the Bible in many Christian communities. The Latin oracle was Vergil ; we have instances of his being consulted before the close of the classical period, and that practice was not extinct in the seventeenth century, though the ancient method was not, apparently, the random opening of a book but the picking up, at a shrine, of one of a number of slips or counters on each of which a Vergilian passage was written. This is but one form of divination (not counting astrology) which has come down from antiquity, as witness the following instance. In A.D. 371, the emperors Valens and Valentinian, badly frightened by information of a conspiracy against them, made vigorous enquiries, assisted by the utmost cruelty towards the accused. One piece of evidence which the judges were offered was this. Two of the culprits, Patricius and Hilarius, after performing certain elaborate rites, had placed on a table a metal dish having the letters of the Greek alphabet around its edge. Over this a diviner held a ring hung on a linen thread, and the consultants noted towards which letters it swung. The consultation was highly success-ful, for it spelled out answers to their questions in Greek hexameters. Thus encouraged, they boldly asked who the next Emperor was to be, and the ring obligingly spelled out TH-E-O-D, which satisfied them, for they made sure it was Theodorus, one of the Imperial secretaries. Doubtless the apparatus, if allowed to go on, would have undeceived them and explained that it meant Theodosius, who actually became Emperor in 379 along with Gratian and sole Emperor not many years later. But the interesting feature for us is that the device is one of the many varieties of what is now called a ouija-board. A simpler form of it is still used, not for grave matters of State, but for the more modest end of discovering whether a given egg will hatch a male or a female chicken. It is one of several modes of divination which depend on the accidental movements of some object suspended from a string or laid on a smooth surface where a slight force will push it one way or another ; the planchette is an allied method.

Still commoner, perhaps, are the charms which are still to be found up and down Europe and once were widely and firmly believed in. All their most characteristic features—words of power which are partly foreign names (Biblical and other), partly gibberish, narratives of the doings of some holy or powerful person, with an application to the needs of the operator ("as such-a-one mastered this disease, so may it be cured in the present case") and so forth are to be paralleled in antiquity. Besides these verbal spells, some of the best-known features of witchcraft descend from antiquity, for instance *envoûtement*, or harming a person by making a wax or other figure to represent him and injuring it. The powers attributed to witches and other uncanny beings are much the same whether we get examples from ancient superstitions or mediaeval and post-mediaeval treatises on the subject. For example, their reputed power of turning themselves or someone else into the likeness of a beast is attested by several ancient stories, and was so widely believed still when Reginald Scot printed his *Discoverie of Witchcraft* in 1584 that, as he says,

these examples and reasons might put us in doubt, that everie asse, woolfe, or cat that we see, were a man, a woman, or a child.

For which reason he spends not a little space in heaping up arguments from the theology and science of his day to show such changes to be impossible.

But such survivals as these are really of little significance. They are not specifically Roman beliefs and practices which passed to a later age, hardly even Graeco-Roman, for they contained many foreign elements in antiquity. It is more to the point to ask if in the religion of Western Europe there can be detected any features which can reasonably be traced to Rome, other than the circumstance that the most numerous Christian communion has its headquarters at the Vatican and uses Latin as its official language. I think such characteristics can be detected. The main stream of Western Christianity, Catholicism in its wider sense, seems to me to have not a few inheritances from the spirit of ancient Rome and its most normal ways of thought and action. To begin with, it is a disciplined body, holding fast to certain doctrines and rites which it regards as fundamental and indispensable and claims to have inherited from the earliest times. It is therefore legalistic and conservative, characteristics which have more than once made for obscurantism and resistance to natural and inevitable change, but have on the whole contributed to its great stability and its power to outlive one rival after another. Its conservatism has not prevented development, for new doctrines have from time to time been approved, although the theory is always that they were implicit from the beginning and the innovation is simply their explicit statement. Ritual has shown, always within certain bounds, a like elasticity. All this might, with very little change, be asserted of Roman law and custom, both sacral and secular, for novelty in both those fields was apt to take the outward form of mere interpretation. Another shape which its legalism has taken is insistence on proper established form ; in the administration, especially, of its sacraments it prescribes, and from very early times has prescribed, a right and approved way of doing and saying what is necessary, and denies validity to any different method, save within very clearly fixed limits. There is always a written text to appeal to, and that text is guaranteed by the express approval of competent authority. The College of Pontiffs, could it be brought back to see its successors, would heartily agree, for it also had its texts, whereof not one syllable might be altered without vitiating the whole rite ; the very term "vitiate" is adapted from the technical Latin word *uitium*, signifying a flaw.

But there is perhaps even more in it than that. Beyond all the definiteness of dogmas and creeds and the exactitude of rituals and prayers, the ceremonies of historical Christianity leave room for a mind perceptive to such influences to feel the presence or influence of something not to be caught in meshes of words or more than hinted at in actions. Here, then, after the centuries of development, we are in a sense back where we started ; the pious worshipper at a Pontifical Mass may still feel, with the Roman farmer of pre-Republican days, that *numen* is present.

BIBLIOGRAPHY
(A) General Accounts

English is well supplied with these. They include : F. ALTHEIM, *A History of Roman Religion*, translated H. Mattingly (original, often very unorthodox, in its views), 1938; C. BAILEY, *Phases in the Religion of ancient Rome*, 1932; CARTER, JESSE BENEDICT, *The Religion of Numa, and other Essays on the Religion of ancient Rome*, 1906 ; FOWLER, W. WARDE, *Roman Festivals of the period of the Republic* (standard English work, now slightly out of date), ed. 2, 1908 ; HALLIDAY, WILLIAM REGINALD, *Lectures on the history of Roman Religion*, 1922.

(B) Interpretative

BAILEY, *Religion in Virgil*, 1935 ; CARTER, *The religious life of Ancient Rome*, 1912 ; FOWLER, *The Religious experience of the Roman People*, 1911 ; *Roman ideas of Deity*, 1914 ; WAGENVOORT, H., *Roman Dynamism* (treats the idea of *numen* especially), 1947 (for this book the Dutch edition, *Imperium*, 1941, was used).

(C) Particular Points

Oriental and mystery-cults ; CUMONT, F., *After Life in Roman Paganism*, 1928 ; *Les religions orientales dans le paganisme romain*, ed. 4, 1929 (excellently annotated ; the English translation by Grant Showerman, 1911, is from an earlier and less well documented edition). Calendar festivals ; FRAZER, SIR J. G., *The Fasti of Ovid*, 5 vols., 1929 ; numerous points are discussed, with ethnological parallels, in his other works, notably *The Golden Bough*, ed. 3, 13 vols., 1911-1936. Miscellaneous problems ; ROSE, H. J., *The Roman Questions of Plutarch*, 1924. Survivals of savage customs in classical times ; same, *Primitive Culture in Italy*, 1926. Survivals of Roman customs, etc., into post-classical times ; HALLIDAY, *Greek and Roman Folklore*, 1927 ; SPARGO, JOHN WEBSTER, *Virgil the Necromancer*, 1934. On the history of Christmas there is no good work in English.

INDEX